"The impact of the women's rights work of Elizabeth Cady Stanton and others in my family was profound. It also carried over to generations of descendants in my own family. This is a strong point of the story told by Marguerite Kearns. Generations into the future will be changed permanently by those who have come before us."

— Coline Jenkins, Founder and President, Elizabeth Cady Stanton Trust

"Edna and Wilmer Kearns's story resonates deeply today both as a slice of history and as a rare glimpse of the kind of domestic relationship, based on equality, that helps move society forward. The women's suffrage movement was a determined drive for liberty, and women like Edna were engaged as in battle. They needed backup and critical support to keep going, and men like Wilmer were there to give it. He was Edna's partner and his story reflects the experiences of men across the country who quietly shared women's long campaign for freedom. *An Unfinished Revolution* is a revealing personal journey that reminds us that love and cooperation are necessary elements to empower changemakers and shape a better future."

— Robert P. J. Cooney Jr., author of
Winning the Vote: The Triumph of the American Woman Suffrage Movement

"This book is the intimate account of several generations of a Quaker family actively involved in the extension of women's rights. The author collected the family stories, including those of her grandfather, a man fully committed to his wife's social activism. A valuable addition to the women's suffrage canon, this memoir offers a rare glimpse into the ways a movement can define a family."

— Susan Goodier, coauthor of *Women Will Vote:*
Winning Suffrage in New York State

"All the great issues of life have been the outcome of 'small things,' wrote Edna Buckman Kearns. This book illustrates that truth, showing how one Quaker family contributed through their daily choices to the largest nonviolent movement for social change in US history, the movement for women's right to vote. Intertwining fascinating details about personal experiences over generations, this story uses the lives of Edna and Wilmer Kearns to show how individual actions formed the basis for a national movement for equality, offering an inspiration for all of us today."

— Judith Wellman, author of *The Road to Seneca Falls:*
Elizabeth Cady Stanton and the First Woman's Rights Convention

An Unfinished Revolution

An Unfinished Revolution

Edna Buckman Kearns and the Struggle for Women's Rights

Marguerite Kearns

excelsior editions

AN IMPRINT OF STATE UNIVERSITY OF NEW YORK PRESS

Cover image: "On to Albany"—Jones' Army 1/1/14, part of the George Grantham Bain Collection available through the Library of Congress. Suffrage activist Ida Craft is to the left of the man holding the flag with Edna, Serena, and Wilmer Kearns to his right.

Published by State University of New York Press, Albany

Excelsior Editions is an imprint of the State University of New York Press

For information, contact State University of New York Press, Albany, NY
www.sunypress.edu

Library of Congress Cataloging-in-Publication Data

Names: Kearns, Marguerite, author.
Title: An unfinished revolution : Edna Buckman Kearns and the struggle for women's rights / Marguerite Kearns.
Description: Albany : State University of New York, [2021] | Includes bibliographical references and index.
Identifiers: LCCN 2020048644 (print) | LCCN 2020048645 (ebook) | ISBN 9781438483320 (paperback : alk. paper) | ISBN 9781438483313 (ebook)
Subjects: LCSH: Kearns, Edna Buckman. | Suffragists—United States—Biography. | Women—Suffrage—United States—History.
Classification: LCC JK1899.K43 K43 2021 (print) | LCC JK1899.K43 (ebook) | DDC 324.6/23092 [B]—dc23
LC record available at https://lccn.loc.gov/2020048644
LC ebook record available at https://lccn.loc.gov/2020048645

10 9 8 7 6 5 4 3 2 1

March 4, 1919

Dear Daughter Serena,

. . . If I am arrested tonight (just carrying a purple, white and gold banner), I need not hunger strike here in New York. Dad can call on me in jail and I can get good food—so don't Thee worry . . .

Lovingly, Dearie

Contents

Part III

Part IV

Illustrations

*Unless otherwise indicated, photographs in this book
are from the author's private collection.*

The Story Behind the Story

This is the story of one family in the context of the votes for women struggle, a pivotal US social justice movement. It brings to life my maternal grandparents, Edna and Wilmer Kearns. They were activists in the latter part of the early women's rights movement in the United States from 1908 through 1920. More than a straight historical account, this history of a Quaker family traces a trail of resistance and action that started with prior generations of determined men and women.

The long effort continues with a spirit passed down over the decades to me in the present day. It tells a tale of patriotic protest and of the urgency of passing a torch to future generations. My mother passed on to me a substantial archive of primary documents revealing the details of what it took to win support for the Nineteenth Amendment to the US Constitution. Many similar archives of activists documenting change on the local, state, and national levels have been lost or destroyed.

Some suffrage history scholars believe that not all descendants of suffrage activists realized the significance of these collections. Activists then and now have discovered that if they don't assemble evidence of their efforts and write their own history, the understanding and appreciation of their accomplishments may be incomplete, marginalized, or invisible.

The narrative I'm presenting here reveals in one family unit the cost and sacrifices of organizing for social and political change, as well as the impact of a social movement on several generations. The stories we tell, or leave behind for descendants, make a difference in defining the future. This saga addresses more than the social movement activity in a family that is often squeezed into the larger context of life. Particularly for Quakers, the successful outcome of the early women's rights movement was fueled by the energy and inspiration of a divine Inner Light and the values of connection. Their activism survived in the context of a polarized nation of individuals, many of whom were contaminated by the emotional fallout of living in the hierarchy of a patriarchal social and economic system.

It took over a hundred years for the significance of many events and the internal and external processes of those involved in suffrage campaigning to be recognized. For most of the twentieth century, the effort was neither visible, nor taken seriously. Now this period of history is not only surfacing, but this part of our past can build confidence about how nonviolent organizing and change is within the reach of everyone. The victory of the Nineteenth Amendment not only guaranteed voting rights, it also opened the door to millions of regular citizens participating in a major social revolution.

My quest started as a child of ten years listening to my grandfather's stories about his late wife, Edna Buckman Kearns, my grandmother. I deepened my understanding as an adult through research, the exploration of scholarly works, storytelling, and a close examination of family legends. I felt like an amateur detective fitting together pieces of an enormous puzzle.

Like the conservator who restores historic works of art, there are places in the text where I wove together fact, vintage photos, oral history, and an understanding of the broader context of the period in which my grandparents and ancestors lived. I painted a portrait of my grandfather Wilmer as a storyteller and best friend to my grandmother Edna in an account consistent with historical reality.

Edna was committed to the cause of women's rights, although the complications of daily life intervened. She traveled a path requiring courage and an intolerance of injustice. Edna considered herself a "new woman," a term referring to those who didn't fit traditional gender stereotypes. Wilmer labeled himself a "new man," someone in support of women's rights and the changing social order. Together, they faced many challenges along the way, including a family secret and a scandal.

Wilmer was dependable, well liked, patient, and supportive of the family activism. Edna was an earnest young person, anxious to achieve independence and leave the protective control of her parents behind. She did this by marrying Wilmer Kearns and moving with him from Philadelphia to New York City. My grandfather Wilmer supported Edna in her goal of becoming a women's rights activist, even marching in the men's division of women's rights parades. When Edna attended suffrage meetings and conferences out of town, he covered child care and answered the phone. He was uneasy about Edna's unconventional friend Bess, who believed the voting rights movement was a tenuous reform and not a social revolution. After Edna's death in 1934, Wilmer devoted himself to preserving the Spirit of 1776 horse-drawn suffrage campaign wagon she used in New York City and on Long Island.

Support and augmentation in the narrative have been achieved by way of endnotes and a lengthy list of sources consulted. In the course of my research, I uncovered material not previously published. My background as a news reporter led me to gather impressions and deepen my understanding by exploring behind the scenes. Although I was able to depend on the details and observations about so many personalities within a family over several generations, by necessity I bridged unavoidable gaps in the overall story. This involved examining the record and interpreting what I found, as well as deciding what should be included as personal, emotional, and spiritual truth.

My broad sweep of the past poses questions Americans still raise about the values embodied in the Declaration of Independence, the Bill of Rights, and the US Constitution.

Edna Buckman Kearns and her co-campaigners relied on the principles of "life, liberty, and the pursuit of happiness" as they attempted to address what many called an unfinished and continuing American Revolution. They spread this thematic message with the horse-drawn suffrage wagon.

The examination of one family during the early women's rights movement demonstrates the importance of activism within families, the unreliability of treasured legends, and the role tradition and storytelling plays in collective identity and meaning. The narrative of my grandparents highlights how tens of thousands of citizens stepped forward to reinforce democratic foundations on which others built. This story reveals the context of my grandparents' lives and the times in which they lived. This nation was polarized over efforts to achieve equality among diverse populations and cultures in their day. Social change can be equally slow and difficult today.

As the social revolution toward equality continues, the spirit of the early US women's rights movement endures. Tens of thousands of Americans risked their lives, careers, reputations, families, and peace of mind for equality, justice, and voting rights. The accomplishment of the Nineteenth Amendment is built on and reinterpreted today. Shoes may be scuffed from the steps of so many volunteers, but the momentum is clear: onward.

Part I

Parade memorabilia used by Edna Buckman Kearns.

Chapter 1

The March of the Women

No framed photographs of my maternal grandmother Edna Kearns hung on the walls of my childhood home. Family members spoke about her in soft tones or a murmur—and seldom. My mother told me that, as a child, she called her mother "Dearie." This was scandalous, she said, because many people believed "Dearie" was a name associated with a "chorus girl."

My grandmother's names didn't matter to me. Edna was a mystery, the grandmother I never knew who might have lifted me out of my isolation. Clues about Edna's life were found in what she left behind. At age ten, I couldn't wait to find out more about the horse-drawn suffrage wagon she used in women's rights campaigning, known as the Spirit of 1776, stored in my grandfather's garage. Edna's archive of letters, speeches, and newspaper articles about women demanding the right to vote found a home in an old travel trunk, and my mother opened a box of Edna's protest parade outfits for me to play dress up.

I dug into the assortment of musty-smelling fabric, lace, and long skirts packed away after my grandmother's death. One summer afternoon I pulled a gauze ivory dress over my head to bond with my sweat, along with a purple, white, and gold sash fitting across my chest. I listened for Edna's voice with my eyes closed and heard her faint voice in the distance.

"Hurry. They're waiting for us to join the march down Pennsylvania Avenue in Washington," she called to me from the mist. Hundreds of parade participants belted out a suffrage song to overpower taunts from the sidewalk. Edna fixed her eyes straight ahead while rough voices hollered: "Women shouldn't vote. It's not in their nature," or "If they vote, they won't have children," and "Soon girls will be wearing long pants."

The singing lowered to a whisper as I rubbed my eyes when my mother called me for a snack of celery sticks. I drooled over the possibility of lemonade and butter pecan cookies. On a day like this, though, nothing compared with wearing Edna's dress—the same fabric that once touched her skin. I dragged her long skirts through the mud while marching with my knees lifted high.

"Here's a photo of your grandmother," my mother Wilma told me. Since I'd never seen a likeness of Edna, I lunged toward the image. It took me decades to find out that her photos were stored away because family members couldn't process the grief

Edna Buckman Kearns, "Dearie," Rockville Centre, Long Island, circa 1915.

of her death. They loved her. So did I. As my eyes caressed the waves of her hair, I stood before Edna in my pink halter and faded plaid shorts. In that moment, one word described her—stunning—even if her haunted eyes left me feeling unsettled. I sensed my grandmother was both frail and strong, engaging, and someone to be taken seriously.

I picked up clues about Edna being determined and persistent, a sensible writer, and a quiet but forceful speaker.[1] Her writing style was informed and direct. Few of her sentences, either spoken or written, were out of place. Her words moved without effort across a newspaper column. She could be both funny and perceptive in daily conversation. And according to my grandfather, she listened to others speak before contributing to a conversation.

"I didn't make up the part about marching with Edna," I said silently as a way of convincing myself of an authentic connection with my grandmother. I asked my grandfather, mother, and aunt the same question. "Do spirits of dead people return to earth?"

When I posed this and other unexpected questions, usually I got the same answer. "Why does it matter?"

"Just checking," I said before disappearing into the shell where I resided as a child.

I pried out of Granddaddy that he considered Edna "borderline shy," although he said this didn't fairly describe her. "I'd also call her modest, thoughtful, someone who settled easily into silence and reflection. She liked socializing with others, but talking and sharing was mostly one to one."

So Edna was reserved, like me, I said to myself. In my bedroom at home I pounded the palm of my right hand against the closet door in frustration. Words in my little-girl pink diary couldn't bring my grandmother back. No matter what I did, the questions I asked, or the stories my grandfather told me, I couldn't include Edna in my ordinary reality. I sensed her in a branch breaking on a dogwood tree outside

Marguerite Kearns, during the 1950s.

my bedroom window. I counted my inhales and exhales when estimating how long it took her to march down Pennsylvania Avenue in Washington, DC, in 1913.

Shadowlike images of Edna standing on a soapbox on city streets followed me as patches of sunlight spread across my bedroom floor. I detected outlines of Edna's face and hair falling lightly on her shoulders when a crescent moon came into view. I ran down the hill and up to my bedroom to visit with Edna under wool blankets after being dropped off daily by the school bus. It's fair to say that my grandmother came to occupy much of my waking awareness as a child. I had to listen carefully to my mother and grandfather, though, if I ever expected to understand the complexity of Edna.

Because my grandmother died before my birth, I wondered if she ever suspected an unknown young person like me would take an interest in her someday. Perhaps I'd grow up and write like Edna. I'd tell the world about her, but I wasn't sure if I could manage such a project. I wasn't much of a storyteller, but I practiced on my sister. No one offered me a guidebook for how to survive to age ten and beyond. This translated to me taking everything my grandfather and mother said seriously.

Close family members like Edna's mother, May Begley Buckman, might have predicted that Edna was headed in the direction of a job in a settlement house, a school, or library. May believed that if Edna found a husband with a serious interest in practicing equality in marriage, it would be possible for her to have a family, as well as make a contribution to history. Edna's preference during her teens, however, was not to marry. She wanted to be free. When I heard this, I had no sense of myself or what marriage and freedom meant. Wilmer held the key to my understanding, or so I believed.

"Are your clothes clean enough to visit Granddaddy?" my mother asked when I was about to leave the house to hike the ten minutes to Wilmer's.

"Absolutely," I assured her.

After I arrived at Wilmer's, he opened an overhead garage door to reveal the suffrage campaign wagon used in parades and as a speaker's platform. Granddaddy repeated the story I'd already heard about the horse-drawn wagon Edna used in New York City and on Long Island in 1913. He called the wagon a "symbol" of freedom, a missing link between 1776 and the unfinished revolution of women's rights.

"The wagon was groundbreaking for women," he said, adding, "Sure, the votes for women movement wasn't what it might have been if it had been centralized and well funded. It was mostly volunteer." I had no idea what this meant. Granddaddy's accounts of Edna and the wagon kept me spellbound during summer days when I wasn't typing his novel and work in progress, *Queen Bee, the Refugee*, a tale of immigrants on a journey from the east to the west coast. I wondered if Edna kept certain things about herself a secret. Did she ever question whether Wilmer Kearns was right for her as a husband and partner? I wanted to find out.

On one of my visits, Granddaddy stared at me with one of his classic expressions with his lips closed tight. He swallowed hard, as if a golf ball were stuck in his throat.

Spirit of 1776 suffrage wagon, circa 1980s.

Occasionally he used a magnifying glass to read. When he did, his lips moved slowly. My grandfather didn't always tell me what he was thinking, even though his chin and facial expressions sent a message of sadness. Wilmer missed Edna. I could tell this much. His relationship with her must have represented the deepest and most meaningful period of his life. How did I know? I figured this out from his sighs, the hints of tears gathering in the corners of his eyes. He didn't marry again after Edna. And he definitely wanted to talk to me about her.

I glanced over in my grandfather's direction as he tipped back and forth in his rocking chair when telling me that, for Edna and himself, the women's suffrage movement was no "snooty" affair with fancy ladies in low-cut gowns drinking tea, eating angel food cake, and engaging in old lady talk. Many activists took personal risks by marching in demonstrations and putting themselves on the line for women's rights, just like Edna.

For many like my grandparents, entire families were involved in the agitation. "We were ordinary folks," Granddaddy said. His worn reading glasses slid down on his nose. He might have changed lenses over the decades, but it seemed like he wore the same circular frames he purchased as a young man. He told me Edna spoke with her eyes—except when singing the English suffrage anthem, "The March of the Women": "March, march, swing you along, / Wide blows our banner, and hope is waking."[2]

Women sang and marched together for good reason. There was a sensation of feeling strong and safe together when facing opposition. This thought caused my stomach to curl into a knot. I was shy, awkward, and felt like an outsider, a strange child in love with her invisible grandmother. I joined in with the marching songs, sat straighter in the chair in Granddaddy's kitchen, and kept tune with the stanzas, the rhythms of feet tramping, and anxious hearts in thousands of throats.

"Edna and votes for women was the most glorious time in my life," Granddaddy said. Then he became silent. He must have been picturing Edna in that moment, I decided, because he smiled.

Chapter 2

Wilmer Meets Edna

$\mathcal{E}$dna Buckman met Wilmer Kearns on Logan Circle in the warm weather of 1902, not far from Center City in Philadelphia. I remember Granddaddy Wilmer telling me his breath collapsed in his throat when he noticed her. She more than caught his attention with a stream of sunbeams flooding her shoulders.

She carried a stack of line drawings of portraits and landscapes in her arms. And, he recalled, she wore a Quaker bonnet. After this radiant being dropped her drawings, they landed with a smack on the pavement and flew across the hard surface. On hands and knees, Wilmer retrieved every sketch and returned them to Edna, the opening he needed to introduce himself.

Edna May Buckman and Wilmer Rhamstine Kearns, circa 1903.

After Wilmer returned her drawings, Edna blushed and suggested something he never expected. "I'd love some company. I'm headed in the direction of Market Street."

This was certainly an unusual woman, Wilmer decided, as the two walked along city streets, starting not far from where Wilmer shared lodgings with other business students at 235 East Logan Square. After classes, he and the other students played Parcheesi and rode bicycles in the direction of Independence Hall. They dressed in striped blazers and tight cycling pants.

Edna and Wilmer hiked toward the city's center where a bronze statue of William Penn, Philadelphia's Quaker founder, wearing a broad-brimmed hat, towered over them from the top of City Hall. As they walked, Edna and Wilmer spoke of their favorite authors. Edna liked newspaper reporter and columnist Margaret Fuller. Wilmer was fascinated with the naturalist Henry David Thoreau.

Wilmer kept his pace even with hers. He'd traveled this street before, but hadn't fully experienced the coolness under trees lining the boulevard. As he glided along, he was aware of how Edna enjoyed leading as they covered the city blocks laid out by William Penn generations before. Walking together seemed natural. As Granddaddy related this to me, he said he didn't feel his usual reserve. He presented himself as thoughtful and concerned. Edna came across to Wilmer as mature and aware.

She spoke in the Quaker plain speech to him—"thee" and "thy." And she told him that this plain speech tradition started back in England when Quakers didn't speak differently to those above them in social class, like kings and queens, or those below them. Quakers spoke to everyone in the same way. I was learning at my Quaker Meeting that all life forms on Earth were spiritually equal, including men and women as well as humans of all religions and backgrounds. To express in plain speech that everyone was equal was a radical practice in England during the 1600s. Granddaddy would learn to speak this way freely if he decided to spend more time with Edna.

"Philadelphia is an informal place where I don't feel pressured," Wilmer told her. Of the three big cities lined up in the East—New York, Philadelphia, and Washington, DC—a country boy like Wilmer Kearns found Philadelphia the least intimidating. At age sixteen, he had traveled from Beavertown, the town of his birth in Pennsylvania near Harrisburg, to Philadelphia, to study at Peirce, a business college.

I heard from Granddaddy that many historic buildings from the city's earliest days were still standing on Market Street, a major thoroughfare in 1902. William Penn's city plan fit between the Delaware and Schuylkill Rivers, a grid laid out in 1682 when Edna's Quaker ancestors arrived in Philadelphia from England with Penn on the ship *Welcome*. Their vision for a population center Penn called a Holy Experiment was rooted in ideals of religious freedom, an opposition to slavery, and peaceful relations with native peoples—all goals difficult to maintain over the long term in a city bursting with new residents from all over the world who didn't necessarily share Quaker values. The Buckmans were the largest family group on the *Welcome*, and family descendants were determined to remember their roots by holding annual family reunions.[1]

Statue of William Penn, 1894, before installation on the top of Philadelphia's City Hall. Mechanical Curator Collection, Library of Congress.

Since moving to Philadelphia, Granddaddy said he noticed few Quaker women in traditional dress walking the streets. Unlike Edna in her bonnet and long gray dress, an increasing number of female descendants of early Quaker settlers wore conventional clothing. Quaker men also followed contemporary styles that gradually replaced their conservative dark coats and hats. Quaker plain speech was also on the decline. Because Edna wore her bonnet in public, it represented a gesture to convince her mother of her intent to live according to Quaker faith and values.

"Will thee stay here after finishing school?" Edna asked Wilmer after they reached Market Street.

"I'll be off to New York where the pay's better," he told her.

Wilmer didn't know much about Quakers, so he trained his ears to listen to Edna's soft voice. The United States had been changing dramatically, she told him. Philadelphia took second place in commerce compared to New York, the nation's largest city and what my grandfather called a "window on the world."

Granddaddy told me that when he was young during the 1880s, most Americans lived on farms or in small communities. Wilmer and Edna grew up during a transition period of industrialization after technology and machines made inroads across the nation. Wilmer and his friends socialized after business college classes, which meant they usually mentioned William Penn and the Pennsylvania colony as an example of utopian visions.

"There are many stories about Edgar Allan Poe living here too," she added, pointing out that William Penn encouraged a range of diverse citizens to settle in the section of the city known as Northern Liberties. This became home not only to Poe and his family but also to Quakers, working people, artists, poets, and writers. Many were attracted to Philadelphia because of its reputation as a hub of creative activity and publishing during the 1840s. I wondered if Edna and Wilmer might someday live in Northern Liberties, or if they'd set up a household in Center City. I used my imagination to visualize my grandparents. Why not? If they hadn't married, I wouldn't be listening to family stories in Wilmer's kitchen.

"The city oozes with history," Granddaddy told me as I paid attention with an interest I didn't have in school. The names of streets, highways, and inns he mentioned reinforced my sixth-grade social studies units featuring historic figures and locations of note. Tourists to Philadelphia mailed home postcards with illustrations of the Liberty Bell, the Betsy Ross house, and art museums. Granddaddy said he liked Philadelphia, but not so much that it interfered with his plans to find a job in New York City.

"Let's stop by the Market Street teahouse," Edna suggested the day my grandparents met. Wilmer said his lips quivered when his hand accidently touched hers when opening the teahouse door. They could have window shopped at Philadelphia's department stores—Gimbel Brothers, Strawbridge & Clothier, and John Wanamaker's—but delivery wagons and shoppers packed the streets. Philadelphia, a seaport, was no longer the green country town of Edna's ancestors with residential neighborhoods of two-and three-story brick houses contaminated over the decades by steam and smoke congestion. The Market Street teahouse was located several blocks away from where Thomas Jefferson drafted the Declaration of Independence at Seventh and Market Streets in 1776.

"So much changed here after the railroad came in," Edna told Wilmer. He agreed. The railroad made it possible for my grandfather to study business at Peirce College in Philadelphia, an institution founded in 1865 with programs for both men and women. Train travel opened the way for Edna's father, Charles Harper Buckman, to work for Boll Brothers, a firm manufacturing brass beds and accessories with its headquarters in Harrisburg, the state capital.

I collected more facts, and realized that many Buckman family members and ancestors had been farmers in Bucks County near Philadelphia. Farming had its limits. Young Quaker men gradually left rural areas for jobs and small businesses in Philadelphia. The railroad opened up other choices for Edna and her generation. My grandmother's goal of someday participating in women's rights organizing was associated with locomotives. Trains made it possible for activists like Susan B. Anthony from Upstate New York to speak nationally on behalf of temperance, the abolition of slavery, and women's rights.

At the teahouse, Edna and Wilmer added to their exchange with a mutual appreciation of literature. They'd both read Charlotte Perkins Gilman's short story "The Yellow Wallpaper." Even more telling, the pair agreed that it was the isolation many married women felt, together with the few civil rights they enjoyed, that led many to experience depression and mental illness. That's what writer Gilman's short story was about—how the top-down social system didn't contribute to a balanced state of mental health.

"I would have done anything to spend the entire afternoon with Edna," Wilmer told me. He described the light freckles scattered across her cheeks. Silky lashes dominated her face. When Edna brushed away a wisp of hair close to her chin, he swore the aroma of French talcum powder filled the space between them. Edna's soft hair tumbled onto her shoulders when she removed her bonnet.

"Where was thee raised?" she asked him, again in Quaker plain speech.

"In Beavertown, out in Pennsylvania Dutch country," Wilmer replied. He told her about the parlor at home where family members and friends gathered for playing the piano, violins, violas, tubas, and trumpets. He emphasized that he was a musician, a category of young man she wasn't familiar with. Many Quakers then believed music was a distraction from spiritual practices. Edna liked music. Wilmer also shared impressions of Snyder County where he'd been raised. Their lively exchange survived two rounds of scones with orange marmalade, plus a pot of oolong tea.

Wilmer told me how much he loved being the center of attention, whereas he said Edna gravitated to speak to women at special events, asking others to share their personal stories. She listened patiently while Wilmer worked the room. He was comfortable with business accounts and numbers, in addition to being a storyteller. Edna made her opinions known about the urgency of winning women's voting rights with an amendment to the US Constitution. He would just as soon marry and fill a household with boisterous children. Wilmer's ancestors had marched off into the unknown wearing military uniforms during the American Revolution, the War of 1812, and the Civil War.[2] Edna's family of Quakers believed in nonviolence. They refused to participate in war and bloody conflicts.

As Wilmer and Edna lost awareness of anyone but each other, the teahouse server carried a pastry canister to their table filled with crumpets, almond biscuits, and sponge cake. They sent her away and made the scones and marmalade on their plates last. Granddaddy didn't have enough money in his pocket for more than was set before them. And he didn't want to refer to himself as a "starving student."

Wilmer said Edna's collection of artistic street scenes puzzled him as much as they intrigued him. The plain people—also known as Quakers, Mennonites, Amish, Hutterites, Moravians, Brethren, and other religious nonconformists—led him to view Edna's sketches as more associated with spirituality and prayer than representing secular landscapes. Edna studied art, a choice she made that caused awkward silences at her family's dinner table. Her mother May would have preferred that her daughter travel as a minister, like Quaker Lucretia Mott, and minimize her curiosity about music, art, and dancing.

Edna hummed under her breath the next morning so her mother wouldn't hear. She was usually conflicted or distracted by one issue or another. This included her husband extending his business trips to Harrisburg a day longer than expected. She worried about the accumulated clutter in Edna's bedroom, as well as Edna's brother Smythe talking back to a teacher at a Quaker school. One incident had been so serious that he'd been expelled. Mrs. Buckman was concerned about Edna reading too many "worldly" books, unsuited in her opinion, for her daughter's spiritual development.

Edna decided to study art that, in her mother's view, was the ruin of many young women. "Ruin? I don't think this applies to the spiritually motivated artistic expressions of folk painter Edward Hicks," Edna responded. Hicks was a Bucks County Quaker minister and artist who had commercial success painting religious subject matter until his death in 1849. His canvases featured William Penn, native peoples, and over fifty versions of an oil painting referred to as *The Peaceable Kingdom*. This Quaker vision of peaceful coexistence was based on the concept of a shared "Inner Light" inherent in all life forms.

Edna said nothing to her mother about meeting Wilmer Kearns. May would find fault with the couple not being "properly introduced." Wilmer exhibited perfect manners at the teahouse, but Edna could tell from the expression on his face that he longed for an opportunity to see her again. She told him about the Quaker boardinghouse on East Fifteenth Street in New York City, the Penington, where he could rent a room after moving to Manhattan for his first job. Edna liked Wilmer, but he wasn't the type her mother would support as a boyfriend. Or at least she didn't think so.

A copy of Margaret Fuller's *Woman in the Nineteenth Century* fell from Granddaddy's kitchen bookshelf. Edna liked reading Margaret Fuller, a transcendentalist and writer. Granddaddy encouraged me to think for myself like Fuller. So I wasn't surprised when a piece of paper fell out of the Fuller book, along with a paragraph in Edna's handwriting dealing with the importance of "small things." It had no date.

Although Swiss psychiatrist Carl Jung developed a theory of synchronicity relative to meaningful coincidences, I didn't hear about it until after reaching adulthood. That's how I realized there must be underlying reasons why fireflies flash in unison, birds have the ability to fly in formation, and grandmothers send messages to granddaughters like me by way of a book or a piece of paper falling onto the floor. When Edna spoke or wrote, Wilmer said his breath froze in his throat. Mine did too, but it was too soon to mention it to anyone.

SMALL THINGS

All the great issues of life have been the outcome of "small things," they forming the steppingstones by which such issues have been reached. Even the cup of cold water extended to a fellow wayfarer has been the means of helping and encouraging him on his way, and at the same time ennobling and elevating our own moral natures . . .

Edna Buckman Kearns.[3]

Chapter 3

Granddaddy Wilmer

I asked Granddaddy twice to tell me the story about him standing in front of a German restaurant on the Lower East Side of New York City staring at pastries on a display case shelf. He paused one evening to decide if he had enough cash for dinner and a beer. The restaurant window facing the street didn't muffle vibrations from a ballad played inside on an off-tune piano. The aroma of potatoes with butter served with schnitzel drifted with the opening and closing of restaurant doors.

Granddaddy moved from Philadelphia to New York for his first job as an employee in the accounting department of T. J. Dunn, a cigar manufacturer. Wilmer told me that his insecurities about his job and Edna could be numbed with an order of red beet soup. Even at my young age, I picked up on how nervous and insecure he must have felt. Edna liked Wilmer, but she must have also wondered if they were compatible. Granddaddy studied the restaurant menu before choosing a platter of sauerbraten, parsley potatoes, and a stein of dark lager beer. Then he visited the water closet before checking a nearby shelf for pamphlets or a copy of the Sunday *New York Times*. An accordion player performed traditional German melodies to accompany raucous oompah songs performed with loud baritone voices.

When the young Wilmer Kearns strolled through Manhattan's streets toward the German restaurant and beer hall, he passed by buildings on the Lower East Side of Manhattan housing thousands. Many were new arrivals from around the world, processed through Ellis Island. Residents on some streets were neighbors from the same villages in Europe. The buildings were, for the most part, without adequate lighting and sanitation. The Penington was located in a brownstone building on East Fifteenth Street, operational since 1897. Named after Isaac Penington, a prominent English Quaker, the boardinghouse offered rooms at a reasonable price and was exactly what Wilmer needed. He hoped that living there would give him a better understanding of Quakers.

Granddaddy found solitude on the other side of the Meeting House door at 15 Rutherford Place. He chose an empty bench and settled into meditative silence to reflect on the impact of falling in love with Edna May Buckman, a ninth-generation Quaker from Philadelphia. She must have other eligible men interested in her, he thought, no doubt Quakers. Granddaddy said he asked himself, "What does Edna see in me?" And then the reminder surfaced. She insisted they become "just friends."

Wilmer Kearns, who'd been raised and churched in Pennsylvania Dutch country, faced the fact that Edna and her Quaker ancestors refused to engage in violence, whereas his Lutheran ancestors and extended family members thought little about joining the military. I knew Wilmer as my Quaker grandfather. Edna fell in love with him in her late teens and eventually he married her, but not before he became a Quaker himself. I did the math and counted on my fingers. "That makes me an eleventh-generation Quaker," I said. Granddaddy nodded in agreement.

My grandfather left his kitchen curtains open for light to come in from a winter sky filled with clouds of snow prepared to fall on the Montgomery County, Pennsylvania, landscape of my childhood. Some days when I visited Wilmer, he agonized over what to do with my grandmother's horse-drawn suffrage campaign wagon.

"It should be in a museum," he said.

I stared out of Granddaddy's kitchen window as snowflakes fell, faster and thicker. They stuck against his garage walls. I raised my right eyebrow like Granddaddy did when speaking about Edna. By his response, I could tell that I'd pulled off a poor imitation. Wilmer wasn't always serious when telling me stories about Edna. He also played with words and teased me with affectionate jokes.

"Did Edna ever get tired of marching in parades and riding in that old horse-drawn wagon?" I asked.

"Edna didn't like to admit it, but she did—though rarely," he told me. "She could be impulsive, like a volcano ready to explode. I was there for her when she stood on soapboxes to speak about voting rights. Edna was like her mother. Determined to be seen and heard."

Granddaddy told me Edna demonstrated her skill when recruiting others. She rarely wanted anything for herself personally. If she asked someone to march in parades, attend lectures and protests, or sign petitions, they didn't refuse. Many friends and neighbors signed her petitions for state and national suffrage special elections, and they offered financial support by making donations.

I sensed Edna in my grandfather's living space. She followed me to elementary school. I reached for a copy of Mary Wollstonecraft's 1792 work and feminist classic, *A Vindication of the Rights of Woman*, on my grandfather's bookshelf. I tried to read Wollstonecraft, but the text made no sense. "Too ancient," I thought.

I was sure Edna placed her soft hand on my shoulder, reminding me of warm silk, as if to suggest that she counted on me for something. I had no idea why I bonded with Edna early in my childhood, other than the emotional impact of dressing up in her votes for women parade dresses and sashes. I closed my eyes when listening to Granddaddy and filled my lungs with the imagined scent of the pink and red roses pinned into my grandmother's hair. I struggled to peek beyond the backdrop of my limited vision and wasn't sure if I disappeared into a trance. Haze filled the empty spaces of my awareness with an unfiltered light. I settled into deep breathing. If I mentioned any of this at school, a teacher might suggest I was delusional and should concentrate instead on reality—the present, not the past or future.

Edna May Buckman as a young woman, circa 1903.

Edna didn't say much to Wilmer at first about her "leading," a Quaker reference to combining her spiritual practice with action. Quakers closely examined their leadings, with the idea that these impulses should be linked to divine realms, rather than hobbies or projects grounded in ambition and pride. Granddaddy agreed to Edna's condition of "just friends," although it was clear to me that he was already in love. A reading of Edna's glances at him suggested that the curiosity might be mutual. Wilmer Kearns, however, couldn't take this Quaker woman for granted.

"Of course the votes for women campaigning wasn't all it should have been," Granddaddy told me as his eyes lowered. The way he stared at the kitchen floor, I couldn't meet his gaze. I continued to be mystified by a great deal of what he told me. Wilmer was opinionated. This much I knew. He wrote poems to protest the social and economic order, also well over my head.

"Sure, there will always be those who will say the US movement to win voting rights was about some women and not others. And we were called on the carpet because the Nineteenth Amendment to the Constitution in 1920 barely passed under

VIEW FROM THE BATTERY.

Statue of Liberty in the distance from Battery Park, New York Harbor, late 1800s.
Library of Congress.

the wire," Granddaddy said. "I never claimed to be more than a regular guy who stood up with his wife and daughter and demanded equal rights for everyone."

This sounded logical, although I had no confidence in telling this to others with the same enthusiasm of my grandfather. Listening to him with my eyes closed involved me falling through darkness. My ears popped. I bounced against interior walls to slow a forward rush into the unknown. Moonlight crept up hillsides, and stars showered light on mountain peaks and the marching suffrage sisterhood. Granddaddy explained that Edna worked from dawn to dusk on freedom issues for more than a decade while he was busy at an office job. Volunteering for a social cause became a labor of love.

Granddaddy was convinced little would change in the larger society unless the "dirty fish bowl" of the social system was replaced with what many Quakers called an ocean of free thought and unity. When listening to Wilmer's stories, I paid attention, but not as carefully as, years later, now, I wished I had. Winning women's voting rights impressed me as a long, uphill, and complicated drama.

Granddaddy told me about Bess, Edna's close friend, and how she belonged to what he called the "soapbox generation." Young women like Bess turned their backs on gender limitations and spoke out in public about their impatience with a social system of men at the top, with women and others lined up in descending order in the direction of the bottom. My grandfather wove Bess into his narratives. Bess grew up with Edna, next door, on Rubicam Avenue in the Germantown section of Philadelphia. Edna was practical and steeped in the tradition of being a Quaker—understated and quiet. Bess could be described as a loud and opinionated rebel who tried to jump through the traditional female hoops but failed.

Bess and Edna were critical of their contemporaries who didn't question the social and economic hierarchy. An increasing number of young activists ventured into the public arena to speak to anyone who would listen about civil and human rights.

This is believed to be Edna's best friend, Bess, who grew up with Edna in the Germantown section of Philadelphia, circa 1907.

They represented the restless citizens of the nation, those convinced that American women couldn't win the franchise if they persisted in addressing the issue state by state and quietly, behind the scenes.

Bess and others like her raised the eyebrows of their fathers, brothers, and other male relatives. These discontented young women grew up in large and small cities, as well as on the prairies, in the South, New England, and communities in the far West. Many enrolled in colleges and programs established for females after administrators in mainstream male institutions of higher learning refused to allow women to sit next to men in classrooms and lecture halls.

Those in the emerging soapbox generation discovered quickly that speeches challenging the top-bottom social hierarchy could be risky. Support for equal rights and the franchise for women set them up for being splashed with buckets of water, pelted with eggs, assaulted with tobacco plugs and derogatory labels, including "crowing hen," "shrieking sister," and worse. Bess didn't believe in marriage because a young woman after a ceremony was transformed into her husband's property and then denied basic rights, including the right to vote.

"Aren't you afraid for your safety?" one man called out as he passed an activist lecturing from a park bench the afternoon Granddaddy took me to Battery Park by way of his storytelling. When she approached Wilmer with a suffrage petition, I felt no compelling need to return to my so-called ordinary reality of childhood. I loved the predictable twirling descent when I left Granddaddy's kitchen and headed toward the unseen dimensions of lower Manhattan. There, the soapbox speaker could be described as spontaneous and free-spirited. Granddaddy put it this way: "Young women like this knew their own minds, and they were determined to push ahead rather than stay in their own female sphere."

"I have every intention of being a modern woman," the young activist lectured from a bench platform. Women with their hands pressed firmly around their escorts' elbows avoided walking too close to the speaker. Most Battery Park pedestrians considered this new type of woman brazen, undignified, and confrontational, unworthy of even a glance in her direction. I cheered on the young woman from the chair in my grandfather's kitchen. She represented a role model for me, just like Edna.

Granddaddy told me that an increasing number of young women in the soapbox generation had the courage to say "no" to being treated like girls under the age of twelve. Those coming of age like Edna and Bess refused to tolerate jokes and anecdotes implying that females had no sense of humor because they didn't consider their secondary social standing something to kid about.

Edna considered direct action an appropriate response to injustice, according to Granddaddy, although her friend Bess insisted on immediate, not gradual, change. Edna believed in more education about the importance of women taking a meaningful role in political decision making. She supported women's voting rights, a reliance on petitioning elected officials, and the exercise of freedom of speech. If this didn't prove to be effective, direct and militant action would be justified, according to my grandmother.

Bess defined herself as pessimistic about working within the existing social and economic system. As far as she was concerned, women activists in England were ahead in terms of challenging elected officials directly.[1] Edna didn't approve of tactics she considered violent, whereas Bess demanded that the entire US social and economic system be replaced, by whatever means necessary. Edna supported working within the social and economic framework. Bess didn't see any value in patriarchy and capitalism continuing, either in substance or form. "It just doesn't work," she was fond of saying. "And as soon as there's reform, a new opposition springs up to destroy it."

I imagined Bess wearing a shirtwaist frock and riding a bicycle through Philadelphia's city streets where onlookers admired her as tall and well proportioned. Her small waist and a tumbling waterfall of brown curls down her back gave the impression of her being elegant and eligible. Then Bess shifted her attention to spreading a message about how equal rights wouldn't be possible without radically changing the social and economic system.

"Bess had pluck," Granddaddy said, using a term common in that era when describing a feisty young person with spirit and courage.

Bess experienced a rush of freedom when feeling the soft push of the wind on her back when riding a bike. She drew the line at wearing clothing designed to limit women in movement and, by extension, thought. Her bedroom closet at home had one "bloomer" outfit, a combination of a dress and pants style, convenient for sports, bike riding, and standing on platforms to speak in public. Granddaddy said Edna and Bess didn't hesitate to ask anyone to sign a petition in support of votes for women. And Bess didn't hide her preference for expressing herself personally in a manner many found offensive. She shouted, argued, and resisted her father's tight control.

Granddaddy hadn't thought much about women's rights until he met Edna. Out in Central Pennsylvania where he'd been raised, social stratification wasn't as institutionalized as in urban areas. Wilmer had acquired little information about the larger organizing campaigns for women's voting rights. Of course he'd heard about Elizabeth Cady Stanton's death a few years before and the imminent retirement of her Quaker activist associate, Susan B. Anthony, but little else. During the visit to Battery Park, a suffrage soapbox speaker invited Wilmer to accompany her on a walk where she filled him in about those stepping into leadership positions such as Carrie Chapman Catt, Anna Howard Shaw, and Harriot Stanton Blatch. She called them a preview of the next stage of national votes for women leadership.

"I don't know much about Catt, Shaw, and Blatch," Wilmer told her.

"They're carrying on The Cause," the activist explained. "More women than ever are stepping forward. It's a gradual uprising. We're organizing in our own neighborhoods and communities before taking on the state and nation."

"Opening a few doors to women doesn't include real access to the halls of power. A few rights granted by all-male legislatures can always be taken away. What do you think is next?" Granddaddy asked the activist.

"Younger and different kinds of women joining us," she answered with emphasis. "We need men allies like you, those who aren't afraid of being called names. We're ready to push all the way to an amendment to the US Constitution to guarantee a woman's right to vote."

"How can you be sure the ballot will make a difference?" Wilmer responded.

"It's about time we're invited to sit at the table of power. So we'll keep on speaking on street corners, passing out leaflets, writing letters, congregating in lecture halls and teahouses. Sign our petition. We're standing up and doing whatever it takes until freedom, justice, and equality are ours. We're getting ready to finish the unfinished revolution of 1776."

"Privilege, sadly, is embedded in many human brains," Granddaddy told her.

It was more complicated than this, and my grandfather didn't expect me to grasp the mores and traditions of an era different than mine.

"The men at the office weren't much different than others walking the streets. They were convinced females were irrational, inferior, and emotionally unbalanced," my grandfather told me when describing his associates working in the New York City accounting division of T. J. Dunn. He said his coworkers pontificated over puffs on cigars and shots of whiskey during evening gatherings in saloons and cafés. Granddaddy told me he'd heard the same justifications in support of the status quo, including: "It has always been this way—with men in charge—as far back as the Bible and then some. Nothing will change because women operate with half a deck."

My grandfather said many men spoke about the necessity of females continuing to fill roles as companions to men, instead of viewing them as independent agents in pursuit of their own interests and ambitions. Women's lifestyles were expected to be supportive to men, with occasional rewards, including instances when men eased awkward situations by opening doors or giving up their seats to women on trolleys and trains.

I didn't realize that many anti-suffrage speeches and leaflets featured positions stating that women shouldn't concern themselves with voting and "corrupt" politics. Some men of Granddaddy's acquaintance placed women on pedestals, worshipped them in these elevated states, and assigned them to be in charge of moral and ethical matters or a woman's "sphere." Men were viewed as qualified to vote on behalf of the women in their families. Women weren't expected to complain. This crash course in the social and economic system wasn't easy for me to grasp. My strength was in my perpetual little-girl smile that covered over my innocence and inability to believe that such a social situation existed.

Wilmer told me he couldn't tolerate listening to remarks from his work colleagues justifying second-class citizenship for women. Edna and Bess kept a distance from those who used condescending and caustic remarks to devalue women of all backgrounds. Many men neglected to mention much about the females in their families, other than the size of womanly waistlines and whether or not females nagged their husbands or fathers. The majority of males, according to Granddaddy, presented themselves as logical and responsible. In private, they viewed women as overly emotional and immature. No one had ever expressed the situation to me as clearly as Granddaddy. I couldn't adjust to the idea of growing up in such a world, so I decided that if I listened to enough stories I'd discover later that my grandparents' generation fixed all of these issues.

"Won't voting add to women's burdens and responsibilities?" Wilmer asked Edna. "And what if women graduate from colleges, serve in public office, and then hold jobs in offices and factories where they lose or forget their moral influence?"

"Voting should be a choice," Edna told Wilmer. "Right now, we have no choice. It's said that our movement is stuck, that our supporters and strategies are rigid and resemble deadwood."

Only after accumulating more life experience would I later realize that the opposition to equality included some women themselves, those who sucked emotional juice from men instead of working from within themselves to build personal power. And all of this turned out to be even more complicated. Most everyone had been contaminated by the limitations surrounding them, he claimed, and they were damaged by it. Many in my grandparents' generation worked to reform the social and economic social system, not replace it. So they lived with the limitations, just as they were branded and contained by the social and economic factors they'd inherited.

Granddaddy told me that Edna had noticed a trend under way whereby more suffrage organizations were in formation, rather than fewer. She disliked the infighting among voting rights activists and predicted that women's campaigns wouldn't get anywhere if activists continued working within a loose coalition that resulted in factional divisions.

Granddaddy said Edna told him on more than one occasion, "It boils down to taxation without representation. This is tyranny. It must be resisted."

I clenched my teeth and gripped the armrests on a chair next to Wilmer's kitchen window when hearing more about what my grandparents faced. I got the impression that they might not have succeeded in changing the situation enough to make it clear sailing when I came of age. If only my grandparents would set the record straight, I might be able to navigate the rocky journey to high school and beyond. But I was young and inexperienced in my attempt to understand how the outside world might not receive me, as a female, with open arms. My learning took place in Wilmer's kitchen where one part of me traveled by way of storytelling into the unknown where I had the ability to create the environment I longed for, instead of what my grandfather suggested waited for me.

I assumed that Granddaddy had accepted Edna's condition of "just friends" and then he satisfied himself with her letters. I opened my eyes and stretched before returning to a time warp where Wilmer Kearns, as a young man, wore his pinstriped suit. He passed by sunny Manhattan shop windows to check on the reflection of how his trousers, jacket, and vest fit. Aron, the Polish tailor, gave him a good price for the outfit, but the garment had become snug around his waist since the final fitting.

"Bread, butter, and beer at the German restaurant were my downfall," Granddaddy told me when reflecting on how he scolded himself about gaining extra pounds. Visiting the restaurant and beer hall represented one of Wilmer's few pleasures. After skimping on the noon meal, he treated himself to a stein of dark stout during evenings when residents of Kleindeutschland, Little Germany or Dutchtown, crowded into restaurants and beer gardens located in lower Manhattan. Patrons played billiards or chess. They read the works of Schiller or Goethe, told stories, drank, and listened to music.

Granddaddy filled in empty parts of his tale with the anarchists, atheists, agnostics, union organizers, and freethinkers marching in New York City's annual May Day parade. Misfits to maniacs and scholars pounded on café tables to protest injustice, an end to private ownership, and a commitment to redistributing wealth. They argued over whether Theodore Roosevelt should explore an independent course after taking over the Oval Office following the assassination of US president William McKinley on September 6, 1901.

"I raised my fist and clapped until both hands turned red during rallies and demonstrations," Wilmer admitted. He shared concerns with me about the increased strength of monopolies and trusts, bank failures, government policies of imperialism, and efforts to control the excesses of capitalism, even if Granddaddy felt pessimistic about his own ability to change any of it.

"I couldn't see how we'd dig ourselves out of this mess," he told me. He found New Yorkers to be credible, in addition to being "quirky rascals." Granddaddy couldn't imagine how overcrowded city buildings could ever be made livable for the generations of humanity arriving daily in New York City. I followed Wilmer's accounts about leaving his hat and jacket behind in his rented room at the Penington boardinghouse.[2] Then he hooked his right thumb into his vest pocket and headed out for a hike in the direction of the Brooklyn Bridge. I couldn't wait to find out when he'd meet Edna again at the Market Street teahouse. Granddaddy no longer mentioned to my mother the details of the afternoons we spent together.

Chapter 4

"Dish Rags" and "She-Men"

"*D*ish rags."

"She-men."

"Clear the way," the Washington, DC, police officers shouted.

"Who's gonna fix dinner tonight? You, a husbandette?" roared more voices from the sidewalk opposition with their disparagement and slurs spit out with jets of raw tobacco juice.

"Get a shave, you suffering dish rag."

I would have liked it better if my grandfather had moved ahead in his storytelling in a chronological fashion, continuing after Wilmer met Edna in 1902, although I didn't complain. For all I knew, too many special requests might make Granddaddy retreat to his beloved flower garden.

"Traitor. Sissy," hecklers bellowed as the women's demonstration inched forward. Men marchers and women students from Howard University, an African American private university in the nation's capital, stood out as targets for taunts, assaults, and accusations. From the moment Wilmer Kearns took his place in the men's division on Pennsylvania Avenue, Granddaddy said he sensed the resistance and pushback. The women called it a "procession." Others called it a march or demonstration. My grandfather said he hadn't expected the opposition to have such a presence. He said resistance to women voting wasn't new, but Black activists and men marching in public to reach a national audience in support of the expansion of civil rights—this was unprecedented.[1]

I glanced at the clock. My mother would arrive within the hour to take me home for dinner. There we were—Granddaddy and me—preparing to march by way of storytelling. I would have preferred that my grandfather start from where he left off, back after he met Edna in 1902. I clenched my fists. The name calling and yelling in Washington, DC, worried me. I tried not to look frightened, although I was.

"A riot," Granddaddy told me. "I felt one on its way."

My grandfather said he sensed attack from all sides, from so many pushers and shovers on the sidewalks, spilling into the street, to internal conflicts within the parade organization. One reaction was ingrained in him, as it was for many men, to respond to opposition with force. He'd promised the parade organizers, however, that if he marched in the men's division, he wouldn't exchange violence with violence. This was basic in Quaker faith and practice, exactly what I'd been taught.

Crowds on Pennsylvania Avenue overwhelming the March 3, 1913, women's suffrage procession due to inadequate crowd control by local police. The resulting injuries led to congressional hearings. Library of Congress.

The parade problems piled up. Word spread about white women from Southern states threatening to withdraw if a contingent of students from Howard University marched down Pennsylvania Avenue. After this threat, Granddaddy Wilmer told me he'd heard word from other marchers about attorney Inez Milholland's warning. She'd refuse to ride her horse, Gray Dawn, at the front of the procession if the Howard University students didn't participate. The situation became clearer. My grandfather called it a "paper trail." This meant assembling a record, an archive, proof of what later could substantiate patterns. "When things seem tough, Quakers become a 'witness.'" Granddaddy showed me what Edna had preserved in writing in the *South Side Observer*, published on March 14, 1913:

Down in Washington, I spoke to Miss Alice Paul, chairman of the parade committee. She is a Quaker, a Swarthmore College girl and suffered imprisonment in Holloway Jail [in England] six weeks, undergoing a hunger strike. Miss Paul said that when Rosalie Jones and her hikers reached Washington, she realized that the parade would need more protection than they at first supposed, so she went to President Taft, who referred her to Secretary of War Stimson. Mr. Stimson, who is an openly acknowledged anti-suffragist, refused to provide troops, but said if there was any disorder the troops would be sent out.

I understand the troops from Fort Myer were called out, but I saw six men on horseback mowing the crowds down, and after they had passed by, instead of the policemen keeping the crowd back, they allowed them to fall right back again. I must confess I thought troops meant soldiers, but I have much to learn . . .[2]

If Edna admitted she had a great deal to learn, I was right there with her in what I needed to understand. Granddaddy said that Quakers played an essential role

Serena Kearns participated in the early women's rights movement with her parents, circa 1915.

in standing up for peace when strident patriotism pressured usually calm people to become aggressive and occasionally violent. He told me: "Concerned people must stand firm and make sure peaceful tactics are kept alive."

Oh, that's how it works, I thought. I tried not to react when Wilmer told me about onlookers spilling out of taverns and saloons anxious for a confrontation. Granddaddy said that those like himself in the men's division took twelve steps along Pennsylvania Avenue and then stopped, followed by fifteen steps, and then fifty before waiting again. The district police didn't control verbal abuse from the sidelines. And without specific orders from their superiors, many police officers stood off to the side, passive.[3] The marchers started out four and six abreast. Within several blocks, hostile crowds closed in again on the avenue, and they bumped up against the protesters.

"Do you boys expect your mommies to change your poopy diapers? They're more into voting than punishing traitors like you."

Granddaddy winced when telling me this, adding that he'd never been in such a tight space with no exit. At least he wasn't reluctant to say that everything didn't always turn out in a predictable way. He said the crowds on Pennsylvania Avenue were like branches with barbs surrounding him in all directions. Critics jostled with their shoulders, mouths open, spitting and spewing words of contempt and sarcasm.

"I could barely breathe. I had to do something," Granddaddy said.

"Will you she-men have dinner ready at home?" the street venting continued.

"Hurry and get out of there as fast as you can, Granddaddy," I sputtered. I felt my own defensive reactions building inside me. Would the marchers get out of Washington, DC, without being attacked? And what about the students from Howard University? Would they survive pushback from the sidewalks? And would the parade organizers straighten out this mess?

"The women marchers, across the board, didn't roll over easily in the face of resistance," Wilmer said. "I had to respond. So I hissed."

My grandfather reached for my hand, and his fingers soothed mine. His arms were covered with dust and dirt from planting daffodil bulbs. He smelled of sweat as he stared at me with raised eyebrows. I pulled away, but he kept on rubbing my fingers. I hoped my grandparents' generation was determined enough to respond to these challenges. And little Serena Kearns, my mother's older sister, was the same age at the 1913 parade as I was the summer I listened to Granddaddy's stories in his kitchen.

"The women must have been sick and tired of demanding their rights," I told my grandfather.

"I was sure the parade would end badly," he said, "but I couldn't do much about it, penned in as I was with the men."

"But Granddaddy, you were a witness."

"Thee is right," he responded. This was typical of us, with Granddaddy speaking in Quaker plain speech while I responded in conventional conversation.

My grandfather told me that men over glasses of port predicted the women's march wouldn't add up to more than a few attention seekers performing in public for newspaper reporters. Inside barrooms, parlors, and drawing rooms all over the nation's capital the night before the parade, the resistance accelerated. As dawn arrived on March 3, 1913, thousands of protesters arrived at Union Station, the city's train terminal, from all over the US and other parts of the world. Wilmer, Edna, and little Serena were among them. Some put the total of procession participants at five thousand. Area newspapers published figures as high as ten thousand individuals determined to attract attention to this demonstration of women's public power.

"Sure, the drunken mobs howled," Granddaddy told me. "They threw burning cigarettes and matches at us men. Those sluggards were roaring drunk and furious, while I sweated in the freezing March air and didn't stop hissing."

"Politics is a filthy business. Go back to the kitchen, girls," one of the street critics shouted. "Henpecko." My grandfather bit his thumbnail when telling me this. It wasn't the kind of story grandchildren liked hearing. The narratives led back to Edna, and I was learning how to be quick on my feet. I couldn't wait to hear about the day Edna purchased her wedding dress. And unless Granddaddy expanded the tale again, I could still be waiting until Labor Day to find out about the wedding dress.

The Kearns family had arrived on the train from New York City the morning of March 3, 1913, to join those filling the Washington, DC, streets with march participants and their delegations, floats, bands, horses, automobiles, and banners. Wilmer stood straight in the parade formation with the other men, on edge about responding to the street opposition. Only the cavalry's arrival from nearby Fort Myer broke up what might otherwise have turned into a full-scale unmanageable protest.

"Saved by the liberty bell," I said in my most grown-up sixth grade voice, and my grandfather made a face before moving to the end of the story.

"Finally, we men moved ahead on the line of march," Granddaddy said, emphasizing that he shouted, "Get out of our way."

I had no idea that the 1913 women's march on Washington represented a major turning point in the votes for women campaigning. I wasn't familiar with the symbolic significance of such a high-profile demonstration in the heart of the nation's capital and how it would impact the strategic and tactical decisions of other protesters in the future. I didn't realize that this particular event in Washington, DC, was the first large protest of women in the nation's history. Until then, Wilmer and Edna had joined with smaller versions of suffrage marches prior to 1913 in New York City. This was news to me.

This demonstration of women's power was significantly different in size and significance than ever before. Organizers scheduled the parade for the day before US president-elect Woodrow Wilson's inauguration. Some observers went so far as to claim the women upstaged the incoming president. An elementary school kid like me wasn't able to grasp all the challenges facing a divided movement of votes for women organizations and supporters in a fragile coalition lacking overall agreement on values, strategies, and tactics.[4]

Granddaddy told me the suffrage campaigners weren't monolithic. I had no clue what he meant. From what I heard, the march participants seemed orderly and organized when concentrating on the single theme on which they agreed—that women should

Serena Kearns (*far right*) was a seasoned movement poster child. She is shown here in a suffrage pageant at the Metropolitan Opera in New York City, 1913.

have the right to vote. When and how legislation granting women the ballot should be enacted became contentious as the twentieth century progressed, according to my grandfather. Passing laws to fix this problem was new to me, but it seemed logical. I had to rely on adults to help me figure this out.

Some suffrage supporters believed only white women should vote and the process of reform should be confined state by state instead of being shifted to a national level. Others insisted that all women should vote, period. Many, like Edna's friend Bess, were of the opinion that the entire social system should be abolished so women could start over. I realized only later how much polarization haunted early women's rights activists. And the day of the parade in Washington, DC, the polarization was close to the surface. The so-called national suffrage movement didn't speak with one voice, and my grandfather made a priority of drilling this into my head.

"Did those on the sidewalks tell Edna to go home and take care of her husband and daughter?" I asked Wilmer.

"It was unusual to see a child like Serena at protests," he said. And it had also been a shock for Americans, he added, to see Black women as well as men in the lineups. Even a young person like me many years later didn't miss the obvious—that a votes for women demonstration in the nation's capital was impressive. It took me years to realize that joining with the men's division was excellent preparation for my grandfather's involvement in other women's rights activities. He told me about one photo documenting his involvement in a New York City suffrage parade in 1913, although I didn't discover it until many years later.[5]

Men marching in a suffrage parade in New York City, May 1913. Wilmer Kearns is believed to be in the center, behind another marcher, wearing a straw hat. Library of Congress.

Edna's writing style when describing the Washington, DC parade was relaxed and formal yet opinionated. And it seemed directed at me so I could understand. Edna had this to say about the large women's procession in early March of 1913:

> Those of us who marched in the Friends or Quaker division wore the Quaker bonnet and garb. Spectators tried to pull our capes off of us, the policemen laughing at their crude remarks and actions. . . . My little daughter's face was not slapped but sapped by drunken men all along the line. They also pulled at her bonnet, and not one policeman I spoke to paid any attention. . . .
>
> Mr. Kearns marched with the men's league and he said that if the men had not had instructions from the parade committee to be dignified, not to talk or resent insults, that there would have been a riot, for it was all our men could do to keep their hands off the crowd. They were fighting mad, with many declaring the next day that they believed in militancy.
>
> Imagine my horror the next day at hearing my husband Wilmer hiss the chief of police, Major Sylvester, and all the men around me also began to hiss him. I understand he was hissed all along the line . . .
>
> Our women, through it all, were quiet and orderly. They marched in silent dignity.[6]

Chapter 5

An Unlikely Couple

"Will I become a Quaker man and marry Edna?" Wilmer told me he asked his pendulum in 1903, a crystal with a hole drilled through so it hung from a string. Granddaddy was finally back to his story, told to me in chronological order. He didn't tell Edna about his pendulum. Quakers listened to a small voice within, not messages from a crystal dangling from a string.

As he waited for his dinner at the German restaurant on the Lower East Side, my grandfather held his breath as the pendulum moved hesitantly in the direction of "yes." He was on his way to becoming a Quaker man deserving of marrying Edna. He wondered if his new pocket watch affected the pendulum's ability to perform properly.

Edna wouldn't approve of a pendulum. She would advise him to choose silence and search for answers to his questions by consulting the internal Inner Light. Granddaddy hadn't reached this stage of spiritual development, he told me. Some days it seemed as if the crystal had a mind of its own, as if it suggested a power beyond earth-based reality. On other occasions, the pendulum vibrated in its zeal to deliver an answer, even if the outcome ended as an affirmation of indecision.

Wilmer hung the pendulum on a nail on the window frame in his rented room where he waited until dawn to see if the object absorbed beams from the outside light. It did, but a basic question remained. What about the future? Would Edna and Wilmer get together? I had myself as proof. If they hadn't married and birthed children, I wouldn't be in my grandfather's kitchen. Quakers spoke often about divine light. Wilmer told me he vowed to tap this source of spiritual strength, if only he could figure out how.

Edna relied on her own sense of internal direction, he said. Seasoned Quakers also referred to divine spirit as the "internal teacher" or the universal light or life force. Granddaddy longed for a handy supply of this for himself. He asked the Quaker men boarding at the Penington to help him understand this source. Few could assist other than suggest that Granddaddy's search include "plowing." In this, the hard soil of his soul could be turned over and the seed of the divine might sprout. No one could be converted to the Society of Friends like in other churches, the Quaker men at the Penington emphasized. A seeker had to be "convinced" of the Truth of an Inner Light, which might lead to membership, but only after reflection.

I followed Wilmer to the German beer hall by way of his story. In the restaurant he moved a breadbasket aside to make room for a hot platter of German sausage and fried potatoes. Granddaddy said he couldn't brush aside doubts about Edna's friend Bess and the fascination she had with the French woman writer who published under the man's name of George Sand. Bess said otherwise Sand wouldn't have been taken seriously as a writer.

Bess and Edna made promises to each other as teenagers to remain single and not marry. This carried with it a not-so-veiled conclusion that a young woman didn't need a man to marry for her to feel whole, creative, and content. Edna would never become wholly his, nor would Wilmer want her to be. This was heady material to tell a youngster like me. Once Granddaddy started sharing tales, the memories could pour out of his head so quickly he might forget the impact it might have on me.

Another nagging thought surfaced. What would life be like if Wilmer didn't spend his life with Edna? With her by his side, my grandfather would be in the front lines of action in a new century. Without her, he might suffocate in the boredom of a conventional relationship with someone else. Another sip of lager beer at the restaurant relieved him of the pressure of stale air at T. J. Dunn's factory sites in Manhattan. Experienced cigar rollers insisted that workroom windows be closed so tobacco leaves wouldn't dry too fast to roll cigars into custom-made shapes. Without Edna, Granddaddy might face decades of stale air if married to a woman without Edna's inner resources.

Wilmer Kearns ordered another serving of hot rolls. He had every intention of treating Edna as an equal. If being in love with her meant he'd become a Quaker, it made sense for him to seriously consider such a commitment. If she insisted on volunteering as a rights activist, he wouldn't stand in her way. He lit another five-cent cigar. Edna might change her mind about marriage, but then again, she might not. He agreed with her views about men and women working together and was convinced that those in their generation were capable of committing themselves to partnership, openness, and honesty. Like-minded people should work together, she told him, not against each other. This made sense in the abstract. Wilmer told me he hoped Edna was right.

The aroma of German sweet and sour sauces from the restaurant's kitchen, the full tones of the accordion, and the loud laughter of men and women filling every seat in the restaurant left Wilmer feeling drowsy. He yawned. In Little Germany in Manhattan, a night out on the town like this demanded that he savor every bite of sausage and potatoes as well as empty his stein of beer. If he became a Quaker, he'd have to set aside an acquired taste for extravagant foods and alcoholic drinks. Would it be worth it to make Edna a priority in order to build a future and a family with her? In my mind, there was only one answer to this. Yes.

"For heaven's sake, I'm moving forward," Wilmer said he repeated to himself as he set out his shaving brush and bowl one morning in his rented room after returning from visiting Edna in Philadelphia. He'd set aside a 1903 Sunday afternoon with her at the Market Street teahouse before returning to Manhattan. When he referred to the last day of the weekend as Sunday, Edna reminded him she called it "First Day," another peculiarity of Quakers he'd have to remember. Granddaddy considered himself close to putting drinking beer behind him. But he wasn't ready to cross the line to the point of mentioning marriage. I gasped and longed to ask, "What about the wedding dress?" But I didn't, as my grandfather mulled over another issue surfacing in his awareness—if women deserved freedom, what about the freedom of men?

Granddaddy didn't like being an outsider among his peers at the accounting office. He didn't tell most men of his acquaintance in New York about the woman-owned teahouse back in Philadelphia or the lectures he attended with Edna about gender equality at Plymouth Meeting. I figured he'd work through the difficulties of supporting Edna financially, assuming, of course, they became engaged and married. My grandfather told me he didn't dare hope. The flames of a desperate courage eluded him. Better to keep such expectations to himself and not reveal any opinions at the office that might later result in shame, embarrassment, or guilt. His college colleagues might label him a traitor to his gender because of his support of women's rights.

Wilmer couldn't tell Edna much without revealing how many evenings he spent at the German beer garden. After hours there, Wilmer avoided contact with the Quaker men at the boardinghouse. He couldn't open his mouth without beer odor merging with the air they breathed. He couldn't lounge in the first-floor sitting area without cigar smoke on his suit leaving a lingering aroma behind. Wilmer reassured himself about being a tenderhearted soul, even if prejudice and condescending attitudes surrounded him most everywhere he turned.

I held tight to the arm rests on Granddaddy's kitchen chair before he changed the subject and told me how he appreciated the longer days close to the summer solstice. When getting ready for bed, he said he washed his face to remove city street smoke. He wiped away the stench of spoiled fish spilled from street carts contaminating his shoes. He congratulated himself on an almost a perfect weekly record of attending Quaker worship in New York, except when he traveled to Philadelphia to visit Edna.

And then one Sunday morning, Wilmer said he woke up with a hangover from all the beer he'd consumed with dinner at the German restaurant the evening before. He vowed this wouldn't happen again and then questioned if he should share his uneven progress with Edna. When reflecting on not having made enough effort, he blinked—the same sort of fast and tight blinking three Philadelphia physicians hadn't been able to diagnose or treat.

When mulling over the possibility of returning to live in Beavertown and assisting with the family business, Wilmer said he blinked quickly again. He examined the many ways in which New York City advertised its message that men were better than women, whether he agreed or not. He prayed that what he considered "garbage thoughts and actions" not contaminate his resolve to do the best he could at whatever he set his mind to do. He felt sorry for those girls and women either trained to assume the victim role or who embraced conventional styles of feminine behavior. In short, Granddaddy felt no closer to making a decision about Edna and their future together.

If he left New York and moved back home to Central Pennsylvania, he'd find a woman to marry. Of this, my grandfather had no doubt. He didn't have a job waiting there unless he changed his mind about working for his father in the family horse and buggy shop. He could collaborate with his brother Max on a new scheme of his—building an automobile factory in Snyder County. If the idea had any substance, he'd invite Edna to move to Beavertown with him. After all, she liked his stories about the town where he'd been raised.

At home, Granddaddy changed into his red flannel shirt, tan corduroy trousers, and old garden boots where the sole of his right shoe flapped on the way to his garage. I wondered how often he thought of Edna. He seemed distracted occasionally, as if he remembered her touching his hand and the light violet scent of her skin. When he turned his head toward the kitchen wall, I caught a glance of his mouth moving. He must be talking to her, I said to myself. It seemed to me that my grandfather was bonded to the past with his shoulders weighed down with thoughts.

Bicycle shop owned by Wilmer's older brother, John Kearns, in Beavertown, Pennsylvania, circa 1900.

Even though Edna had never visited Snyder County, Granddaddy told me she could imagine Beavertown's main street and businesses, including the bicycle and typewriter repair shop run by his older brother John Kearns, not far from their father's carriage business. The train station wasn't far from the family home. Wilmer's mother Henrietta Kearns painted in oils on plates and canvases. His brother Max played the violin, as did Wilmer. Oil landscapes painted by family members hung on walls throughout the Kearns home in Beavertown.

The five Kearns children were gregarious and expressive. Granddaddy's parents—Henrietta and John P. Kearns—made sure their children took advantage of all the schooling available in rural Pennsylvania. They modeled positive qualities for their offspring, including how to trust one's intuition and accept tenderness, strength, and vulnerability as gifts to nurture. But a rural community, Wilmer sensed, wasn't fertile territory for a young woman like Edna, someone determined to devote her life to women's rights organizing.

Wilmer's brother, Charles Maxwell Kearns, decided to live in Beavertown. In 1903, Max sketched his first designs of a horseless carriage he planned to manufacture himself and utilize the skills and talents of both his father and older brother John.

Wilmer Kearns (*back row standing, with violin*) with friends in Beavertown at the family home before Wilmer left for Philadelphia to study, circa 1895.

They'd collaborate when transforming horse-drawn wagons into gasoline-powered automobiles. If Wilmer could contribute to a family business, it would be in the area of business management. An attorney family friend, however, warned Wilmer against becoming involved in a commercial venture with family members. This made sense. His brother Max had a temper, and Wilmer concluded that a distance between them improved their relationship. He might find another job in accounting, although his bosses at the cigar firm in Manhattan kept signing checks for bonuses. This made it difficult for him to apply for another position. Granddaddy told me: "I put off too many decisions until later."

The senior Mr. Kearns convinced son Max that he'd be willing to invest in the automobile manufacturing venture Max proposed. A transition was already under way from horse-drawn carriages to motorized vehicles with internal combustion engines. It wasn't long before Wilmer's brother Max founded the Kearns Motor Car Company, with the manufacturing plant located in Beavertown. Wilmer planned to assist in launching this commercial enterprise as a family member, not as a partner.

While Wilmer contemplated a possible future with Edna, she wrote in her diary about a new development at home, something she couldn't explain. Her father, Charles Buckman, had been acting in an unusual way after arriving home from one of his business trips. He didn't rush around but relaxed in the garden and helped his wife with dinner. If Charles had signed a contract to supply beds for an Atlantic City hotel, he didn't share the news. Granddaddy said Edna's father no longer knocked on May's bedroom door late at night, even if the frigid wind outside swept through cracks in the window frames.

Charles Buckman was home with the family and sleeping in his own bed for several weeks when not on the road or at appointments with his boss at company headquarters. He left during the day to attend what he called "conferences in Philadelphia" and was at the head of the dinner table each evening. Charles clearly acted out of the ordinary. Edna, her brother, and mother couldn't figure out what might be going on behind the scenes. They accepted the changes in Charles, however. He had his own agenda, and the rest of the family had theirs, even though the odds against Edna and Wilmer deepening their friendship troubled my grandfather. He predicted that his ancestors' military history wouldn't impress Edna's extended family of Quakers. And he suspected that Edna's mother, wouldn't support his acceptance of an accounting position at T. J. Dunn, a cigar-manufacturing firm, either.

It wouldn't matter to May that one of the company's offices was located at 182–190 Avenue C, within walking distance from where he'd rented a room in New York City. May hated tobacco and cigars. She considered dancing "vain." Tobacco and alcohol had no redeeming qualities, except for medicine, and only then in tiny doses.

May described herself as having a "hungering" mind and soul. She embraced the "peculiar" label generally associated with Quakers that translated into describing her own son, Smythe, as "misguided." She believed he'd fallen victim to "frivolous" dancing and a love of "sinful" entertainment. Mischievous activities like street dancing translated, in her opinion, to "evil" and "wicked" activities. Oh, dear, I told myself. Falling in love with Edna and getting along with the extended Buckman family might be beyond my grandfather's ability.

"Will and Purpose." Granddaddy taught me about these qualities.

Edna's mother loved these two concepts. I didn't realize until decades later that my great-grandmother May stood up to be counted about how Quakers, of all people, forgot their history. Perhaps they never learned how their founding in England had been a reaction to authoritarian theology and a devotion to power politics from within an established church structure. There were other reasons too. "Quaker history is complicated," May told her son and daughter.

When May challenged both husband Charles and son Smythe about materialistic and cultural influences on Quakers, she assumed they respected the sacrifices of Quakers, also known as the "first spreaders of the truth" or the "Children of the Light." Members and attenders at the Religious Society of Friends, or Quakers, referred to themselves with these terms after being stuck with the label of those who quaked in the presence of the divine. Smythe and Charles showed few signs of identifying a divine leading or expressing activist heroism involving original thinking based on spiritual commitments.

Quakers, like everyone else, had to deal with the fast-changing world around them. May questioned if many Philadelphia Quakers did much more than hide behind their Quakerly cloaks. Her husband, Charles, fell into this category. He may have walked through certain doors because of the Buckman family name associated with William Penn and the migration from England to Pennsylvania. But from Granddaddy's perspective, Charles couldn't have cared less about the concept of "primitive Christianity" of Quakerism and if it had had any internal or external significance in the priorities of family members.

Wilmer's first reaction to Edna's mother was to label her as "strict" and uncompromising. Quakers weren't always easy for outsiders like my grandfather to understand. May opposed obedience and an allegiance to external secular rules that, in her opinion, left her and others in an impure state to do the challenging activism for which Quakers, and those identifying with the Hicksite branch, had become well known. The Hicksites relied on the Inner Light. Orthodox Quakers preferred their Bibles as the authority. My mother told me that May respected Hicksite Quaker Lucretia Mott for her determination, as well as for her spirited style. May had good intentions, my mother told me. "However, she couldn't change the outside pressures on Quakers who, in some ways, were like everyone else."

May Buckman noted that even Quakers like herself made mistakes in judgment. Lucretia Mott, for example, admitted her errors and claimed to have learned from them. She believed Mott's accomplishments were both remarkable and astonishing. Although Lucretia Mott didn't claim total responsibility for organizing the Seneca Falls women's convention of 1848 in Upstate New York, she did everything she could to make it happen. Lucretia Mott knew how to network and get things done. Activist Elizabeth

Edna's mother, May Begley Buckman, circa 1900.

Cady Stanton couldn't say enough about how Mott had encouraged and supported her in the direction of becoming a women's rights pioneer.[1]

I kept my face as expressionless as possible so Granddaddy would continue telling the story. He told me that if Edna were to choose one word to describe her father, it would be that she believed he was "backsliding." Charles switched back and forth, without warning, from a devil-may-care bloke to a responsible Quaker family man. Edna didn't write much in her red Wanamaker diary about her father's actions and beliefs. I heard plenty from my mother and grandfather, however. They said it took patience to practice the faith of Quakers and then translate it into action.

"I believe in moderation and responsibility," Wilmer reassured Edna, who raised questions after hearing what he had to say about the availability of cigars and beer in shops and business establishments throughout Manhattan. If Edna had passed on this information to her mother, Wilmer might have faced an ending of the couple's friendship. I wanted to be fearless and passionate like Edna. She had personal power and acted on it. That's what my grandfather loved about her. I showered him with questions about Bedloe's Island in New York harbor where once he'd climbed a wooden staircase to the Statue of Liberty's head.

The Statue of Liberty had power, Granddaddy told me, especially the strength of emotional symbolism. People wept when they arrived in New York's port from around the world where war, poor living conditions, and the lack of religious freedom defined generations. Young Edna wasn't as accepting of the Statue of Liberty as my grandfather. He told me Edna was cynical when pointing out that Lady Liberty's feet had been cemented to the ground. When the Statue of Liberty was dedicated in 1886, women's rights advocates rented a boat to be visible in the harbor when protesting the denial of their right to vote. If I learned little else, it was that the issue of gender inequality wouldn't soon disappear.

As Granddaddy's tale of the Statue of Liberty wound down, his black rotary phone rang. My mother asked my grandfather when I'd be ready to head home.

"Right away," I said when passing on the message. I rarely argued. I could have been called "Pleasing Peggy," the childhood nickname I imposed on myself later in life. If a youngster like me acted pretty and pleasing, an authority figure patted me on the head, if not literally, then with verbal praise. "Pleasing Peggy" lived for the compliments generated by dusting living room surfaces at home. She ran the vacuum cleaner, cooked for the family, and washed dishes—not daily, but often.

I headed over to Granddaddy's house to hear more stories whenever possible. When describing Manhattan of the early twentieth century, I was left with the impression of a cold overcast sky or a sticky summer day. From New York, Wilmer wrote letters to Edna about the city streets and noisy urban landscape. What he told Edna mattered less than the sense of connection he must have felt when exchanging letters with her. My grandfather said he couldn't forget the impact on him of the firm lines of Edna's jaw and cheeks.

Edna had a gentle way of being. Granddaddy definitely considered her a "catch." He admitted to me once, and only in passing, about his premarital loneliness. Edna made him forget his insecurities. She loved books. About social standing, she seemed indifferent. My grandfather said he resonated with Edna's nature. He concluded this by the glow emanating from her face even when her mother May spoke about the world's injustices. A quiver ran down my spine as I reminded myself of my ability to project myself into the past by following Granddaddy's example. During moments like this, I could sense the blood flowing into my face, like Edna must have felt, from my grandfather's constant gaze at her from across the table at the Market Street teahouse.

Life didn't happen without problems to fix, issues to address, and complications to consider. This was part of life, I gathered. I hung on to my grandfather's every word. And as a result of this, I learned about patience. Eventually I'd find out everything about my grandmother's wedding dress. I longed to say: "Edna was falling in love with you, Granddaddy, from the very beginning." It should have been simple to work things out, but the questions remained. Was Wilmer good enough for Edna? And was she good enough for him?

Chapter 6

"When Is Papa Coming Home?"

The day Edna became a woman was preserved in our family's collective memory as a hot muggy Philadelphia summer day about 1895. A cooling thunderstorm might be expected to deliver a sudden drop in temperature, but on that afternoon, no clouds were in sight. This story was, like many others, out of order. I didn't stop Granddaddy when he jumped around. He might lose momentum.

One day Edna was outside with her brother playing street games on Rubicam Avenue. She must have been twelve or close to thirteen years of age when Thomas Smith Buckman, also known as Brother or Smythe, informed the entire neighborhood of his sister's condition by walking up and down the street yelling, "Edna's bleeding."

For years, Edna couldn't release the embarrassment bonded to her bones. She raced into the house, convinced that her mother would confine her to bed with a terminal condition. Instead, May told her daughter about becoming a woman. For May Buckman and what many called the Victorian generation, sexual expression was mentioned only to a few people, and then, only when absolutely necessary.[1]

The day Edna became a woman, May had spent the afternoon sweating over a spice cake recipe from Mrs. Hattie A. Burr's suffrage cookbook.[2] She planned for roast chicken, mashed potatoes with gravy, freshly baked bread, and greens from the garden. All of this would be ready when Papa arrived home on the afternoon train from Harrisburg. When Charles didn't show up when expected, his empty chair at the dinner table sent a message that expectations for men were different than for women.

Charles Buckman's absence from the dinner table heightened the awareness for his wife that the man of the house was out in the world surrounded by those she labeled as of "questionable moral character and influence." She told Edna in a whisper about her suspicion that Papa ate rich foods in excess when on the job. He drank alcoholic beverages, and who knows what else. How much did Charles identify with the dominant secular culture? Why wasn't his loyalty devoted entirely to his Quaker family?

Papa Buckman loved his job from what Edna could tell. And as far as her brother Smythe was concerned, Edna barely tolerated his rebellious attitude that boiled down to "the hell if I care if Quakers believe if I'm a good boy or not." The breakdown of traditional Quaker culture wasn't a new worry for May and her only daughter. In 1901, Edna prepared and presented a paper for her Quaker spiritual community in Plymouth Meeting. The topic raised was: "Are young Friends deviating from the old customs of Friends?"[3] Just as May believed the older generation was succumbing to temptations and "worldly" influences, some in the younger generation like Edna also aired broader issues, such as: What about Quakers marrying those who've been raised in other churches or faiths? And what was the best reasoning needed to "elder" those influenced by the dominant commercial and materialistic culture?

"Did Papa stay over an extra day to meet with his boss in Harrisburg?" Edna asked her mother.

"Dear, I don't know what to think anymore," May reportedly replied.

I heard more about the Buckman family conflict from my mother when piecing the story together years later. Granddaddy's prior critical and condescending remarks suddenly made sense. He'd also skillfully changed the subject if the Boll Brothers company, where Charles worked, was raised in general conversation. I remember my mother saying something like, "Charles worked for a brass bed company. What could you expect, other than him fooling around?" It was predictable that he'd experiment, she told me. "Folks, even mature fathers, pass through rebellious phases and midlife crises."

Edna and her mother were familiar with early feminists in England like Mary Wollstonecraft, a writer who believed that women's nature, equal to men, required the female gender to stand up and be heard about family and community issues. Wollstonecraft was fearless. Some of her contemporaries in England during the 1700s described her as mentally unbalanced, even as her advocacy in support of gender equality spread to the United States and around the world.

Granddaddy told me that Philadelphia Quaker and activist Lucretia Mott kept a copy of Wollstonecraft's book, *A Vindication of the Rights of Woman*, on a table at home for easy access. Mott was said to have memorized relevant passages, and she consulted Wollstonecraft's other writings. She also liked philosopher John Stuart Mill's essay, *The Subjection of Women*, published in 1869. Many social commentators around the world labeled the double gender standard as unacceptable. The prevailing mainstream attitude was that women should retire to their kitchens and remain invisible within the larger culture.

May Buckman admired Lucretia Mott as a role model for change. But Mott had her troubles, too.[4] Conservative Quakers believed an individual like Lucretia Mott had no business sticking her nose into issues beyond her sphere of influence. One of Lucretia's strongest assets was her husband, according to those who had an opinion on the subject. I remember Granddaddy saying, "James Mott was a prize package." He said he listened carefully when Edna spoke about James and Lucretia Mott, who raised six children. They also worked together as a team on social issues lodged in a larger context.

Lucretia Mott's contemporaries described her as a darling, and also a terror when she lost her temper. She hated slavery, as well as discrimination against women and native peoples. Both Lucretia and James considered each other essential to the physical health and emotional well-being of their family. She lived her life as an example of spirit-led advocacy and committed action. Edna admired this.

As a Quaker minister, Lucretia Mott took to the road to speak in public. James cared for the household responsibilities like his wife did when he had his own business affairs to attend to. This wasn't unusual in many Hicksite Quaker households. When Lucretia advocated for an 1848 women's convention in Seneca Falls, James agreed to be the gathering's facilitator because many women did not believe they were qualified. James Mott also signed the Declaration of Sentiments—the women's version of the Declaration of Independence—along with Lucretia and many others.

Some in the larger world claimed that James "allowed" Lucretia to be a gadfly in the world instead of the sweet Quaker matron she appeared to be when wearing her bonnet, shawl, and long linen dresses. Lucretia refused to wear cotton because its production relied on the labor of enslaved workers. James closed his cotton distribution firm and founded a business specializing in wool. Once, when Wilmer asked Edna about James Mott, she emphasized that James didn't "allow" Lucretia to do anything. Her actions were based on her own spiritual beliefs and priorities.

Daguerreotype portrait of James and Lucretia Mott. Original photograph by William Langenheim, 1842. Library of Congress.

"James and Lucretia supported each other totally," Edna told Wilmer.

"Oh," he replied, using the word I copied from him. "Oh" served as a placeholder rather than me responding with a reaction instead of a seasoned point of view.

Granddaddy told me that when Edna spoke about early feminist writers like Mary Wollstonecraft in England, her message was simple and direct. Friends and family members took Edna seriously. They respected my grandmother's commitment and gravitated in her direction to hear what else she had to say. Edna presented her own opinions clearly. She tested her outer actions with considerable spiritual reflection, according to Wilmer.

May went even further. She'd noticed the signs of weakening spiritual commitments in other Quaker families, including the consumption by some of unnecessary commercial goods, as compared to Quaker values of upholding simplicity and practicing responsible spending. Rich foods and alcoholic drinks weren't considered Quakerly. The accumulation of wealth as a goal was held in high esteem as signs of power in the dominant culture, but not among Quakers. As they developed reputations as honest merchants, many Quakers became wealthy. The spiritual emphasis on equality, as modeled by Quaker founders George Fox and his wife Margaret Fell, eroded over the decades, according to my great-grandmother May.

Edna appeared both young and innocent from where I witnessed her from the other side of a plate glass window, staring into the past through storytelling. When Edna complained to her mother about her brother announcing to the neighbors about the blood dripping down her legs, I swallowed hard. Edna's red diary preserved her reactions to life's events on five lines reserved for each day of the year. She didn't include a response to her mother's embarrassed explanation about the purpose of menstruation. Instead, Edna made an effort to record in her diary the comings and goings of her father Charles, when he arrived home from one business trip, or left for another.

Although Edna's entries about her father were relatively few, she made the point for future generations. The atmosphere in the Buckman household depended on her father's mood and whether or not he returned home as promised.[5] And my grandmother had noticed that after Charles started working for Boll Brothers, his behavior shifted in the direction of reflecting the mainstream culture.

When questioned by May or Edna at dinner about arriving home from the job later than expected, Charles explained to family members that he'd been pressured into sharing dinner with his boss, Charles S. Boll, who'd moved to Harrisburg from Baltimore in 1885.[6] Within several years, Mr. Boll owned and operated his own bed and bedding manufacturing company in Harrisburg. It was advertised as one of largest companies of its type in the nation. Charles Buckman worked his way up to be one of the most productive employees on Mr. Boll's sales force.

May interpreted her husband's advancement in the brass bed company ranks as a reinforcement of the effect of external social climbing that, in her opinion, led to an inevitable spiritual decline. She believed many Philadelphia Quakers, as a result, were no longer willing to put themselves on the line to strengthen their values and

Edna's father, Charles Harper Buckman, circa 1900.

way of life. She used as evidence the ministry of visiting Quakers at weekly worship on Sundays or what Quakers called "First Day." A lengthy preparation for a Quaker ministry qualified both women and men for a divine calling. It wasn't a matter of attending a seminary or theological college. Serious candidates could prepare themselves by reading, reflection, and questioning or acting on a spiritual leading.

Many Quaker ministers offered gems of wisdom in their spoken ministry as well as the spiritual pamphlets they wrote and distributed. If a traveling minister spoke about "waywardness," for example, May listened carefully to the presentation. She, like many other Quaker women, had witnessed family members singing "vain" songs, or wandering far from the salutary highway of true religion, or taking delight in the "running of horses." May associated all of these alleged sins with the work environment of the Boll Brothers Company in Harrisburg. She even disliked the name of the concern.

Edna reported on her father's absences from home on diary pages facing shoe and gown illustrations of products sold by John Wanamaker's department store in Center City

Philadelphia. His employment with Boll Brothers involved spending extended time on the road selling beds. With Charles away, Buckman family members spent hours wrestling with an answer to the chronic nagging question, "When is Papa coming home?" When no one could be sure of the answer, the woodwork at Echo Dale appeared dull without May's persistent polishing. After Papa sent word with the exact hour of his arrival, the living room curtains stood wide open and the window glass sparkled.

Mamma Buckman could be described as a robust and sturdy woman, someone who wrote often in her spiritual journal about her relationship with the divine. Edna didn't ask her mother what she wrote about, although she hoped the godhead of the journal was strong and with an intensity enough to remind members of the family of their responsibility to care about the future of Quakers in the United States. This may have seemed unnecessary to someone like Wilmer when first hearing Edna's concerns about her family. He didn't have a personal investment in the topic, yet he realized that he represented, in his own Kearns family, an early generation of a young person leaving home to seek education and employment in an urban area.

Charles Buckman once told his wife that he needed more quality time with his son and daughter, but regrettably his absences were necessary because of his job requirements to negotiate and sign contracts. Boll Brothers Manufacturing Company shipped its mattresses and iron and brass beds to every state in the US and to nations around the world. After a fire destroyed the central Harrisburg plant in 1903, insurance inspectors estimated damages to have been over $100,000.[7] The company's policy of expanding its markets had far-reaching implications for employees and their families.

"I'm not going to Quaker worship this week," May told Edna on more than one occasion.

"How could thee think of such a thing?" Edna responded.

"I can't stand seeing the pity on Friends' faces," May said to her daughter.

May stayed at home many First Days because she didn't want anyone at the Quaker Meetings in Germantown or Plymouth Meeting, where they worshipped, to ask, "How is Charles?" Then she'd have to admit he'd been traveling again. Mamma was proud. Edna suspected there might be more to her father's employment than he shared with family members. He spent overnights in expensive Harrisburg hotels, for example. When at home, he succumbed to May's pressure to attend Quaker worship with the family but he didn't hide signs of his frustration and impatience either.

Granddaddy told me that "traveling men" like Charles found it necessary to juggle business catalogs, price lists, and advertising brochures for novel items, such as one Boll Brothers product, "Weaving Wire Bed Springs." Charles Buckman packed product brochures in his traveling trunk next to changes of suits and starched ironed shirts. Members of Boll Brothers' sales team distanced themselves socially from door-to-door salesmen, well known for their off-color jokes, flashy outfits, and proffering of free alcoholic drinks in saloons and hotel bars. The distance Buckman family members lived from Harrisburg didn't prevent family members and others from speculating what might be taking place there.

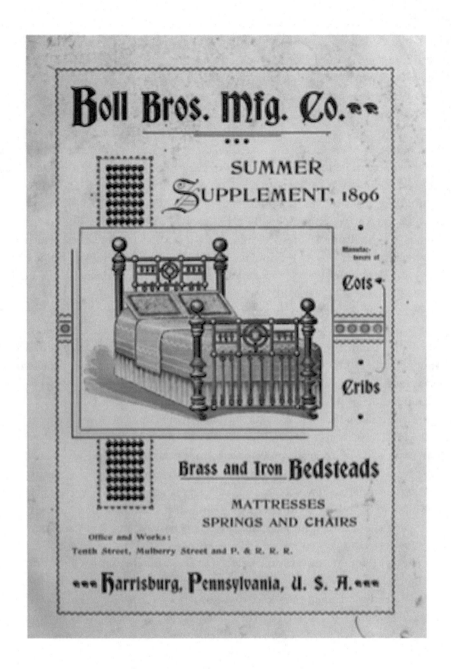

Boll Brothers, 1896 Summer Supplement.

My mother claimed that business trips involved high living that Charles failed to mention to his family. He neglected to say, for instance, that the serving tables at the Hotel Bolton in Harrisburg sagged with tasty dishes with plenty of butter, meat, and oil. He learned to censor his remarks after describing to his wife once how the banquet tables had been loaded with prairie hens, wild duck, venison, chicken, and oysters for company functions. May read between the lines of her husband's explanations and wondered if what he told family members contained a grain of truth.

"I've heard thee trot out the same excuses about entertaining and closing a deal in a bar," she told Charles after one of his business trips.

"Take my word for it—I drink only cider and coffee," he said.

May didn't believe Charles. Edna didn't either. And May made it clear to her daughter that men in general didn't mind making promises to women before marriage. Then she claimed they took opposite positions after the wedding ceremony.

Granddaddy told me those Quakers arranging their lives to reflect the external culture were quicker to dispense with plain speech and purchase stylish outfits. Still, many Quakers valued simple lifestyles and spirit-led activities. Since she had lived next door to the Buckmans on Rubicam Avenue in Germantown, Edna's friend Bess also noticed how Charles tended to "slip and slide," as she described deviations from what she observed as basic Quaker faith and practice.

At home, Charles stopped mentioning how champagne seemed to spring from hotel fountains at Boll Brothers' functions. He'd learned his lesson after telling his wife about one banquet featuring exotic dishes. He'd never do that again, according to Granddaddy, because May imagined serving tables groaning with the weight of rich and exotic foods. She could even recite menu highlights, including Long Island Neck Clams, turtle soup, Deviled Crabs a la Baltimore, Saratoga Chips, Sweetbreads a la Périgord, steamed peas, beef filet, spring chicken on toast, lettuce and tomato salad, and finally, lobster with mayonnaise.

The expression of anguish on May's face reflected her expectation that the hotel's final course featured champagne, white wine, strawberries, assorted cakes, vanilla ice cream, Roquefort cheese, crackers, coffee, and—last but not least—cigars. The banquet food, dreadful in my great-grandmother's opinion, tested the limits of her patience, especially when she heard about alcoholic waterfalls flowing in a hotel setting immersed in a cigar smoke fog.

Whenever temperance events were held in Philadelphia, whether associated with Quakers or not, May arrived early and chose a seat in the front row of the audience. If friends and neighbors said anything about Charles Buckman's wife, it was that she didn't hesitate to emphasize the grim reality associated with the unregulated use of tobacco and alcohol. If Charles were to discuss his situation with non-Quaker friends, they would have supported him when he told of long work hours and travel to distant venues such as New York, Boston, Baltimore, and Chicago. He would have been persuasive about defending his need for a stiff drink now and then. Not so with any Quaker friends Charles might have had.

May prevailed on family members for hours with lectures about how alcohol destroyed families, communities, and nations. She pointed out how factory workers left their jobs on Fridays and headed for saloons and taverns. By Sunday, their empty pockets spelled doom for wives and children facing empty pantry shelves. May relied on the rhetoric of the period emphasizing moral standards. She used phrases like "truth and purity," "courage and steadfastness," "sincerity and simplicity," and "grace and quiet dignity," all with themes designed to reinforce Quaker faith and practice.

"Drink leads to forgetting. Alcohol feeds a false sense of confidence," May lectured. "And alcoholic spirits turn humans into ferocious beasts." She detoured into the specifics by citing references to ethics and theology. The most potent examples May reserved for how alcoholic drinks robbed imbibers of a clear conscience. It didn't take much to realize why May's husband and son were singled out for criticism. She used words like "vicissitudes" and "trials." She added phrases like "divine truth," "great fear and dread," "fortitude," and challenges of faith that were "vigorous and virulent."

When Charles returned home from business trips, his clothing reeked of Turkish tobacco. "I can't stand when others smoke around me," he said to explain the stench on his clothing when entering a room. Edna and May weren't convinced that secondhand smoke was potent enough to contaminate his suits and jackets. But they didn't argue. It didn't matter that when Charles left for business travel, the aroma of his traveling trunk reminded family members of a cedar forest. He layered small cedar blocks in with the content of his luggage. After arriving home, bathing, changing his clothes, and presenting himself at the dinner table, Charles no longer smelled like a smokestack. He placed his feet flat on the floor at the dinner table, as if to ground himself and adjust to family routines again.

Charles sat upright in his chair at dinner and answered May's questions about his business trips with clipped sentences. When May called him Harper, his middle name, she spoke with affection. When addressed as Charles, he inhaled slowly to demonstrate his patience. My great-grandfather Charles was accustomed to hearing perspectives from his colleagues at work that girls were to be raised to assume the roles of wives and mothers—what mainstream ministers and church officials referred to as the "natural order of the universe." Men didn't expect their authority to be challenged. Uncomfortable questions weren't welcome. If Edna were to tolerate less than appropriate behavior from her father—someone familiar with Quaker culture and tradition—what could she expect from someone like Wilmer Kearns?

Charles loved when Edna called him Papa Harper, a family naming tradition originating with Robert Harper, a Scots-Irish immigrant fleeing Ireland due to discrimination in 1727. He signed on as an indentured servant to John Buzby, a wealthy Quaker from the Philadelphia area. After Harper married Buzby's daughter Sarah, the Quaker descendants passed down the surname of Harper in one form or another until family oral history suggested that the Harper and Buckman family branches eventually joined hands through social and business interactions.[8]

To anyone who examined Charles Harper Buckman closely, his knuckles appeared gray at the dinner table. Sweat came close to gathering steam on his temples and chin. He forced his baritone voice into service to assist in changing the subject from business trips to his son and daughter's school reports. Charles relied on forced gentle but firm laughter to steer attention away from himself and avoid questions about his job. It was one of those rare occasions when Charles Buckman would have preferred to have been invisible.

Chapter 7

The Secret

"Some stories can't be forgotten," Granddaddy whispered to me in a low voice.
"Which stories?" I asked.

"The ones with secrets."

I gasped. Few young people would let an opportunity pass after being presented with an opening to a realm of secrets. Before I heard about the "family secret," I'd been wondering why Edna continued seeing Wilmer. It must, I decided, have been because of the stories he told, especially about the summer afternoons he spent in the kitchen at home, as a boy, watching his mother prepare pickles, dumplings, and rhubarb pie.

Wilmer Kearns at his Beechwood Drive home near Lansdale, Pennsylvania, circa 1960s. Photo by Wilma Kearns Culp.

Folks from miles around in Snyder County praised his mother Henrietta's cooking. When Wilmer took center stage at social occasions in Philadelphia, he assumed the role of a walking and talking guide through Pennsylvania Dutch cuisine. He excelled as a dinner guest among those curious about a region of the state that produced someone like my grandfather.

In spite of all the stories Granddaddy told, it didn't seem logical that he would include secrets. He avoided parts of ordinary life few spoke about that included, for instance, the how, why, and when females were no longer "girls" from age ten or twelve on and they were transformed overnight into women. Other forbidden topics included how some families had rebellious youngsters in their midst, such as Edna's brother Smythe. This fascinated me, as much as studying the photographs of Edna as a young woman when waiting to hear about our family's secrets.

It didn't take much for someone my age to figure out that certain traditional country recipes from Pennsylvania Dutch country, such as Shoo Fly pie and dried beef gravy fueled Granddaddy's playing of the piano, flute, violin, banjo, guitar, and mandolin when he was young.[1] Songs he performed for friends included ballads he learned from the Juniata Valley, sung in both German and English. They provided a context to my grandfather's stories.

Wilmer told me he had introduced city listeners to rural farm women, blacksmiths, and distillers. Iron ore miners and shoemakers were included, along with mill workers, free blacks, and native peoples. Wilmer squeezed stonemasons, undertakers, and the railroad day watchmen of Pennsylvania into story folds, while I held my breath waiting to hear the family dirt. Granddaddy showed me a photo of himself as a young man. "Handsome," I thought. If he played things right, Granddaddy would make a terrific husband for Edna. I simply had to know the secret he'd been carrying around, something that Edna's mother had possibly done and felt guilty about it, so much so she'd only told her daughter. I wondered how often Edna had passed on the Buckman family secrets to Granddaddy.

Granddaddy told me about playing musical instruments as background for his tales about the homespun Yankees, their extravagant lies and legends. And I yawned throughout his verbal journeys about Pennsylvania barns to their hex signs and the many settlements of those who loved comfort food and plenty of it. If Granddaddy mentioned scrapple, the storytelling ritual included hearing about what went into producing it. Hog brains and stomach linings. How dreadful, I thought. When Granddaddy laid sticky buns out on his kitchen table to accompany the storytelling, I made sure I didn't miss out on hearing everything he had to say.

"But what about the family's secrets?" I wasn't shy about asking my grandfather, who considered himself a cross-country specialist in narratives—someone who jumped onto a bucking bronco tale, sunk his teeth into it, and wouldn't let go in spite of how often he told it. If his stories required a magician and prophet, my grandfather assigned Merlin a role. If he needed a knight-errant like Don Quixote roaming the landscape in search of justice, Wilmer Kearns placed this character on a horse and

Kearns family in Beavertown, Pennsylvania after Wilmer Kearns married and lived in New York City." *Left to Right*: standing: Wilmer Kearns, Lulu Kearns, John Kearns, Marie Kearns, Charles Maxwell Kearns. *Sitting*: John Preston Kearns and Henrietta Rhamstine Kearns. Circa 1922.

turned him loose. He tended to be stingy when it came to sensitive topics his listeners might repeat to others. They'd tell someone else, he predicted, and the tale might be repeated like the childhood game played across the nation, "Whisper Down the Lane." By the end, stories were dramatically different from what the first whisperer intended.

I waited patiently while Granddaddy's verbal wanderings led to details of the moon's phases and related advice about when farm fields were ripe for planting. No matter how many anecdotes Wilmer shared, sooner or later he left some individuals out of starring roles. Edna's friend Bess was one of Wilmer's first story critics. Bess hated domestic life. Frustrated and annoyed at the possibility, she repeated her refusal to become the property of any man, whether her father or a husband. This was no secret.

"Marriage is unnatural," Bess added when arguing her position with my grandfather. "If women would only stop being wives and mothers, inequality would end overnight."

Because her own father made a point of putting her down, Bess didn't have faith in trusting a husband whose name she would be expected to take after promising in a public ceremony to honor and obey him. When Wilmer dared challenge Bess to come to terms with her father's position on gender inequality, she was blunt in her response.

"Understand my father? Look at our family problems from his point of view? There's no compromise from where he stands. He's right, and I'm wrong. He's a good guy the way he supports his family. I'm a bad girl because I don't do what he says."

Wilmer listened. He didn't comment.

"You're giving men permission to make women invisible when you don't include more of us in your stories," Bess suggested to Wilmer. "You benefit from how things are. Admit it, why don't you? You're not taking the proper steps to do your part."

Wilmer told me he bristled at Bess's accusations. He believed they were based on the assumption that he hadn't considered the emotional impact of entrenched male political control over generations, as well as the dominance of men in social and economic relations. He was further affronted because his friendship with Edna had already steered him in the direction of questioning the social and economic status quo. To Granddaddy, Bess posed a major obstacle to his dream of Edna falling in love with him and accepting his marriage proposal. Wilmer said he understood Bess's point about marriage being advantageous for men, but this didn't make him sympathetic to Edna's close friend when the stakes were so high.

I waited and then reached for one of Granddaddy's freshly baked brownies. He didn't notice. My grandfather may have been caught up in a memory about Bess and it didn't register that I sat straight in the kitchen chair, waiting for the moment when the secret finally would be released. Someone in the family must have done something terrible. I decided not to interrupt the flow of Granddaddy getting around to telling me. And if the family secret involved Bess, I could hardly wait to hear it.

"It's your job to separate the bad apples from the good ones," Bess told my grandfather. "Men like you should lead the way and do the heavy lifting for women's rights on the front lines."

While Bess had every right to speak her mind, her use of the term "bad apples" annoyed Wilmer. It bothered him that she viewed him as both an enemy and a savior. He hated the way she related to him with a wide glide of her right hand through the air as she spoke. Once Bess started expressing herself, she didn't stop until she ran out of breath. Would women gain power, he wondered, by taking it away from men? Or did they want only power sharing and equality as Edna insisted? If the answer to this involved a momentous revelation, I thought, so much the better. But what about the secret? It had to involve Bess and if it didn't—why did Granddaddy let Edna's friend Bess interfere with a cover-up of a family secret?

"Oh, I'll admit there are a few good men out there, but most are like Philip, who my father pressured me to marry," Bess told Wilmer. "Philip's a man who pretends. Maybe you're one of them. Maybe not. Philip has two faces. One for his friends, and the other for those he calls his 'girls.' Sure, he might admit that sooner or later women will vote, but don't get him started about equality. That's where Philip draws the line."

Many of Edna's contemporaries, like Bess, viewed the votes for women campaign as "stagnant" by 1900.[2] The state-by-state strategic approach to woman's suffrage turned out to be more challenging and time-consuming than many expected. The Market Street teahouse was convenient for Wilmer and Edna's visits, and Edna had nothing but praise for the establishment's bathroom geared to the needs of its female customers. At that time, public bathrooms weren't readily available to women, only men. The direction was clear. Relatively few young women were willing to devote fifty years of their lives working for gender equality and the rights of American women.

Susan B. Anthony and Elizabeth Cady Stanton may have set aside fifty years to winning the ballot, but the twentieth century impressed many as a great time to be alive. Debates about marriage, its advantages and disadvantages, weren't new. Bess could cite chapter and verse of instances of activism involving American women. Over the decades many had voted illegally. They refused to pay taxes on owned or donated property without political representation. They chose not to marry, refused to take their husband's last name, or protested about the requirement of becoming a man's personal property. Bess backed up her opinions with personal observations. With Wilmer a captive in conversations, she wouldn't leave him alone.

"Oh, I picked up right away on Philip being the kind of husband who'd hit the ceiling if dinner ended up on the table five minutes late," she went on. "Naturally he'll give his wife her due, praise her beef stew and how well she dresses the little ones. Philip is the type who hides an ugly part of himself, covered over by a pasty smile on his face. As if he's a victim, puzzled because he can't get all the respect he believes he deserves as a man. The kind who figures women might complain, but in his mind all the talk about equality will sooner or later blow over."

Wilmer said that when he was in a situation like this, it took all his strength to listen. I persisted in hearing about the secret. Was my grandfather avoiding me? Attempting to change the subject? Was he forgetting his promise to tell me a secret? Granddaddy was the storyteller, not me. I didn't want to hear any more about Bess. My grandfather kept his storytelling removed from mentions of sex, violence, and swearing. When I was about to surrender and accept Granddaddy keeping some memories to himself, the protected past must have leaked into his throat from a hidden location in his belly. And there it was, finally—the hidden drama revealed as only my grandfather could tell it.

After the day Edna became a woman, Wilmer said Mamma Buckman had climbed the stairs to her bedroom once the dinner dishes were washed and stored away. When Granddaddy introduced this story to me, Edna's mother, not Bess, was the focus. I held my breath to make sure I didn't appear overly interested in what came next. I closed my eyes as May shut the door and stood before her bedroom window to listen to leaves rustling on the lawn as the standing clock downstairs chimed.

Granddaddy speculated that May must have thought through her next move carefully. It led her to dressing in a robe and tiptoeing down the hall to her husband's bedroom. Once there, she slipped a leather wallet out of Charles's jacket hanging in the bedroom closet. Then my grandfather elaborated on the waves of guilt May must have felt as she did this, even as Charles soaked in the bathroom tub's steaming water down the hall. Granddaddy told me May examined her husband's wallet quickly, as if she expected him next to burst into the room unannounced.

If Charles observed his usual routine, he wouldn't step out of the claw-footed porcelain tub for at least an hour. He'd supervised the installation of the tub, pedestal sink, and toilet to replace the chamber pots and outside privy the family used when they spent summers at Echo Dale when it was only a summer home. Charles Buckman's employment as an agent for Boll Brothers translated into extra income for home improvements after they moved to Echo Dale permanently. This included the bathroom tub, in addition to a kitchen range and plantings for their backyard garden.

I agonized during the next few minutes it took for May to open the billfold. A train ticket receipt fell out, round trip to Boston, just as Charles told her. That wasn't all that fell out. With the train ticket, out dropped a theater ticket for a Gilbert and Sullivan performance. Charles hadn't mentioned this, and May wondered if he'd attended alone.

After the train receipt and theater ticket revealed themselves, a pickup receipt surfaced in the wallet from a Harrisburg laundry dated during one of her husband's recent business trips. It was folded next to a restaurant bill for not one, but two dinners. All this would have been alarming enough, but Granddaddy described how May gasped when she noticed a scribbled addendum to the invoice confirming the purchase of two glasses of champagne. That's when May must have realized, with a jolt, that her worst suspicions about Charles were justified.

No doubt Wilmer had promised Edna not to tell anyone about this episode, and there he was, passing the story on to me. Did dead folks have privacy and confidentiality rights? I didn't ask this question back then, but it occurred to me decades later. In a moment of revelation when Edna related the story to Wilmer, she may have been testing him to determine what sort of partner he might make someday. Could he keep a secret? And if the dinner tab was on one invoice, it suggested that Charles paid for the meal. If so, was the other individual sharing dinner and drinks a man or a woman?

It was possible that Edna decided to release this sensitive information to relieve the burden she felt of carrying it around. If May had confided in her daughter what she discovered, only Edna could have known about her father's wallet and what it revealed to her mother as the evidence landed on the floor.

So there it was—the family secret, now part of the family record. Once this story was passed on to me, I inherited the residual guilt of generations. Would I keep this family drama close to my chest? My mother expected me to bury the details of this family secret. This turned into a major disagreement decades later. "What will people think of us?" she wondered. But by then, I was a newspaper reporter, and I was convinced that the tale was more about a previous generation's values than my own family.

Chapter 8

"Don't Fall in Love with Curmudgeons"

Wilmer was late for his appointment with Edna at the Market Street teahouse. She would be waiting, as usual, at a table near a window. Granddaddy had looked forward to seeing her for more than a week, checking off each day on a calendar. And then, he was late by a quarter-hour as he raced into the building.

"A treat for us," Wilmer announced on greeting Edna. He held out two large, thick-skinned oranges as a gift, something to show that he cared.

My grandfather had heard of Quaker women, like Edna, making statements like, "I have everything I need with my schooling, family, and friends." Edna, he figured, was no different. For a week he'd agonized over choosing the best gift for her. An engagement ring? This was his first choice, but it required a leap of faith. Edna might be the type to hand the ring back to him along with the dreaded words: "We're just friends." Fruit seemed like a safe alternative. He presented one orange to Edna and laid the other on his side of the table.

"Gorgeous oranges," she said. "Where did thee find them?"

"On boats arriving on Philadelphia's wharfs. These are from Florida's temples of sacred groves. They're nothing like the crop in the market last season—pale, small, and as hard as the rocks in Fairmount Park."

Edna smiled, one of those irresistible expressions that made Wilmer's heart beat faster and inspired his words to flow. As he peeled the orange and set aside the ripe pieces, he told her how his father, John P. Kearns, had traveled far and wide throughout the Southeast to purchase some of the best carriage horses for his Beavertown buggy business. He'd returned often with fresh oranges for the Kearns children. After hearing about the family secret, I was ready for him telling me more about oranges. Every Christmas, oranges and tangerines were stuffed into my holiday stocking.

Edna held up her orange and admired its skin with a firm texture and promise of succulent juices. Wilmer hadn't purchased her an expensive leather-bound book, but rather a simple orange. He believed he'd made the correct choice. Edna, as it turned out, adored oranges. Her favorite painting, Wilmer later learned, was Sandro Botticelli's *Primavera*, featuring an orange grove loaded with ripe fruit, with ethereal dancers stepping gingerly on the ground.

Primavera, or "Allegory of Spring," by Sandro Botticelli, circa 1482.

Edna had studied art at Samuel S. Fleisher's Graphic Sketch Club in downtown Philadelphia before enrolling in an art course at the museum school.[1] Her early artistic expressions featured oranges, viewed from several angles on paper for canvases destined to hang on her bedroom walls. She didn't feel compelled to tell Wilmer that the competition among women art students was fierce. She had difficulty coming to terms with this. If she were destined to become a women's rights activist, it would have to be a "Quaker leading," as her mother reminded her. May was convinced that the divine Inner Light might also illuminate other directions for Edna, who had considered organizing in support of women's rights full time.

Wilmer had enough to consider, starting with resistance from college friends at Peirce College. They hadn't been supportive of his move to New York or what he told them about Edna. On his weekend visits to Philadelphia when Wilmer made the rounds of associates from Peirce, they were of one mind in warning him about his love for a Quaker woman. They suggested that Wilmer might feel inadequate, that he may have sensed he was nothing until he met her.

"Are you out of your mind?" Wilmer's college friends asked him after he revealed the extent of his feelings about Edna. "Don't fall in love with curmudgeons." But what was a "curmudgeon"? I had no idea. As Granddaddy's stories about Edna cast her life as dramatic, I felt myself shrinking in stature like the little girl in the book *Alice in Wonderland*. I doubted if I could ever measure up to Edna.

"Face it. Her parents will block you," Granddaddy's friends said when confronting him. "Don't get involved with crackpots who have no paid ministers. They believe anyone can speak divine truth, and they make decisions together. Don't fall into Edna's spider trap because you won't like it when we say—'We told you so.'"

Wilmer wasn't sure how to respond to his friends' remarks. Any number of Quaker beliefs proved incomprehensible to many non-Quakers, not the least among them the notion that women were equal to men. This included the idea that decisions should be made cooperatively. Some women in the mainstream culture looked to Native Americans as an example of functioning matrilineal social structures and democratic decision making. Quakers didn't vote on their own internal issues. They relied on a shared spiritual process to reach community decisions. Wilmer's friends challenged my grandfather as to why this Quaker woman, Edna, required so much of his attention.

"She's into women's rights. All women. Not just a few," Wilmer stuttered.

"Good luck" had been the sarcastic response to Granddaddy's explanation that the Iroquois Confederacy or Haudenosaunee, the Inuit of the far north, and Quakers

Wilmer Kearns (*center front*) with business college friends, circa 1900.

subscribed to the concept of cooperative decision making and inclusive attitudes about humanity. This included respect for humans of all backgrounds, the natural surroundings, and more. Humans working together, not against each other, made sense to my grandfather.

An inner divine light was present, regardless of gender, age, class, religion, or any other differences, according to Edna and her mother. In practice during this era, rural American women tended to be more liberated than their urban counterparts. This was due, in part, to a division of labor on the frontier requiring everyone to contribute to the survival of the family. Quaker women conducted their own meetings for worship for business within a larger spiritual community that valued democratic decision making. So it wasn't a matter of Quakers simply believing in the equality of males and females. The concept existed within a larger theological framework.

Granddaddy told me he could imitate Edna in her repetitive insistence that he understand what she meant about an Inner Light. The term suggested a spiritual force in every living being to greater or lesser degrees. To help make her point, Edna reinforced the role of the Inner Light in her shifting direction from art student to women's rights advocate.

"The Inner Light wasn't at the top of my list as a young man," Granddaddy said in an aside to me. It didn't take much for me to figure out that a different kind of spark interested my grandfather—love.

Edna told him about Quaker founder George Fox who, in the 1600s, organized a visible and viable dissenting spiritual movement back in England.[2] She didn't hide the fact that Fox was controversial because he believed in the equality of all humans and life forms. Wilmer described Fox as someone who expected beatings and repeated stays behind prison bars because of his radical spiritual beliefs. Fox inspired an increasing number of dissenters, even as English state and church authorities branded him a dangerous traitor and a loathsome dissident.

Wilmer didn't consider Edna a traitor or an ill-tempered troublemaker. She'd simply decided that she would carry on Quaker faith and practice in her life, even if her brother Smythe and her father Charles didn't. From what Granddaddy told me, Quakers would be on the decline in the United States if they continued to avoid proselytizing. Most didn't believe in strong-arm methods of recruitment. If they didn't do something to attract new members, my grandfather was convinced their numbers might someday lead to extinction.

At their teahouse rendezvous, Edna set aside the orange Wilmer had given her when she ordered a pot of oolong tea, her usual choice. Lucretia Mott loved oolong tea. Then my grandmother decided on a crumpet with lemon marmalade. After Wilmer started working in New York City, he had more loose change in his pockets. He preferred to take responsibility for the tab, as was expected in dating rituals. But this wasn't a date. Edna had insisted more than once that they share the costs of getting together at the teahouse.

Wilmer loved crumpets. His mother never made them, so he ordered one. Henrietta Kearns believed crumpets were "fussy." She liked to prepare Funny Cake, a special Pennsylvania treat she described as a light chocolate cake baked in a pie shell with only fresh country eggs and butter. To Wilmer's mother, crumpets couldn't compete with Funny Cake. Crumpets also wouldn't elicit praise at the breakfast table from John P. Kearns, Wilmer's father. The flat wheat-based buns had firm exteriors and soft centers. Crumpets required baking yeast. Then they were cooked on a griddle and served toasted and buttered, a treat but not substantial enough for hardworking farmhands and automobile workers.

Edna had an agenda she was determined to stick to. While Wilmer liked to weave oranges and Funny Cake into their conversations, Edna chose instead to mention more about Quakers. Wilmer said he asked himself: "What do Quakers have to do with me?" He wasn't interested in knowing more about Quakers if he and Edna continued in the manner of casual friends. Then he realized that Quakers not only referred to themselves as "Friends" with a capital "F," but the term also had other meanings.

"I understood what Edna meant. We are all friends in terms of searching for spiritual truth. That's what we Quakers are saying in so many words," my grandfather told me. But friends with a small "f" seemed less of an invitation to him than a rejection. And Granddaddy winced at Edna's reference to friendship. This set a boundary, and Edna didn't spell out many guidelines. I figured out that my grandfather was expected to act properly without much coaching. The Buckmans were Hicksites, those firmly insisting on the importance of consulting an Inner Light for making decisions.[3]

Wilmer, like his college friends, had heard of Quaker women's participation in women's rights organizing. If non-Quaker women, like Elizabeth Cady Stanton, needed moral support, they asked a Quaker woman like Lucretia Mott for advice. Quaker women stood out among their contemporaries as believing that men and women, and all humans, were equal. And in disputes with the local, state, or the national government, many Quakers—both men and women—put their lives on the line and accepted prison sentences, if necessary, to affirm their beliefs and fundamental spiritual commitments.

Granddaddy continued talking about himself while I listened. He admitted that he might have been afraid of loving Edna too much, that he might lose his identity in hers. Compared to my own experience, the story of George Fox and the Quakers— related by Edna to Wilmer, and then he to me—seemed remote. It wasn't beyond the understanding of my grandfather's generation though. Even then, Quakers were considered peculiar due to their beliefs about equality and their distaste of war.[4]

Edna didn't hesitate to explain to Wilmer about how George Fox memorized his biblical scriptures back and forth, up and down, and inside out. Fox supported establishing more Quaker buildings for worship, called Meeting Houses, in England during an era when no shrines, religious paintings, or stained glass windows were permitted in Quaker houses of worship.

When questioned by his friends at the Philadelphia business college, Wilmer was able to suggest that without Martin Luther and the Protestant Reformation, spiritual dissidents like George Fox and his followers might not have survived the English civil wars and religious controversies. And while Quakers were viewed as "strict," in fact

George Fox (1624–1690), founder of the Religious Society of Friends. Library of Congress.

their lifestyles were, in several ways, progressive when compared to the doctrines and practices of many established churches during the seventeenth and eighteenth centuries.

Granddaddy told me that Fox refused to gamble, drink, overeat, fornicate in brothels, or indulge in many activities other than praying, preaching, singing psalms, and—as the result of his efforts—being run out of town by angry crowds and church authorities. Wilmer said Fox relied on personal experience when he referred to the Inner Light that was viewed as a radical spiritual belief.

Fox and his wife Margaret Fell defended the right of women to become ministers, and they were equally passionate about finding solutions for social issues. Opponents jeered George Fox for his ministry. Rowdy crowds beat, whipped, tortured, and kicked him out of churches, cities, and towns. He was treated as a misguided blasphemer and punished. State and church authorities in England dumped him for extended stays into dungeons and prisons that were filthy, disease ridden, and full of crawling vermin. This could kill or at least permanently damage the bodies of anyone confined in them.

Because so many Quakers faced imprisonment as a result of their beliefs, it wasn't surprising that prison reform became a concern of many participating in the Holy Experiment that William Penn envisioned for Pennsylvania.[5]

When hearing so much background in Granddaddy's stories, I felt like I stood on the edge of a mountain cliff. I could better understand my grandmother only when hearing how the spiritual experiences of Quaker girls and women were rooted in a mystical experience. As Edna reached out for education and interaction, her independence and unique perspectives impacted others.

It seemed logical that Granddaddy had to decide whether or not he'd become a Quaker in order to make points with Edna. And, her responsibility was to determine how and when she'd become a women's rights activist, and if she would marry or not. Later I came to understand that Edna's spiritual journey was rooted less in habit and personality than a reliance on Quaker values and testimonies.

Granddaddy told me that he gradually came to understand why George Fox got in trouble for refusing to take his hat off to his so-called superiors and reject the ideological doctrines of an established church hierarchy. I questioned if I could ever become used to the punishments dealt out to George Fox and his wife Margaret Fell. They suffered from persecution willingly and without complaints. It apparently didn't matter that they considered themselves peaceful and ethical individuals steeped in integrity. Fined and imprisoned often, Fox didn't see his wife for extended periods of time. When they married late in life, Fox and Fell agreed that she would keep her own name and personal property, a highly unusual arrangement for a married couple during this period of history. From what I could tell, becoming a Quaker was daunting to contemplate.

As I watched Granddaddy sort his junk mail from bills in his kitchen, he told me about those in England who labeled George Fox as a heretic and organizer of political resistance. Fox denied the accusations and insisted he was interested only in spiritual matters. He refused to carry a weapon but was imprisoned and discriminated against just the same. Establishment churches with their cadres of priests and ministers weren't sympathetic with Fox's perspective either. In fact, when William Penn's father, a former English admiral, heard that his son had joined the Quakers, he was furious that his own flesh and blood would associate with individuals with such unconventional views and questionable reputations.

My primary childhood goal turned into an insistence that my grandparents marry for love. And as soon as this happened, then the emotional bridge between Edna and me might shrink. I might be able to learn to love her, too, like Granddaddy. The more I understood about Quakers, the closer I would come to moving closer to my grandmother Edna.

While English church authorities held firm to their position that religious seekers required the spiritual direction of ministers, priests, scholars, and an all-powerful and centralized church, Quakers disagreed. As a result, a considerable number of Quakers suffered and died in prison. Many left England, including Edna's Buckman ancestors, who'd sailed on the ship *Welcome* with William Penn and others to live in Pennsylvania and elsewhere along the Eastern seaboard of North America. Later Quaker ministers like Lucretia Mott kept Philadelphia's history and founders in the news.[6]

Thoughts like this filled my head as Granddaddy spun his tales, and my young mind wandered. I noticed how Granddaddy's eyes were a luminous brown with dark streaks of caramel, depending on the light pouring in from his kitchen windows. When there was a knock on the door one day, it turned out to be the newspaper carrier collecting cash for the weekly delivery. The door opening resulted in a draft in the room, and I shivered as Granddaddy was distracted paying the bill. I wondered if my grandfather, when he met Edna as a young man, really had much of an understanding of Quakers, much less Quaker women like Lucretia Mott.

An epicenter for Quakers, Philadelphia had been home to many independent women, including abolitionist and women's rights advocate Lucretia Mott, a visible and outspoken activist. Mott founded a female antislavery society during a period when many abolitionist men wouldn't permit women to serve in the movement in other than supportive roles. Women were expected to defer to the men and not seek leadership positions.

Philadelphians had heard of Mott's Society in 1838 when the organization sponsored an interracial women's abolitionist convention, a major affront to many white city residents. An angry crowd gathered and hurled rocks at Pennsylvania Hall at Sixth and Haines Streets where the convention delegates met. As the ire of the mob, estimated at fifteen thousand, accelerated, an integrated line of women linked arms to escape the building. The hostile crowd burned Pennsylvania Hall to the ground. Three days of violence targeting African Americans followed in the streets, with even an orphanage falling victim.[6]

"This sent an unwelcome message about mixed groups struggling together," Granddaddy told me. Wilmer kept me on the edge of my chair as he stuffed his tales with heroes and scoundrels. When he piled his own lunch plate with tuna salad and hard-boiled eggs, Granddaddy made forays into other creative spaces. This included telling me about the Pennsylvania Dutch tradition of "bundling." In this example of the folkways of a previous era, unmarried couples slept overnight in bed together, cuddling and staying warm together with a board separating them. Granddaddy's stories, like this, made the long Pennsylvania winters bearable as I waited for the return of spring.

Chapter 9

The Spirit of 1776 Wagon

When I hiked over to Granddaddy's house, I'd find him standing next to an open mailbox with his name painted in red bold letters—Wilmer R. Kearns. He waited for the postal carrier to deliver his mail, including packages of fenugreek seeds and peanut butter from his organic supplier, Walnut Acres, in rural Pennsylvania. Sometimes I carried a bouquet of daisies for my grandfather, as he adored wildflowers. Although his garden brimmed with cultivated plantings of iris, dahlias, lilies, roses, peonies, and tulips, he was always pleased by the gift of a handpicked wild bouquet.

One day my mother, brothers, and sister stopped at Granddaddy's on their way home from an appointment with our family physician. They piled out of the car near Wilmer's mailbox. After agreeing to unveil Edna's suffrage campaign wagon, Granddaddy reached for a handle to the overhead garage door to show us the suffrage movement artifact. As he ran his hands over the wagon's axles, oak wheel rims, and side wood panels, my grandfather told the same story I'd heard throughout my years in elementary school.

"George Washington loved this wagon. So did your grandmother Edna when she used it as a platform for giving freedom speeches in New York City's streets and on Long Island."

My pulse settled and then revived again. I felt blood rushing to my fingertips. I hadn't uncovered all the mysteries associated with a woman's spirit yet. I was clueless about finding a way to rid myself of anxiety about gender injustices. My grandfather claimed that patriarchy didn't end after women legally won the right to vote in 1920 by way of the Nineteenth Amendment to the US Constitution. At night I sensed the full moon in the sky, not because I could see the moon out of my bedroom window. I couldn't. I sensed the moon's tug on my chest. Young people didn't have many rights, a topic I should have brought more vigorously to Granddaddy's attention. The girl-boy situation made no sense to me either. I believed that the solutions to gender imbalances depended on education, and that once the facts were presented, we'd all agree and change course.

"That's not really how the world works," my grandfather told me.

I winced when he included the word "reality" in our conversation. I didn't ask any more about this so-called state of being because this top-down social order didn't sound logical to me. Who came up with the idea of some privileged people at the top and others stacked under them, down to the basement? If my grandparents found themselves in the position of airing their complaints in public, the situation must have been serious. And Granddaddy gave no indication that social conditions had changed dramatically over the decades since 1920.

"It's better than it used to be," he said, and changed the subject to the suffrage campaign wagon stored in his garage. I hoped all of the injustices and misunderstandings might be resolved by this wagon that my grandfather doted over. I questioned if the old wagon was like a pill young people like me could swallow to solve the problems of the planet. I hoped so, and waited to hear more about this wagon that even had "spirit" in its name.

Spirit of 1776 suffrage wagon on its first organizing journey from Manhattan to Long Island, July 1913. *Left to right*: Edna Buckman Kearns, Serena Kearns, and Irene Davison.

Granddaddy was certain that George Washington used the old wagon to inspect troops before the Battle of Long Island. So I created a mental construct of General Washington, the father of our nation, giving a pep talk to his soldiers when surrounded by clouds of cannon and gun smoke. My brothers, sister, and I were secure in the knowledge, passed on by my grandfather, that a patriot, Ebenezer Conklin from Huntington, New York, built the wagon in a Long Island barn in 1776. I was sure that, after completing the sanding and polishing, Mr. Conklin painted the words "Spirit of 1776" on the sides and rear of the wagon, a theme of the American Revolution and one rationale for the women's rights movement.[1]

"And what exactly was this spirit of 1776?" I asked Granddaddy.

"Everybody wanted some of this spirit," he said. "It was a protest against taxes and oppression."

If it hadn't been for the wagon, I might not have thought much about the history of the tea tax boycott of 1776. I added to this mental muddle a grandmother I never met, the source of her woman's power I didn't fully understand, and a horse-drawn vehicle I sat on summers when my mother took photos of us kids with a Brownie camera. I didn't realize then that "taxation without representation" was tested in 1913 with the campaign wagon promoting a link between the American Revolution and the early women's rights movement.

Many women's suffrage supporters identified with the early colonists in revolt. Some Long Island residents fiercely defended their loyalist backgrounds, in particular the descendants of former Tory sympathizers like the Jones family of Long Island. This family was divided on women's voting rights. Edna's friend Rosalie Jones aligned herself with the suffrage activists. Her mother and sister supported the opposition, or the "antis."[2]

From what I could tell, the wagon was a trigger releasing emotional expressions of noble values, principled ideals, and patriotic sentiments. It was generally viewed in 1776 that the concept of the spirit of 1776 had the power to break fragile bonds between England and its colonies. And then, later on, it also had the potential of affecting power relationships between men and women.

That's what Wilmer suggested to me with his stories. For him, the wagon evoked images of hearts and minds filled with courage, bravura, and defiance expressed in forceful speeches and proclamations. Abigail Adams, the nation's second First Lady, referred to the Spirit of 1776's tenacity when she wrote in a letter to her husband John Adams: "The flame is kindled, and like lightning it catches from soul to soul."[3]

My grandfather explained to me that the American Revolution represented a major conflict involving mostly men, many of them plantation owners who didn't take seriously appeals to extend human rights and freedom to women, native peoples, and African Americans. Some in the women's movement promoted the patriotic protest theme as far back as the 1848 women's convention in Seneca Falls. The underlying significance of this revolutionary spirit relied on a belief in the power of patriotic protest that competed with an interpretation of patriotism as "my country right or wrong." If a conflict needed solving, those subscribing to the patriotic protest rationale considered it a necessity to fix whatever injustice deserved attention rather than justifying or continuing it.[4]

It took decades for me to be exposed to historians who argued that the reliance on patriotism as protest shifted during the First World War to a more conservative interpretation of patriotism consistent with war. Some scholarly researchers have pointed out that the patriotic protest perspective was tested in social initiatives that included the abolitionist, civil rights and gay rights movements. Patriotic protest was also used to justify other movements in US history, including the antibusing, antiabortion, and Tea Party campaigns of the twentieth century.[5]

Scholar Simon Hall argues that there is sufficient evidence to support the patriotic protest theme when Elizabeth Cady Stanton and others edited the nation's Declaration of Independence in 1848 to read that all men *and* women were created equal. The US women organizing for voting and other rights numbered their grievances and complaints in their own freedom declaration, just as the revolutionary colonists did something similar in 1776.

Not until I was older did I understand that the organizers of the Seneca Falls women's convention tied their demands to the Declaration of Independence so that it stood as evidence of the nation's unfinished revolution. The women of New Zealand, Australia, and four western states in the US had approved women's voting rights by the turn of the twentieth century.

Edna and her mother viewed the prospect of winning US women's voting rights as difficult, but not impossible. The addition of martyrs strengthened the visibility of the long suffrage movement effort. The campaigns for women's voting rights had martyrs in both England and the US. The king's horse during the 1913 derby in England, the traditional horse race, trampled suffrage activist and protester Emily Wilding Davison. And by 1916, the US also had a martyr—Inez Milholland, who died while on a women's rights speaking tour of the western US. Edna B. Kearns had worked with Inez on women's rights issues in New York State.

Granddaddy told me that many activists within the decentralized early women's rights movement were not in agreement about continuing a state-by-state campaign as compared to a conviction that voting rights could be best achieved by way of an amendment to the US Constitution. That's when Granddaddy told me his version of what had happened with the old wagon.

"After the Brits won the Battle of Long Island in 1776, they captured New York City and the wagon. General Washington hightailed it south so he wouldn't get captured," Wilmer told me as part of a long-winded explanation.

"And then?"

"After the revolutionaries rescued the wagon, they hid it away for safety."

"Where?"

"In a Long Island barn—until Mr. Remson found it in 1884."

I discovered later that Granddaddy's version of the old wagon's history wasn't confirmed by primary sources. If the wagon had been built about 1820, as later transportation scholars have claimed, this would have placed the wagon's construction several decades *after* George Washington's death. My grandfather wasn't aware of this, and I wasn't either at a young age. A happy ending for Granddaddy's wagon story relied on Isaac Remson, founder and owner of the I. S. Remson Company.

After Mr. Remson's death, company president A. F. Wilson donated the horse-drawn wagon to assist women activists organizing for the vote. The donation came with a perk for the Remson firm. This came in the form of advertising painted on the wagon after a series of letters was exchanged between the wagon company and representatives of the state suffrage association in Manhattan. By the fall of 1913, suffrage association president Harriet May Mills, nearing the end of her term in office, presented the campaign wagon to Edna Kearns in a letter so she could continue its use in votes for women organizing.

It took decades for me to learn the difference between academic scholarship and my grandfather's storytelling, especially when his version of history proved to be infinitely more fascinating than what I learned in school. In all fairness, Granddaddy might have said, "For all I know, George Washington may have traveled in this wagon," or, "I bet Nathan Hale would have liked this old buggy too." If Wilmer offered disclaimers, he may not have shared them with a reporter from a Philadelphia area newspaper, the *Ambler Gazette*, when on August 19, 1943, the vehicle was again associated with the Long Island patriot cause.

To me, Harriet May Mills, I. S. Remson, and A. F. Wilson had earned their laurels as the wagon's saviors. And based on what Granddaddy told me, the vehicle survived cannon balls, rifle shots, and capture by the British. In later years, some of my family members were convinced the wagon was worth a million dollars or more. They believed our family would become famous someday because of the wagon's caretaking and preservation. But this wasn't to be. The commitment and belief in the ideals the wagon represented inspired Granddaddy, who following Edna's death in 1934, spent the rest of his life preserving and advocating for the old wagon. As an adult, I followed in his footsteps by recognizing that the wagon's value was in the ideals it symbolized rather than its monetary value.

"The full history of the wagon is not known, but it is believed to have been used to transport troops for George Washington," the 1943 *Ambler Gazette* feature article noted when citing Granddaddy as the source of the claims he circulated when driving the wagon in the Philadelphia area. "Nathan Hale is said to have used it in his expedition to gather information for the colonials behind British lines" was one of Granddaddy's featured newspaper quotations.

The 1943 newspaper coverage of Wilmer Kearns and his friend M. J. Guthrie highlighted their wagon tour of Philadelphia-area towns and villages. The journey brought scores of residents out of their homes to fill sidewalks and porches to stare at the wagon and its drivers. It took me years to separate fact from fiction. But when I first heard the wagon story, I wasn't discriminating when listening to speeches about the alleged "oldest wagon in America." My grandfather had no proof of the wagon's age, but he didn't let facts stand in the way of telling a memorable story.

The lack of sufficient horses and wagons to carry food, supplies, and equipment over poor or nonexistent roads plagued General George Washington during the American Revolution. He hired wagons and drivers to transport supplies, food, and necessities. Horse-drawn wagons were also donated or impressed into service. But vehicles used for pleasure, such as the Spirit of 1776 wagon with springs, weren't in use until well after 1800.

Statements that Wilmer Kearns made to the press about the campaign wagon's age and significance raised questions among several of my family members. One example—my mother's remark to Aunt Serena that I overheard: "If George Washington made this wagon so valuable, then why did the Remson Company give it away— free—to the women?" Aunt Serena was young when she first rode in the old wagon. She shared her opinion in later years that if General Washington had carried supplies in the wagon, there wouldn't have been enough room for him, two assistants, and several cartons of bandages.

George Washington was well known throughout eastern Pennsylvania for sleeping in the homes of area residents during the American Revolution, with historic road

Wilmer Kearns (*right*) with his friend M. J. Guthrie on a 1943 trip traveling with the Spirit of 1776 wagon in the Philadelphia area.

markers installed at inns, private homes, and on public highways. It seemed reasonable to me for the famous general to have awarded the old horse-drawn wagon with perpetual distinction by riding in it. In all fairness to Mr. Remson, Mr. Wilson, and the legend they passed on to Harriet May Mills and the suffrage activists, scholarship associated with wagon designs and transportation construction wasn't highly developed in the late 1800s and early 1900s. Wagon owners drafted stories to suit themselves, and reporters didn't necessarily ask to examine primary sources.

"Don't take seriously everything the teachers tell thee about the Revolutionary War," my grandfather suggested after explaining to me how the conflict with England in 1776 had been a messy affair, colonial neighbor against neighbor, with numerous instances of families split down the middle. He said that some colonists found England's administration acceptable, while others supported insurrection. "Those who were taxed were angry, and those who owned little or nothing to be taxed resented those who did," he told me.

My social studies book didn't mention colonial riots, soldier desertions, and a network of women offering support and aid to the rebels. Granddaddy also told me about a population of dissenters who weren't necessarily of one mind about which side they were on. Wilmer got many of his details right, even if I wasn't convinced that George Washington rode in my grandmother's campaign wagon.

The taxation protests reached activists' hungry ears as the federal government in 1913 tightened the network of support for a compulsory national income tax. When Edna Kearns and others hit the road in New York City and on Long Island with their protest caravans, they promoted the "taxation without representation is tyranny" rationale and challenged the right of the national government in Washington to levy taxes on women and others who were prevented from voting.

"At least the old vehicle was stashed away, safe and sound in a barn," I thought back then, especially after hearing that the English captured New York City and turned the seaport into a Tory stronghold in 1776. According to my grandfather, the populations of many communities on Long Island, outside of New York City, relocated to New England and other regions. Edna's Quaker ancestors kept busy milking cows on their Bucks County farms outside of Philadelphia while keeping a distance from the hostilities. Some of Wilmer's ancestors back in rural Pennsylvania enlisted in the Revolutionary Army, while Edna's remained firm in their opposition to war.

"The uprising was more than a couple of gadflies who wrote up a document in Philadelphia declaring independence from England," my grandfather emphasized as he sipped a cup of hot fenugreek tea in his kitchen. "The country's founders had their axes to grind. If thee scratches the surface, a broader picture will come to light."

"Like what?"

"Thee may be surprised about what floats up to the surface."

My teacher Mr. Culbertson didn't include research skills in the sixth grade curriculum. I don't remember a library in my elementary school either. My collection of wagon facts depended on my visits to Granddaddy when he had more to say about

I. S. Remson, who founded his Brooklyn wagon business in 1850. Remson died in 1910, but not before setting out to purchase the oldest wagon on Long Island to add to his vehicle collection.

"Fewer horses and wagons were on the streets when I moved to Manhattan," Granddaddy said when explaining how Mr. Remson told family members and employees the hard facts about automobiles replacing horses and wagons. Remson hurt financially as the expanding automobile industry threatened to force his wagon business into bankruptcy.

This led to more background about how Isaac Remson did the best he could tracking down Long Island's oldest wagon. This enhanced his reputation as an expert specializing in horse-drawn vehicles. Company employees obsessed over new ways to promote the wagon business as gasoline-fueled automobiles became a persistent feature on city thoroughfares and country byways. If the women activists campaigned with the wagon in rural Long Island, the Remson firm might receive valuable publicity for its products, according to my grandfather.

I. S. Remson had been raised on Long Island. When he traveled there with the intention of purchasing the island's oldest wagon, he relied on former contacts to assist him. In 1884, with the help of a scout, he added a sleigh and a wagon, both named the Spirit of 1776, to his transportation collection in Brooklyn.

Both items relied on claims that they'd been built by Ebenezer Conklin, an alleged patriot from Huntington on Long Island. I found no documentation decades later confirming the wagon and sleigh's revolutionary associations with someone named Ebenezer Conklin or anyone else. Remson firm president A. F. Wilson did his part prior to the wagon's July 1913 dedication by contacting metropolitan newspapers to promote media coverage of the wagon's donation to the women's cause. He stressed the vehicle's alleged revolutionary origins. And Remson firm employees did what they could to follow through on the donation's publicity potential.[6]

The claim that a revolutionary patriot built the wagon relied on oral history reportedly provided by the seller, a Mr. Hewlett, who steered I. S. Remson to the old wagon and sleigh stored in a Long Island barn. In 1885, the Brooklyn Daily Eagle devoted almost a half page to the history of the sleigh, possibly the more colorful of the two acquisitions. In this way, the legend of the Spirit of 1776, as illustrated by two items from Long Island, was entered into the newspaper's record.[7] My search for the wagon in public records later never uncovered the fate of the sleigh.

The Brooklyn Daily Eagle article suggested that I. S. Remson may have paid an inflated price for the two artifacts as questions were continually raised about the wagon's origins and significance.[8] Apparently this didn't matter to state suffrage association president Harriet May Mills, a longtime advocate of the taxation without representation suffrage argument.[9] The 1776 spirit rationale defined news coverage when Edna Kearns, Serena Kearns, and Irene Corwin Davison showed up in Manhattan wearing revolutionary-style uniforms and tricornered hats supporting the logic behind "taxation without representation." They traveled in the horse-drawn wagon from Manhattan to Long Island during the July and August heat of the 1913 summer season.[10]

After the wagon's acquisition in the late 1800s, Remson Company officials pressed the wagon into service. They assigned an employee to drive through Brooklyn's streets over the Fourth of July holiday to advertise the wagon and carriage works. In one letter between the Remson firm and the women activists, company officials described their employee as a tall man who wore a colonial period costume advertising the benefits of horses and buggies.[11]

The Independence Day wagon observances attracted some public interest, even if founder I. S. Remson didn't live long enough to observe the intense teeth grinding in his firm's accounting office as company profits dropped dramatically after 1910. That's when Andrew F. Wilson, Remson Company president, proposed the idea of donating the Spirit of 1776 horse-drawn wagon to the state women's suffrage association. Unfortunately, the impact of gasoline-fueled vehicles had already made horses and buggies obsolete.

The following letter from Andrew Wilson to a Mrs. Lee of the New York State Woman Suffrage Association offering the artifact to the women's movement demonstrates the carriage firm's commitment to donate the wagon:

I. S. Remson Manufacturing Co., Manufacturers Importers and Dealers in Carriages, Harness, Blankets, and Iron Stable Fixtures, 740–750 Grand Street Brooklyn, New York

June 19, 1913

Mrs. Lee, N.Y.S. Woman Suffrage Ass'n, 180 Madison Ave., N.Y.

Dear Madam,

In going through our stock the other day, I discovered an old style vehicle which, according to the records that Mr. Remson obtained some twenty years ago when we secured the wagon, was the property of Ebenezer Kellum on Huntington, L.I. (as I remember it) and which has been used by our house for advertising purposes at different times in various parades. Usually when it was sent out we had a large man, Amos Veritan, who wears his hair long and is a splendid representation of the familiar Uncle Sam . . .

Chapter 10

Getting to Know the
Family on Edgar Allan Poe's Chairs

*W*ilmer Kearns would have been relieved to hear a bluebird's tweets coming from the foliage on the day of his visit to the Buckman family home. Soaked limbs drooped over the lush lawn when climbing rose bushes were in bloom. The landscape near Echo Dale filled with the songs of wrens as the country air cleared with a light mist evaporating on the lawn's grass cover. He traveled on the train from Philadelphia to the Buckman family residence near Norristown and arrived fifteen minutes earlier than what Edna suggested.

Echo Dale was so named because of an echo in the valley, a location near Sandy Hill Road in Plymouth Heights, northwest of the city. My mother once told me that on a clear day she could see all the way to Philadelphia from Echo Dale. This might not be possible today, but it was then.[1] Taking Edna's stated desire seriously that they be "just friends," Granddaddy told me he supported Edna reaching her potential and finding contentment being unmarried, if that suited her.

"This was the job of a friend," he told me. "To support Edna's happiness."

Granddaddy said he was tempted to reject Bess as Edna's best friend. He'd never faced a situation where a young woman like Edna relied on another woman's friendship to prevent romance from entering the picture. And he'd never encountered a circumstance where a legend, such as the Buckman's association with a famous literary figure like Edgar Allan Poe, played such a pivotal role in family affairs.

Granddaddy told me about the first visit to Echo Dale with such intensity, I sensed myself there with him on the day of the tea reception. I couldn't help wondering how Buckman family members would greet my grandfather. Would they accept him? Or would this occasion foreshadow other difficulties in the future? Such thoughts filled my head as I squirmed on Granddaddy's kitchen chair. If I concentrated, I could slide in behind him in the story, as he told it, and observe Edna for myself.

Once through the front door and inside Echo Dale, Granddaddy and I stared up at the staircase rising before us. I hoped for a guide to help me locate Edna's bedroom, as well as the rooms of her brother Smythe and my great-grandparents on the second floor. Granddaddy took me by the hand and steered me to the right,

Echo Dale, the Buckman family home, circa 1910.

toward a living area doubling as a tearoom where Buckman family members waited to meet him. There they'd drink tea and fill themselves with cake and the bite-sized sandwiches May prepared.

I moved close to Edna and studied her hands. They were long, with thin delicate bones. Wilmer grinned, and I realized this expression may have served as a cover-up for the disorientation he felt. I felt like an outsider, a sensation made worse because I witnessed this scene grounded in a narrative told to me by my grandfather.

Wilmer said he had nothing to lose by sitting on the parlor chairs with Edna, her brother, mother, and her great-grandmother—or more correctly, Edna's step-great-grandmother, Mary Ann. I hoped this gathering might lead to Edna changing her mind about marriage. Granddaddy would have loved to notice any signs of encouragement from Edna, but he wasn't bold enough to press the point. He'd already listened to Edna at the Market Street teahouse describing the Buckmans as peaceful Quakers going about their daily routines by thee-ing and thou-ing each other and making decisions based on integrity carried out to the best of their ability.

"I hope thee had a comfortable journey on the train," Edna said to Wilmer.

She didn't appear nervous as she spoke to him, but I couldn't join in with the conversation. Even if I had, Edna wouldn't have been able to hear me from where I sat in Granddaddy's kitchen, my eyes closed in a distant reverie.

"Edna was the perfect hostess. She smiled at the gift I brought her," Wilmer told me.

"What was it?"

"A red rose."

I liked the red rose reference, an item familiar and reassuring. May, Edna's mother, suggested that Wilmer Kearns and the Buckman family members engage in light conversation before unveiling her prize tea wagon loaded with cups, saucers, and plates. The cart stood ready with biscuits, spice cake, tiny sandwiches, and bonbons as anticipation built for tea and conversation. I'd grown up with the so-called Edgar Allan Poe chairs, lined up like a shrine in Granddaddy's living room. And I couldn't leave Echo Dale without facing the journey back to my grandfather's kitchen where I'd hit the dark sides of a long tunnel with shifting shadows of the past.

"Mamma might seem strange, but bear up the best thee can," Edna whispered to Wilmer. "Sit next to me. I've been looking forward to thy arrival since dawn."

Edna's mother poured him a cup of jasmine tea. Some family members used lemon in their tea. Granddaddy liked cream and sugar. He hid his nervousness by anticipating a plate of watercress tea sandwiches headed in his direction. Edna held her cup and saucer steady with her pinky stuck out. She sipped her tea slowly. That day she'd pinned freshly picked roses into her hair, a signature feature for Edna that resulted, as usual, in arousing my grandfather's interest.

Wilmer surreptitiously studied Edna's translucent skin. I didn't miss this opportunity to observe Edna carefully when socializing took the course of predictable small talk. Granddaddy mentioned to those gathered how much he liked Fairmount Park, the thick forests and meadows filled with stalks of swaying red blooms. I could tell that Edna liked Wilmer, especially how he held his own in social situations, a quality Edna hoped her mother would notice. Then May introduced Wilmer to what she referred to as the Edgar Allan Poe chairs.

Wilmer admired Poe's writing, and his expression identified him as a fan of the controversial and innovative bard. But Edna hadn't mentioned much to Wilmer about her family's connection to Poe, whom some Philadelphia residents tagged as one of the nation's literary giants. Others, by comparison, couldn't say enough to cast doubt on Poe's reputation.

"The parlor chairs we're sitting on came from Poe's former home in Philadelphia," May explained as Edna lifted a sugar cube from a serving bowl. Wilmer poured so much cream into his cup, the liquid splashed onto the saucer. Edna sat up straight as her mother referred to the controversial writer's sojourn in Philadelphia from 1838 to 1844. This included the year 1843 when the Poe family rented the rear of a property on North Seventh Street in the Northern Liberties section of Philadelphia.[2] May placed the author's Philadelphia residency in the larger context of his life.

". . . It was the best of times, it was the worst of times for Poe and his family," she said.

Edgar Allan Poe house, near North Seventh Street, Philadelphia, administered by the National Park Service. Library of Congress, 1967.

Wilmer resisted the impulse to point out to May that this quote had been lifted from *A Tale of Two Cities*, the 1859 novel by Charles Dickens. My grandfather didn't want to make a poor impression by correcting Edna's mother. The other facts sounded correct about how in 1843 Edgar Allan Poe, his wife Virginia and mother-in-law Maria Poe Clemm, or "Muddy," rented this structure not far from Spring Garden Street. Philadelphians claimed that Poe had been productive when living there. He wrote poetry, articles, literary reviews, and stories there, including "The Black Cat" and "The Gold Bug."[3]

"Our relatives from the Jones side of our family became Poe's landlord for a spell," May interjected. No one present challenged this claim or disagreed.

Wilmer sat back in his Poe chair after Edna's mother May passed around slices of spice cake. The recipe came from Mrs. Hattie A. Burr's women's suffrage cookbook. May's term for her entertaining style was "spiritual hospitality." She practiced this type of hospitality whenever friends and family members gathered to talk about honoring their Quaker heritage. Edna wasn't certain if the formal stuffed chairs had been used in Poe's rented quarters, or if they'd been part of the parlor furnishings from the red brick house around the corner that she believed had been owned by Poe's prior

Edgar Allan Poe daguerreotype, 1848. Library of Congress.

Quaker landlord, William M. Alburger. I questioned if the chairs were used by the landlord, Poe himself, at both residences—or not at all.[4]

"Make of this what thee wants," Edna whispered to Wilmer. Then she winked.

Wilmer decided that he would. Whether or not these claims had substance, the Buckman family members, except for Edna, spoke as if the Poe chairs represented gospel truth. Granddaddy didn't understand the significance of pinning down the precise identity of Poe's landlord, or if the designation had bounced like hot coals from one set of Quaker families to another.

Edna whispered to Wilmer that whoever arrived to collect the monthly rent had to face the fact that Poe couldn't meet his financial commitments. And so the rumor circulating around Philadelphia for decades had to do with whether or not the landlord, whoever it was, agreed to accept the furniture the poet allegedly offered in exchange for back rent. That was before Poe moved with his family to New York City in 1844.

If the claim contained even a grain of truth, it might suggest that the Buckman family members, and Wilmer Kearns himself, were sitting on the same parlor furniture that the poet used personally to receive guests. Granddaddy emphasized to me that he wasn't a detective. And Poe had the reputation of writing the first detective story in the English language. Rubbing elbows with Edgar Allan Poe was accomplished by sitting on his alleged chairs in the family's tearoom. This connection turned out to be equal in importance to the later family legend linking the suffrage campaign wagon with George Washington and the Battle of Long Island in 1776.

I suspected that these family stories weren't entirely reliable, as evidenced by legends in other families associating them with key players and events in American history. One friend of mine claimed an ancestral grandfather had replaced General George Custer's metal shoes on his horses. Later I decided that those lacking in social status either manufactured or relied on family legends to enhance their social standing. This provided context and direction, as well as suggesting symbolic significance when elevating certain families to higher positions of importance, even if these same legends might later be debunked by descendants like me.

The tea party conversation focused on the commentary about the Poe chairs, as well as the significance of Edna completing her schooling. Even Edna wondered if she had the commitment and skills to devote to a life of social activism.

"Our sweet Edna will make a difference among those paving the way for women's rights," May noted. Her attention focused on Wilmer, who, I suspected, had only a vague idea of what a "Quaker leading" involved.[5] Perhaps it was May's intention to remind those assembled at Echo Dale that Edna had links to a long Quaker history in the Philadelphia area, and he did not.

"Our Edna is called to work for equality. To be in the world and serve," May added. "Whatever resistance she faces only adds to her determination to bring the opposition over to our side."

Edna shifted in her Poe chair, as if uncomfortable with her mother speaking for her. So she added her own opinion to the subject under discussion.

"There's room for new thinking about freedom by young women today," she said.

Wilmer told me he didn't consider himself informed enough to comment. Philadelphia newspapers may not have featured the news of New Zealand qualifying as the first nation to empower its women with the ballot. Word may not have reached my grandfather or Buckman family members of the thirty-three thousand signatures collected in Australia to achieve partial suffrage there by 1902. For women throughout the world, voting rights arrived in one of several ways: slowly, quickly after a momentum developed as a result of organizing, national independence, or as a by-product of war and revolution.

A global tide of awareness touched off equality marches and advocacy campaigns in various locations around the US, especially New York State, which was considered the "cradle" of the US women's rights movement. This was, in part, due to the Seneca Falls women's convention in the Finger Lakes region in Upstate New York in 1848. For all the significance this held for Edna and her mother, Wilmer was more interested in watercress tea sandwiches. And for my part, I wondered if the Poe chairs had secret compartments with coded messages, like bottles thrown from ships. Perhaps Poe's wife, Virginia, had once sewn covers to place over the parlor chairs to make them last longer.

Granddaddy brought me down to earth when he mentioned that Poe couldn't have cared less about women's rights. Poe grew up in the South and didn't question social arrangements, including the institution of slavery and the limitations placed on women and girls. Many early women's rights advocates like Edna understood and appreciated the persistence and accomplishments of the so-called "war horses" of earlier voting rights campaigns.

The advocacy of the suffrage old guard like Susan B. Anthony, Elizabeth Cady Stanton, Lucy Stone, and many others had resulted in a broader female support base by the turn of the twentieth century. Poe lived until 1849. It's likely that by then he knew little or nothing about the increasing dissatisfaction of US women. Poe courted several single older women after his wife Virginia died from tuberculosis at an early age. Some of Poe's later love interests were wealthy widows, and if they wrote poetry, he referred to them as "lady poets."

Few women writers of the period before the Civil War reached the level of Poe's literary stature. He didn't leave a stone unturned when expressing his free spirit. Granddaddy made it clear to me that gossip circulating in Philadelphia characterized Edgar Allan Poe as living modestly. And according to my grandfather, the word "modest" concealed the negative impact of the author's roller coaster lifestyle, the financial and personal challenges he faced, and the difficulty of any writer, male or female, to be able to earn a living with a pen and paper. No copyright laws existed. Publishers were primed to publish articles, reviews, poetry, and fiction. They were less eager to compensate authors for their works.

I wanted to become a writer someday by following Edna's lead. But the situation for Poe and those who followed him wasn't encouraging. Editors and magazine owners paid Poe for his freelance writing and short stories occasionally. More often than not, Poe arrived home intoxicated with empty pockets or in utter frustration, especially after accepting employment requiring an overload of editorial work for little pay. Most women in Edna's generation weren't in a position to set aside their domestic responsibilities to pursue liberty and justice, let alone write treatises and novels. Women's limited access to education, birth control, employment, and quality medical care only made matters worse. Only a handful of women used men's pen names to publish their novels and prose.

If a writer like Poe wasn't able to put food on the table for his family, my grandfather told me he couldn't imagine how Edna, as an activist and newspaper columnist, could manage without a husband unless she lived at home with her parents. Young women faced limited choices, whether single or married. My grandfather wasn't in a position to predict how writing would eventually open up numerous opportunities for women. Newspapers, which were founded with regularity by 1900 in the New York City metropolitan area, provided an outlet for some female writers. But by then, Poe and his lady poets were six feet under the ground.

Granddaddy said he struggled against feelings he later described to me as despondent over Edna's boundary of "just friends" and her hesitancy to make decisions that might interfere with her own personal freedom. When visiting at Echo Dale, I noticed how Wilmer presented himself as enthusiastic about the upcoming twentieth century. Edna, like many aspiring women activists, was aware of the need for a strong and visible national support coalition.

Many women of that era took advantage of the few socially acceptable opportunities available to them, even if they decided later to double their impact in movement work by exercising their rights of free speech, assembly, and the use of bold and innovative campaign strategies and tactics. If the Buckman family's interest in Edgar Allan Poe had any advantages, it was associated with the idea that someone like Edna might write someday for newspapers and utilize media outlets as resources in campaigns for social change.

"Where does thee fit into the next century, Edna dear?" asked great-grandmother Mary Ann Brooke Buckman.

"Wherever I'm needed," Edna replied.

Granddaddy had a knack for filling in the blanks when telling me a story. He said Edna wasn't fully convinced she had the strength and perseverance to respond to a divine calling relative to women's rights. My grandmother must have struggled to overcome persistent excuses to become involved in activism. These could include her mother needing her help at home, the grueling routines of attending art school, or the painful theological schism of 1828 to 1829 that divided Philadelphia Quakers between the Orthodox and Hicksite factions.

Identifying with the Hicksite faction made Edna's decision making depend more on personal experience and reflection, rather than interpreting scripture—like Orthodox Quakers relied on—for insight and direction. Since Buckman family members identified as Hicksites, Edna suggested to Wilmer that someday the obstacles before her would dissolve and "the way will open."[6]

Wilmer said he swallowed hard, even with a piece of spice cake lodged in his throat. He struggled to keep his polite social mask attached, from the corners of his forehead down to his chin. He had his doubts, and not many sources for guidance, other than Edna and those he met at the Penington in New York, about how to relate to and understand Quakers. If he'd asked his mother for advice about Edna, most likely Henrietta Kearns would have said, "Whatever feels right to you, dear. The Lord moves in mysterious ways."

If loyalty was the goal, Edna already had this in friendship from Wilmer Kearns. Granddaddy told me he did his best to hide his feelings for her, holding himself back from revealing how he adored everything about her. This included Edna's loose skirt falling casually around her ankles and the way she didn't bind her waist and chest with a corset. He appreciated how she avoided accentuating her long dresses like former generations of women who forced their wide skirts into hoop shapes.

Edna's eyes weren't trained to the floor, as a more demure woman's behavior would have dictated. She didn't attempt to seduce a man with dewy expressions generated by commercial eye drops advertised to give the impression of availability. According to Granddaddy, Edna didn't fit the profile of a typical woman in search of a husband. He liked this about her. He remained cautious about Bess and her boycott of marriage. If Edna changed her mind about a wedding, she would surely have conditions. Could he meet the challenges?

I worried about the slow pace of the Buckman family tea party. From my perspective, the entire afternoon could pass without any progress leading toward the topic of marriage. Would my grandfather gift Edna with an engagement ring? Would he persist if she returned an engagement ring with her usual response of "just friends"? Or would he use the passage of time to his advantage? The rationale justifying the popular Cult of Blessed Singleness, spread by way of Bible quotes, recommended that young women value an unmarried state, a condition they should celebrate. To an increasing number of those in the soapbox generation, marriage had an unsavory reputation. This included Edgar Allan Poe marrying Virginia, his thirteen-year-old first cousin, when he was twenty-seven.

Vagueness had helped the Poe chair legend gain traction within the Buckman family. Poe wasn't a Quaker, and he never considered becoming one. However, he provided plenty of content for his Quaker neighbors to gossip about. Poe's former landlord, Mr. Alburger, was a member of the Religious Society of Friends, as were the Jones family members related to the Buckmans after Ann Comly married Thomas Buckman. Mr. Alburger may have been identified in city records as a plumber, but more often than not neighbors and others simply referred to him as Poe's Quaker landlord.

"Mamma never tires of reminding us of how valuable these chairs are, even if she doesn't like Poe's writings," Edna added in an aside to Wilmer. Family oral history confirmed the Buckman family's claim to a direct connection to and a stake in ownership of what they referred to as the Poe chairs. My virtual witnessing of Granddaddy's first visit to Echo Dale to meet the Buckman family provoked Wilmer to challenge me again about my role in this family drama.

"If you don't write our family story, who will?" Granddaddy asked me. My grandfather threw down the gauntlet to me. I had little confidence I would ever write well enough to share the drama of the Buckman family and the Poe chairs. Only when sitting in in Granddaddy's kitchen did I have access to what seemed like supernatural powers allowing me to close my eyes and project myself back to the early 1900s. My pulse was reduced to a slow beat. I suppressed any recognizable facial expressions as the Buckman family's tea party resumed.

"Tell us about thy father, Wilmer," May asked after platters of spice cake and watercress tea sandwiches had been circulated for a second round.

"My dad runs a horse and buggy business, back where I was born, near Harrisburg," he said.

"And thy mother?"

"She was educated in a Civil War orphanage."

"And how does thee describe thyself?"

"A Snyder County man descended from pious women, God-fearing farmers, ore miners, and soldiers."

I waited to hear what May said after a pause following the reference to my grandfather's military ancestry. The Quaker testimony about nonviolence represented faith and practice rooted in the belief of the equality of all God's children. If Quakers believed a divine nature resided in all life forms, then war, prejudice, and discrimination were, by their very natures, inappropriate and morally bankrupt. This may have kept the Buckmans from approving of war and soldiering, but it didn't stop some Quakers from owning slaves and marching off to war when living in the early colonial settlements.[7]

Quakers in general didn't operate and own large plantations, but a growing unrest among them developed during the 1700s about the moral and ethical implications of holding human brothers or sisters against their will. Whenever Wilmer asked Edna anything about Quakers, he heard the full explanation of the Inner Light until he could have memorized it and repeated it back to her. Most everything the Buckman family discussed eventually was linked in some way to this inner sparkle. Slavery, in many Quakers' minds, wasn't consistent with recognizing and honoring this shared inner divine light.

I had yet to discover that most Buckman family members didn't waver in their commitment to nonviolence, even if a few men with family military histories had, on several occasions, become members of the Society of Friends in order to marry their Quaker sweethearts. It was clear to my grandfather that he hadn't offered an explanation about his family background to satisfy Edna's mother. So he blundered on, aware that no matter how he explained himself, May would have something to say about it.

"I believe in standing up for what is right—like when a situation is evil and everything else has been tried," he offered. "No one should be shocked if war comes next. Where would we be without men, like those in my family, who served in the military?"

"Live for thy country, Wilmer," May responded. "Thee isn't required to die for thy country. We can solve conflicts other than by shooting each other. And it's possible to kill without even using a weapon. Love—let us love one another."

Everyone in the room set down their teacups in saucers. They waited for Wilmer's reply. He wanted to make it clear that he didn't have any problem with spreading love as far as it could go. This gave Edna an opening to inject another lesson about nonviolence by pointing out that war boiled down to killing others, even when enhanced by the poundings of a drummer boy, stirring songs, and the military rhythms of marching feet.

"Oh, there are battles and politics. Sure. But underneath it all is a bloody business of shattered bones, fragmented guts, fever, and infection," Edna said. For her, the women's rights movement in the United States would continue to be nonviolent. "As it should be," she added. Granddaddy may have bitten his tongue when visiting the Buckmans, but he was less circumspect in what he told me about the boundaries he created around himself in defense when sitting on an Edgar Allan Poe chair.

"I agree it's possible to kill without a gun, and love is top drawer. But what if my family is threatened, or our country invaded?" Wilmer presented this question to represent his thinking, while Edna took a different approach.

"What's passive and weak about going to jail for what one believes in? A quick and bloody response to injustice only leads to more injustice and violence," she said. "We who are committed to nonviolence keep the vision of peace alive. When we take a stand against war, we're strengthening the values of peacetime after the crisis is over."

Wilmer checked the expressions of those in the circle of tea drinkers. Edna had done her best preparing her mother to meet Wilmer. Unfortunately, May appeared close to fainting as the exchange about war and peace headed toward a brick wall. When Edna first told her mother about Wilmer, she'd insisted that the couple had done nothing wrong—not much different than if Edna had met her friend Bess for tea in Center City.

"Wilmer tells terrific stories," she told her mother the previous week. While she didn't reveal this to May, Edna was leaning toward the possibility that Wilmer was the type of man who could be counted on if she were later to commit to and participate in the women's rights movement. This would have been premature to mention at the Echo Dale tea. Wilmer still had to meet Edna's test of what she might be looking for in a partner if she decided to marry. Little about this matter reduced the worry lines deepening on May's forehead.

The day of the gathering, Edna's father Charles Buckman was away on a business trip so he wasn't there to take part in the interrogation of Edna's friend. Papa expected a full report, however, on Wilmer Kearns by the following weekend. The Civil War orphanage, Wilmer's admiration of Poe's writing, and the defense of his own military ancestry would claim top billing on a list of items for Mamma to discuss with Papa.

The tea party atmosphere became even more strained when Wilmer disclosed his fondness for Poe's tale "The Murders in the Rue Morgue." In this classic work of mystery literature, Poe introduced the first hard-boiled detective protagonist in the English language, investigator C. Auguste Dupin, on whom the character of Sherlock Holmes and other fictional detectives were later based. Wilmer mentioned how Dupin's methodical and logical mind wouldn't rest when it came to sweeping a crime scene for clues.

"Poe's literary genius is downplayed when dirt's dug up about his personal life," Wilmer told the Buckman family members in an increasingly confident tone. The reference to Poe's Rue Morgue mystery further distressed Edna's mother. In her opinion, Poe's tale of murder added up to a bizarre and brazen literary invention. It's not as if May had read "The Murders in the Rue Morgue," because she hadn't. Most literature in May Buckman's view fell into the category of distractions from the obligation of Quakers to communicate with the Almighty. The absence of ministers and priests among Quakers made them suspect among the general population, but Quakers believed that the faithful should minister to each other.

May questioned why daughter Edna was so impressed with someone like Wilmer Kearns, a Lutheran who'd been raised in Pennsylvania Dutch country before accepting his first job in New York City at—God forbid—a cigar firm. She didn't hold back from sharing her view that five-cent cigars constituted a gateway to the next step of turning into a slobbering alcoholic.

Wilmer shared pride in his mother's education in a Civil War state-run orphanage and boarding school. This didn't impress May. She was convinced that Wilmer didn't have much potential, even if he attempted to find out a little about Quaker culture and its faith-based lifestyle. May Buckman was a woman who, at every opportunity, told her husband, son, and daughter: "More hours should be spent in worship." She didn't approve of a poet like Poe featuring lovesick lonely men obsessed with death and graveyards in his writing. It would have suited her if Poe, his literary friends, and all remnants of snuff, spirits, and smelly feet were banned from Planet Earth. At least, to his credit, Wilmer wore a clean starched shirt, trimmed his fingernails, and polished his shoes.

My grandfather surveyed the bonbon plate to ease his ongoing discomfort. When studying the Echo Dale tearoom, Granddaddy noticed facial expressions suggestive that Buckman family members didn't approve of him continuing as Edna's friend. I relied on my initial observation that Wilmer respected Edna's practice of not curling her hair or covering her body with silks and lace. I understood how she might prefer men friends who didn't drink wine and whiskey, play cards, gamble, guzzle beer, dance all night, minimize the importance of women, and indulge in superficial entertainment.

When Granddaddy glanced in the direction of Mary Ann Brooke Buckman, Edna's step-great-grandmother, he noticed Mary Ann's supportive nods and smiles. After all, it was Mary Ann's job to keep Buckman family identity strong after Thomas Buckman's

Buckman family, 1890s, at the home of Thomas Buckman and Mary Ann Brooke Buckman in Rydal, Montgomery County, outside Philadelphia. Thomas and Mary Ann are in the row in front of the children, to the right of the center pole.

first wife Ann died. She had prioritized releasing Quaker women to follow the dictates of their consciences. And if the social conditions of the 1800s and early 1900s seemed distant and dismal to me, I wondered if Quaker faith and practice would also become the key to my survival in life as well.

Wilmer decided against mentioning his love of smoking Cuban cigars or how much he enjoyed his pendulum or having his palm read on Chestnut Street by one of Philadelphia's street psychics. Quakers didn't rely on outside sources for basic information—only the Inner Light. Wilmer guessed correctly that he wasn't at the front of a line of young men competing for Edna's attention. But why should he further prejudice his position, whatever it was? Perhaps being a friend wasn't such a demanding position to fill. Edna had, after all, asked him to sit next to her on an Edgar Allan Poe chair.

I studied Mary Ann Brooke Buckman, and then shifted back to my grandfather to assess his serious brow, the strong shoulder bones of his youth, and the sensuous curve of his chin. Wilmer curled his fingers around his teacup to extend the liquid's warmth to the last sip before turning toward me, as if to say, "Don't turn thy back on writing about this someday. For future generations."

I longed to roll my eyes in frustration, but didn't. If Granddaddy counted on me to record this afternoon tea at Echo Dale and other events, family members were in trouble. Their story, and my story by extension, might never be told. Granddaddy was able to share narratives with many different types of listeners. But as a young person, I couldn't. Quaker reliance on the Inner Light was a possibility, although so far any insights to my position were dim.

Wilmer must have realized that if he expected to come to terms with Edna, he had to acknowledge that the source of Buckman family power resided with Mary Ann Buckman. May, Charles, Edna, and Smythe referred to her as "Grandmother." She pulled her weight due to her elder status. Mary Ann could sit in any parlor chair and blend with the wall. She parted her hair in the middle and wore respectable long dresses. When family decisions were under consideration, Granddaddy said that Edna and her mother May made it a priority to consult with Mary Ann, the second wife of Edna's great-grandfather, Thomas Buckman. He died when Edna was about ten.

Infants were named after Thomas Buckman. Extended family members gathered each year at Thomas Buckman's home outside of Philadelphia for a reunion to stay current with local and family news. After my great-great-great-grandfather Thomas Buckman's death in 1892, Mary Ann assumed authority within the Buckman clan. She collected descendant stories going back to 1682. She challenged family members to find out more about the Widow Buckman who organized the journey from Sussex, England, to Pennsylvania with William Penn. Buckman descendants weren't even sure of the Buckman matriarch's first name. Most referred to her as Joan.

Joan died on the trip across the Atlantic Ocean to Philadelphia when a smallpox epidemic swept the ship *Welcome*. She had organized the Buckman family to leave and sail to America. According to oral history, Joan worshipped with William Penn and his

Mary Ann Brooke Buckman, second wife of Thomas Buckman. Mary Ann organized the Buckman family reunion in 1912–1913, circa 1890.

family back in England. Penn believed it would be possible to set up Philadelphia as an intentional utopian community and Holy Experiment specializing in human rights and the freedom of religion.

If Wilmer Kearns expected to make points with Edna, he'd better have a William Penn story up his sleeve to tell. He didn't. Granddaddy said he realized that his success with Edna or lack of it would depend on his standing with Mary Ann. She honored everyone in the family, and in particular, the first wife of Thomas Buckman, Ann Comly Buckman, the mother of Amos Buckman, Edna's grandfather. If Edna expressed a romantic interest in a young man like Wilmer Kearns, Mary Ann would be expected to evaluate him.

The curtains at each of Echo Dale's windows billowed. A roar of thunder followed a flash of lightning. A woman of few words, Mary Ann Buckman made every sentence count. She rarely mentioned her swollen ankles and stiff shoulders, problems minimized when compared to her firm jaw, strong will, and determination that there be no compromises when observing the Quaker testimonies of peace, simplicity, equality, and integrity.

Mary Ann worried, as did Edna's mother May, about how some city Quakers had become financially comfortable and "worldly," whereas those living in rural areas made a priority of emphasizing to their children the importance of Quaker silent worship and the spiritual testimonies. The Quaker struggle to survive in the city they founded became an ongoing concern for Mary Ann as well as May Begley Buckman. Daughters marrying non-Quakers, like Wilmer Kearns, concerned May Buckman. If Quakers had a future, they had to protect their faith and way of life. May fretted over Quakers who didn't take fundamental principles seriously and objected when those she called "fallen Quakers" were viewed as representing the entire Religious Society of Friends. As she invariably noted, "Just because Quakers have high ideals doesn't mean everyone rushes to practice them."

"Would thee like more spice cake?" May asked Wilmer as another crack of thunder rattled the front door's frame. He nodded his head and piled as much cake as he could onto his plate. Granddaddy didn't have the cash to purchase dinner on his way home. He had already exhausted the change in his pockets by buying a round-trip train ticket to visit Edna at Echo Dale.

"Grandfather Thomas loved storms," Mary Ann continued. "He depended on rain for his crops, as long as the thunder wasn't too bad and frightened the dogs."

Mary Ann considered it her responsibility to mention her late husband whenever possible. He'd farmed the same land in Montgomery County for more than forty years. She described Thomas Buckman as a family man who read the weekday and Sunday Philadelphia newspapers. Everyone but Wilmer had already heard Mary Ann's stories about Thomas that she was in the habit of repeating.

Thomas Buckman, I learned, invested in the local limestone industry because of the rich lime deposits in the area of Plymouth Meeting.[8] Even when wearing his best suit, Thomas smelled of smoke from the family's wood-burning stoves. His cheeks were ruddy from outdoor labor, and he brushed his bushy white hair away from his forehead. Family members, friends, and members of the broader community respected Thomas and his first wife Ann Comly Buckman, who died in 1861, after giving birth to seven Buckman children.

This branch of the larger Buckman family had a reputation for strong bones and constitutions. And Mary Ann Buckman didn't hesitate to remind family members that many of the faithful back in England had survived grueling prison sentences after Quakers were arrested for their unconventional beliefs. Hundreds died. Quakers had been fined or punished for challenging the established English church over issues such as abolition, equality, and the necessity of nonviolence.

I was aware of how relocating to Pennsylvania from England hadn't resolved the difficulties of keeping the faithful together. The challenge, Granddaddy told me, was

Thomas Buckman, circa 1890. A Quaker farmer in Montgomery County, Thomas was the husband of Ann Comly Buckman and Mary Ann Brooke Buckman.

of a different sort—maintaining cultural and spiritual values as the "City of Brotherly Love" opened its gates to many who didn't support or respect Quaker democratic ideals. It took effort but I finally realized that Edna's mother, May, wasn't the crab she had the reputation of being. Her concerns about the evils of alcohol were reasonable, although I didn't trust her to support Edna and Wilmer's budding romance.

Thomas Buckman was head of the family for decades. From what Wilmer told me, Ann Comly Buckman provided emotional stability for family members before Mary Ann Brooke Buckman entered the scene after Ann's death. Even Mary Ann referred to Ann Comly as headstrong. At family gatherings before her death, Ann Comly criticized the taboo against Orthodox and Hicksite Quakers courting and marrying each other. For this pairing, Ann Comly and Thomas Buckman had been punished by limited access to the Quaker community.

Ann Comly Buckman, first wife of Thomas Buckman, circa 1850s.

"Mary Ann took over the job of keeping us Buckmans together after Ann died," Edna told Wilmer. She added that Mary Ann hadn't been raised a Quaker because her grandfather, William Brooke, served in General George Washington's high command. Mary Ann's saving grace stemmed from her collection of ancestors that included Quaker settlers who'd sailed before and after William Penn to populate the colonial city of Philadelphia.

At the family tea party, Edna's mother May steered the tea conversation back to women's rights. "This is a priority for us in the Buckman family," she emphasized. Wilmer didn't respond. How Edna defined her life was her decision, he told me. By the end of the tea gathering, the rain had ended. Edna's mother May ushered Wilmer out the front door without an invitation to visit the family's flourishing backyard garden. Edna followed my grandfather to the front gate where five minutes would be long enough to wish him a safe trip back to the city on the train.

"I dropped my spoon and said all the wrong things," Wilmer told Edna at the gate. "I'm sorry to have made such a golden ass out of myself."

"Thee is an open book," she replied. "What is in thy head comes straight out of thy mouth. It isn't a coincidence this happens when sitting on Edgar Allan Poe's chairs."

Edna explained that the Poe parlor furniture forced its captives to sit up straight, affirm the external reality, and engage in superficial conversations.

"If Poe ever sat in our chairs, he would have suffocated, like when he wrote about closets and catacombs," Edna added as she handed Wilmer a rolled piece of black velvet that she claimed contained "something special."

"It's for thee to remember today," she said.

At the station, travelers arrived with suitcases and packages to wait for the arrival of the train back to Center City. Wilmer wondered if all Quakers were like Edna's family members. They weren't the type of plain people he'd heard about who farmed, gathered eggs, spread seed for the chickens, and had few kind words for bishops or church officials meddling in personal spiritual affairs. Granddaddy told me he'd never heard such street gossip about Edgar Allan Poe.

"The two of us are meant for each other. I'm sure of it," Wilmer repeated softly to himself as he cradled Edna's parting gift at the train station that he told me decades later was what Scottish poet Robert Burns called a symbol of love—a "red, red rose."

Part II

Chapter 11

The Telephone Party Line

"Who are you going to vote for? Dwight Eisenhower or Adlai Stevenson?"[1] This was the question my mother Wilma put to her friend on the phone as I settled down with my ear to the metal heating grate upstairs to eavesdrop. My bedroom was directly over the room where my mother Wilma talked on the phone and smoked cigarettes. This habit provoked my father to nag her until she finally gave up smoking before my brother Tom, their fifth and final child, was born.

"I disagree," I heard my mother telling her friend on the phone. "Eisenhower was a military general. Still weird in the head from the Second World War, if you ask me."

Wilma Buckman Kearns (Culp), circa 1950s.

I concentrated on my mother's side of the conversation.

"No, I don't think so. Eisenhower's popular. And Stevenson's an egghead. My husband's a Republican. I vote Democrat. Bud's ancestors were Mennonites who married Quakers near Philadelphia. Then the family on his side went church mainstream a couple of generations ago. On my end, the Buckman family has been around the Philadelphia area as Quakers for ten generations. I'm the tenth. My kids are the eleventh."

When pressed tight to the grate, my ears had red grid lines on the edges. I kept certain questions close to my chest while waiting for my mother to mention Edna. For example, why did I have braids, unlike most other girls my age? Why couldn't I wear Mary Jane shoes? What was the problem with me eating in the school cafeteria where I could buy Sloppy Joes and orange gelatin dessert? My mother handed me a lunch box every morning with a peanut butter sandwich with soggy lettuce and an apple to take to school. I felt different from all the other elementary school kids with their salami and cheese sandwiches. When my mother mentioned Edna, my head almost went through the heating vent to the room below.

Edna Buckman Kearns (*right*) and her second child, Wilma, Marguerite's mother, circa 1921.

"What about me as the second daughter in the family? My mother Edna didn't plan for me. I popped out into the world and turned the family inside out. My older sister Serena wasn't the only child anymore. She never got over it. I was born about a week after US women first voted in November after my family moved from New York back to Pennsylvania in 1920. Growing up, I was always under my mother's feet."

My listening affirmed my suspicion that Nancy Drew, the teen detective, would have persisted in snooping like me. Nancy was a hound for clues.[2] I impressed the girls at school by telling them how Nancy Drew could drive a car around tight corners on two wheels. When she set her mind to solving a mystery, nothing could stop her. Hard-boiled newspaper editors couldn't reason with Nancy either.

"I'll get my story yet," Nancy vowed. "A reporter will stop at nothing to get a scoop."

Both Nancy Drew and my grandmother Edna were comfortable with words. Edna reported women's rights news for metropolitan New York City newspapers. Nancy poked around in dark houses for clues with her friend Ted, who tracked down mysteries with his camera. Ted's younger brother and sister tagged along on the film set of *Nancy Drew, Reporter*. Sneering men wearing creepy hats poked their heads out of closet doors. Good guys chased bad guys on two-lane highways. And in the end, Nancy solved murders. She filed her news articles by the deadline. Edna produced news of votes for women campaigns with her letters and newspaper columns. And I practiced eavesdropping on our family's telephone party line in my relentless search to find out more about my grandmother Edna.

"My grandfather Charles Buckman died about seven years before I was born," my mother continued on the phone, puffing away. "And Lordy, did I hear about him! He looked—well, you'd know what I mean if I said his skin was bronze from working in the garden with him wearing nothing at all. He was a piece of work. Especially the way he turned so brown, hardly anybody recognized him."

With my ear to the floor's metal grate, I could tell when a neighbor interrupted by picking up the phone on the party line.

"Hang up, will ya? I'll be off in ten minutes. Thank you," my grumpy mother scolded a neighbor. She went on to tell her friend about Charles Buckman noticing the difference in the reactions of bank employees when he arrived as a man of color in spring and summer, and then, a pale man during winter and fall. In photos, Charles either appeared white or as a bronze man surrounded by pale family members for the remaining months.

"Is there something you're not admitting?" Charles's sales colleagues at Boll Brothers in Harrisburg asked him repeatedly, according to my mother. Their other remarks were accompanied by smirks and guffaws.

"Are you sure your mother didn't run wild—west of the Delaware River?"

My mother told her friend that Charles Harper Buckman wasn't certain of any genetic ties with indigenous Americans appearing on the limbs of the Buckman family tree. As far as all the other tree branches were concerned, Charles couldn't be sure.

Photograph featuring Charles Harper Buckman and family with his summer skin.
Left to right, standing: Edna, her brother Smythe, and Wilmer Kearns. *Sitting*: Charles
Harper Buckman and May Begley Buckman, with little Serena Kearns, circa 1910.

He hadn't planned on an exterior transformation that some said made him resemble members of the Delaware tribe of Native Americans, also known as the Lenni Lenape peoples in Pennsylvania. When pressed, Charles said he suspected some genetic material responsible for his appearance might have been passed down from Ann Comly, Thomas Buckman's first wife and my great-great-great-grandmother.

"I was forever in trouble as a kid," my mother added on the phone. "I wasn't like my sister Serena. A good girl, after her younger years of being a brat. I came along and caused a disturbance." I felt my neck stiffen and my throat turn dry.

Next to Granddaddy, I depended on my mother to tell me about Edna and the Buckman family. She told me many referred to Ann Comly Buckman's high cheekbones and wide face as the "broad Buckman face." This family characteristic had been passed down to my mother and me by way of Edna. These features, when combined with the hot sun, turned my great grandfather Charles into the shade of walnuts, depending on the season. The Lenni Lenape recognized him as kin, because their ancestors taught my Buckman ancestors farming in Bucks County, Pennsylvania.

"Do you think we're part Indian?" my mother asked me once.

"How would I know? You're the mother passing on stories to me. Anything could have happened with the Lenni Lenape."

My ancestors and native peoples lived in close proximity in Bucks County, near Philadelphia, although this didn't guarantee that we were related by blood to those who met my ancestors when they got off the boat from England. It was possible, but most likely, it wasn't true. Over the generations, many of the Lenni Lenape died from disease introduced by outsiders. They also witnessed the theft of their land by colonists. After Quakers no longer controlled Pennsylvania's government, the impact of negative colonization accelerated. The Lenape were matrilineal.[3] That's what my grandmother Edna liked about them, according to my mother.

"No one would blame thee for forgetting those Indians," remarked Edna's brother Smythe, who visited the garden at Echo Dale and found his father Charles digging to prepare a mound of soil. He planted corn and then, around it, squash and beans.

"Sorry. I can't forget," Charles replied. "I can't think of anything but the Lenni Lenape."

After tamping down a planting mound, Charles started another, a story also shared with a neighbor on the telephone party line.

"How I hate these phone contraptions," my mother added when passing on the family story about Edna's brother, Smythe, to her friend. "I can barely talk a second before an interruption. Now—where were we?"

My mother said that her grandmother May Begley Buckman was wrapped up in the temperance movement and prison reform work, and Charles Harper Buckman was away from home for business often. May accused him of being "in his cups" when staying overnight in high-class hotels when family members expected him to be signing brass bed contracts. "My uncle Smythe was a brat," my mother said, describing one visit he made to Wilmer and herself when he couldn't wait to find a bar to buy a drink.

"Yeah, right," my mother snorted. "May wouldn't walk down the same side of the street as a saloon. And Smythe got kicked out of a bunch of Quaker schools. My mother Edna was the goody-goody child in the Buckman family. She did whatever her mother wanted until my father, Wilmer, showed up. Edna fell in love with him, hard."

After the call on the party line was over, my mother asked what I'd been doing in my bedroom.

"Reading Nancy Drew," I told her.

I didn't mention that I spent hours listening through the heating grate and committing to memory my mother's remarks when speaking on the phone. I remembered almost everything I'd heard from Granddaddy. If I didn't collect enough facts about Edna, I asked Aunt Serena, who was tired of me asking too many questions. Even with all of the stories told to me, I didn't know much about my grandmother Edna. I'd concluded that she was terrific as a votes for women activist, that she wrote well and inspired others around her.

I'd have to wait until I was older, after I learned how to write stronger sentences and decent paragraphs, after I had a better grasp of history and practiced interviewing techniques.

"There's one story I haven't told you," Granddaddy said one afternoon.

"About what?"

"I thought I'd lose Edna for sure because of how she reacted to the offer of my boss to take me to dinner."

"What did she say?"

"She didn't want me going."

"But you were only a friend to Edna."

"I know."

The storytelling was progressing, but I'd have to be patient. I bit my thumbnail and chewed the rough skin on my lips. I had a cramp in my thigh. My nose itched. Granddaddy Wilmer was in love with Edna, and she was in love with him, but neither one had revealed this to the other. I was impatient. Afternoons were reserved for storytelling, and my grandfather might decide to go outside and water his green peppers and roses. I sensed that my grandparents' narrative was about to enter a sensitive phase that might satisfy my curiosity and put a stop to my questioning. Granddaddy noticed this.

"The way will open to more of the story tomorrow," he said.

Chapter 12

Just Friends

*I*t had started snowing, a storm in flashes, melting on sidewalks and street surfaces. It was 1903, I believe. Granddaddy didn't always tell me stories in consecutive order. When he spoke about sleeping under wool blankets as a young man, I assumed he was living in New York. He narrowed my exposure to his tale by saying he stayed awake at night, unable to sleep, upset about his friendship with Edna.

Wilmer didn't like spending weekends alone at the Quaker boardinghouse when he could have been in Philadelphia visiting with Edna at the Market Street teahouse. Once or twice during these excursions south, he'd slip his arm around her shoulder. This never advanced to a kiss or embrace. He could hear her perpetual warning, rarely spoken out loud, defining their relationship. "Just friends." He thought about her constantly and speculated about where their friendship might or might not lead.

I wasn't content confined to a kitchen chair while Wilmer wandered Manhattan's streets until exhaustion overcame him. I wanted to know more, and couldn't get enough of the story. On the next visit to Philadelphia he expected that Edna would inform him of her plans to forge ahead into the future on her own. This might involve volunteering for a women's rights organization, addressing envelopes, and licking stamps. This felt remote when compared to his accounting job.

During one of my visits, I could tell Granddaddy must have been remembering. I stared at the way the muscles on his face gave way to an inward gaze. He said street lights in the vicinity of Stuyvesant Square Park, not far from the Penington, cast a faint glow onto the surrounding neighborhood as he entered a phase of expectant waiting for Edna to come to terms with her future. I could understand why Edna liked Wilmer—his bold opinions, his reliability, thoughtfulness, and support of her commitment to women's rights. He was usually prepared with a joke when they met at the Market Street teahouse. He still didn't have a story about William Penn. Edna finally told him about how oral family history featured the Buckman children on the ship *Welcome* sitting at Penn's feet. Penn had a reputation for being a fine storyteller.

When they were together, Wilmer spoke easily about Henry David Thoreau. Edna made a face when he reached the part about the essays Thoreau wrote about his retreat at Walden Pond in Massachusetts. That's when Edna told him bluntly—she didn't like Thoreau.

"I get the impression he had little use for women. He wrote a lot about the natural world, and the rest about himself," she said.

I didn't care. My main interest was in following my grandparents' trail to marriage. Granddaddy told me about being nervous and insecure around Edna, although I couldn't be entirely sure about what he meant. Perhaps she was examining him to find out if he'd become a good partner. And how did they progress past "just friends"? They were already more than friends, but I didn't dare say this out loud. Granddaddy only wanted to talk about Frederick Douglass. I scratched my head.

What did Frederick Douglass know about my grandmother's wedding dress? Did she save it or give it away after the ceremony? Edna May Buckman was thirteen years old when Frederick Douglass died. She may have heard about him, but their paths never crossed.

Frederick Douglass, circa 1870. Photo by George Francis Schreiber. Library of Congress.

If any one individual changed the course of history, Granddaddy believed Douglass qualified because of his life circumstances as someone who'd personally witnessed and experienced slavery. He proposed and supported a resolution at the Seneca Falls women's convention in 1848 setting a goal of US women winning the right to vote. This defined the direction of the US women's rights movement. And Granddaddy Wilmer wanted to make sure I knew the basics about Frederick Douglass.

"Douglass had more understanding of freedom than practically anybody I can think of," Granddaddy said. I didn't argue. I had no idea if my grandmother had the stamina to be her own person and carve out her own life's path. Edna's wedding dress was proof they'd married, which gave the green light to me to find out more about the silky gown. What happened to it? Did moths eat it to shreds? Did she give it away?

Granddaddy persisted in teaching me history. He said the women and men at the Seneca Falls women's convention in 1848 weren't of one mind about voting.[1] Some believed voting rights would be too difficult to achieve. Others were of the opinion that the election system was corrupt and women shouldn't invest in a limited goal. Frederick Douglass insisted at the Seneca Falls convention that the women of the nation set their sights on winning the ballot. He believed collective power was key when undermining prejudice and discrimination.

The drama of Frederick Douglass supporting women's freedom took center stage. This opened the door to my grandfather telling me more about Henry David Thoreau. Granddaddy didn't agree with all of Edna's positions on civil and human rights and how women might win them, but he felt confident when speaking about Thoreau.

"I didn't have the clearest head myself about women's rights strategy," he told me. He mentioned that often as a young man, he couldn't think straight because of the wretched residue of domestic tobacco permeating the T. J. Dunn building in New York City. Granddaddy said he was barely able to breathe some days in the accounting office.

If most of the tobacco leaf used by T. J. Dunn employees for the manufacture of cigars had been of high-grade Cuban origin, Wilmer might not have reacted as he did. His paycheck and that of other staff members relied on a predictable ritual carried out all over the nation on weekends and evenings. Men gathered in home parlors after dinner for port or cognac and five-cent cigars. The women washed dishes, traded recipes in the kitchen, and left the men alone. Cigars stood at the boundary of the gender divide.

During T. J. Dunn staff meetings, the distinct aroma of cheap tobacco drifted up from the shop floor below and caused Wilmer to sniffle and sneeze. The stench infiltrating the meeting room at the firm's Manhattan headquarters could be traced to the domestic tobacco grown in Ohio and shipped to New York. It irritated Wilmer's respiratory system. The lower-grade tobacco may have been adequate for manufacturing cheap cigars for taverns and saloons. However, it caused my grandfather severe distress when he sat in the conference room waiting for the firm's staff meeting to start.

Members of the company business staff in Manhattan met monthly during 1903 to discuss the business operation. Management's new plan, according to Granddaddy,

Street scene in Philadelphia, circa 1910. The man walking is similar to what Wilmer Kearns might have looked like as an employee of a cigar firm. Photo by Lewis W. Hine. Library of Congress.

involved the firm's expansion of manufacturing operations into Lower East Side neighborhoods, as well as Philadelphia and the surrounding countryside. Firm officials decided to take advantage of cigar piecework, paying less than in unionized shops. Edna and her mother May didn't approve of such profits at the expense of women. So they lobbied Wilmer to find a position elsewhere. He stalled. He had no accounting experience before his job at T. J. Dunn.

The firm produced the popular five-cent cigar, named after a vaudeville actor, advertised on billboards and ads in newspapers and magazines, all exclaiming: "Hello There! Smoke Up With Pete Dailey Cigar, 5 cents. Successful Everywhere." In addition to the Pete Dailey model, Granddaddy said the company also produced both high-

and low-end cigar brands acquired through the purchase of other cigar manufacturing concerns.

Wilmer plastered a fake grin across his face. The specifics of cigar production weren't on the office meeting agenda the day of the staff meeting. This session, scheduled to take several hours, focused on higher profits from cheaper cigars. Snuff, pipe, and chewing tobacco were disappearing from widespread use. Expanded cigar smoking, promoted for the image or implied relaxation value, relied on cigars purchased for five cents and more.[2]

In a quest for higher profits, T. J. Dunn cigar company officials said they expected staff members to scale back their resistance to hiring women workers who would replace predominantly male custom cigar hand-rollers. Many of those skilled workers were German and Bavarian men, union members whose custom-rolled cigars represented an exclusive and expensive line. When cigar company official Theodore Werner introduced the topic of higher revenues and the hiring of women workers, Wilmer said the smirks disappeared from the faces of the company staff. Many of the labor force of women were born in other parts of the world. To many employers, these immigrants were candidates for cheap labor.

"Girls are less likely to organize and strike," Mr. Werner noted. "They need no more than basic supervision to produce cigars with molds and machines. And they're happy for whatever they carry home at the end of the week."

Wilmer didn't share the firm's expansion plans with May and Edna. They would only repeat their reservations. He'd have to hear their complaints about how women's labors were responsible for even more profits for T. J. Dunn. Edna believed that if women employees had any good sense, they should be organizing a union themselves. She believed their interests should be represented over issues of low pay, long hours, and poor working conditions. Issues like these had led to strikes in the Manhattan cigar industry before 1900. Organized factory workers didn't hesitate to walk out and raise their protest signs high on the sidewalks for all New Yorkers to see.

The whispering, paper shuffling, and window glancing ceased as Mr. Werner added to his presentation. Granddaddy painted a picture for me of impatient staff members scraping the legs of their chairs on the hardwood floor. My grandfather's associates rarely asked questions or challenged the bosses. When referring to family life, Granddaddy said the men sitting around the company's conference table occasionally referred to "the wife" or "my daughter" or "my son," seldom any of them by name.

Their attitudes were predictable, talking about how women served families best as mothers and helpmates to men, efforts and contributions taken for granted. Few wives, in their opinion, deserved praise or recognition. Women's performance as domestic workers and marriage partners was taken for granted. Wives and daughters were rarely mentioned as independent agents with needs and desires of their own. Yet Granddaddy's associates at the office claimed to be fond of their wives and offspring. Those women who accepted employment in cigar manufacture, on the other hand, were blamed for forcing men out of decent jobs.

After the meeting, Benjamin Corell, one of the company's partners, took Wilmer aside and invited him to dinner at Delmonico's the following week. Wilmer had been in New York City long enough to recognize the name of the restaurant—Delmonico's—as a fashionable restaurant and one of the most expensive in the city.

"Let's meet at six," Mr. Corell suggested. The invitation made Wilmer feel so unsettled that he mentioned his reaction to Edna. He couldn't refuse the dinner invitation, he told her. Edna objected to him accepting the invitation. None of the other employees in the office, to his knowledge, had been guests of either boss, Werner or Corell. Wilmer viewed the evening as an opportunity to ask for a raise. He couldn't ask Edna to marry him unless he could prove his worth in the job market. In the coming months, Wilmer and Edna exchanged letters as their relationship deepened, as the envelope and Edna's reply suggest. If Wilmer didn't move toward the direction of marriage, he was of the opinion they would forever remain, just friends.

Echo Dale, Plymouth Heights
Norristown, Pennsylvania

My dearest Boy:—

Received thy letter . . . Yesterday morning I felt so badly, I was sent to bed. Dr. Corson happened to drop in for a social visit but Mamma brought him

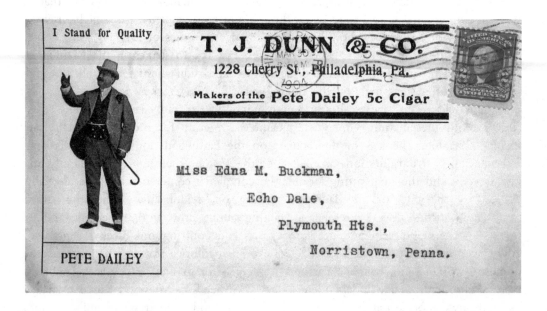

Envelope for a letter Wilmer Kearns sent to Edna Buckman, mailed from the T. J. Dunn office on Cherry Street in Philadelphia, 1904.

up to me. I told him I was not ill, really. "No," he said. "Thee hasn't scarlet fever or pneumonia, but thee is a sick girl. Thee can't feel like jumping around."

He said my skin was yellow and I had a little touch of the jaundice. But I feel pretty well today—only so very tired, in fact exhausted. I stayed in thy room and slept most of the day; thought of thee too, dearest. How could I help it? Mamma was telling me of the shock we gave Mrs. Sheppard on Seventh Day.

It seems Emma said, "Well, I guess we will see 'Billy' there tonight as Edna calls him."

Mrs. S—"Why, Emma, why it looks serious."

Emma—"Well, I guess we shall see him."

Mrs. S—"Why, Emma. Thee startles me."

Emma—"Now, Mother, I didn't tell thee anything, remember."

Mrs. S—"What will Edna Buckman do next? Why, I thought Edna never intended to get friendly with a man."

I feel better after seeing Dr. Corson and wonder if thee is returning to Philadelphia soon.

Faithfully, Edna[3]

Chapter 13

Dinner at Delmonico's

*G*randdaddy told me he followed Mr. Corell's choice of what to order after studying the price range of entrees at dinner at Delmonico's.[1] One of Edna's responses to the invitation, my grandfather said, was to warn him not to agree to be a guest of a T. J. Dunn executive because he might become compromised in the process.

"I have no choice," he told Edna. "Especially if I ask the bosses to give me a positive recommendation for another job."

Did Edna's concern exceed what was expected from a friend? Wilmer wasn't sure. Granddaddy informed Edna by letter that he'd completed the application form for a position at the William McKinley Music Company in Manhattan. He didn't ask Edna about the reasons for her "friendly" interest in having him keep a social distance from his employers. If their friendship evolved into a deeper intimacy, he would agree to their working together, as compared to the conventional expectation that men took charge.

Wilmer told me that he felt awkward during the meal with Mr. Corell at Delmonico's, even though his boss was a likable fellow with an enthusiasm for the most mundane of topics, especially the weather. A storm headed toward New York City and this fascinated Benjamin Corell. He didn't bore friends and acquaintances by speaking about himself other than to include a brief reference to his family. Granddaddy didn't have to pick up the dinner tab. So he didn't feel compelled to mention that a single steak platter at Delmonico's would have been enough to feed the entire seven-member Kearns family back in Beavertown for Sunday dinner.

Wilmer imagined his mother Henrietta Kearns making chicken-fried steak with cream gravy. He estimated that a sizable Delmonico steak could be the main ingredient in a Pennsylvania Dutch beef pie with a buttery top crust sealing in chunks of tender beef, onions, carrots, and potatoes. Wilmer's father, John P. Kearns, may have been proprietor of one of Snyder County's most successful carriage and wagon businesses, but that didn't prevent Henrietta Kearns from juggling limited resources. She prepared a variety of Pennsylvania Dutch dishes for her family on a strict budget.

As the meal drew to a close, Mr. Corell lit a cigar—not a Pete Dailey five-cent special, but a high-end Cuban cigar. He offered Wilmer one. Granddaddy lit up and went through the motions of a cognac and cigar ritual. They'd finished a meal of raw Long Island clams, turtle soup, salad, Delmonico's famous steak, scalloped potatoes,

Delmonico's restaurant, New York City, 1903. Library of Congress.

freshly baked bread, and steamed green beans. Mr. Corell presented his agenda after the restaurant table was cleared.

Both Benjamin Corell and business partner Theodore Werner had registered their cigar manufacturing operations under their own names, as well as T. J. Dunn, a firm they purchased a decade prior. Expanded cigar manufacture fueled the company's expansion into lofts and satellite operations in several Manhattan locations.

"There's something designed for you in our future, Wilmer," Mr. Corell told my grandfather. Some company work sites had employees evenly divided between men and women. This wasn't a result of the firm's equitable hiring policies, but because women could be paid less. Wilmer was well aware of how women workers provided the bridge to automation and five-cent cigars.

In addition to its New York operations, T. J. Dunn operated a factory on Broad Street in Philadelphia. Mr. Corell mentioned how the potential workforce in the rural countryside outside the city could result in additional profits. He elaborated on how he pictured Wilmer serving on the front lines of the firm's public relations. Granddaddy opened his eyes wide and blinked at the suggestion, suggesting that he might not

T. J. Dunn & Co. cigar manufacturing firm, 210–214 North Broad Street, Philadelphia, circa 1900. Courtesy of the Print and Picture Department, Free Library of Philadelphia.

only be interested but intrigued by the possibility. This wasn't my grandfather's intent, he told me later. He said he could feel the cognac and cigar and chocolate mousse combination mix into a muddle of indecision and indigestion. And Mr. Corell wasn't finished.

"Now, I realize, Wilmer, someone like you likes to conduct business up front—direct and honest."

"You have always been fair with me, sir."

"Call me Ben. We appreciate your work on our books. Someone we can trust."

"Which brings up something I've been meaning to ask you," Wilmer said.

"I'm getting to your raise. We'll be sending you out for confidential assignments, especially travel to our operations in Philadelphia and outside the city. Talk to the workers. Be our face to the world. Listen to them. They're like your people back in Snyder County."

"Will there be more work for me with the company audit?"

"None that won't be compensated by a boost in salary, plus traveling expenses when you're on the road. New responsibilities will be involved."

Mr. Corell promised that Wilmer would find the expanded duties satisfying. The new assignment would involve representing T. J. Dunn at trade meetings and conventions. He'd be responsible for finding common ground with the cigar rollers, as well as employees in the company's shops and assembly lines. Intoxicated by the food, the conversation, the cognac, coffee, chocolate mousse, and Mr. Corell's promises, my grandfather said he thought about a larger paycheck and a promising future with the firm. This was, after all, a period of American history when cigar production and consumption was at its height.

A proposal like this laid before my grandfather would remind Edna of how business travel had led to her father's taste for luxuries. Wilmer could suggest to Edna that he'd be in the Philadelphia area on business more often. They would visit at Echo Dale, rather than the Market Street teahouse. Granddaddy said he preferred that his job remain simple. Arrive at work in the morning, do his best, and leave exactly at the closing hour when the bosses locked the doors. Occasionally the office closing was at five, more often at six.

In Wilmer's favorite fantasies, Edna would be waiting at home to join him for a hot evening meal. In my grandfather's imagined scene, his sweetheart would have spent most of the day standing on a soapbox lecturing about women's voting rights before returning home and preparing him dried beef gravy on toast.

But what about Edna's hesitations about marriage? Or Wilmer's anxieties about earning enough to pay the rent and expenses? Mr. Corell made it clear that T. J. Dunn employment involved a generous paycheck as compensation for employee loyalty and initiative. Messrs. Werner and Corell didn't promise him a field of roses. No, sir. Roses grew on bushes, not in fields. What if Edna turned out to be like her mother May? Or her friend Bess? Granddaddy longed for a stage curtain to open and a soprano to step forward and perform an aria that filled the void with a love story. He couldn't decide if the opera should be written by Mozart, Bizet, or Puccini. It didn't matter. Life would be more comfortable if someone like Wilmer served his employers by making sure they earned a respectable profit.

Granddaddy made it clear to me that he couldn't escape from the so-called reality of 1902 and 1903. He had to pay the bills, eat three meals a day, and show up at the office in a business suit. He'd have to set aside extra to purchase a round-trip train ticket to Philadelphia on weekends. Building a future with Edna, he realized, also involved sitting next to her in silence weekly at the Quaker Meeting House. This would provide an opportunity to face the fact that the pink roses in Edna's hair would eventually wilt and crumble. When he tried to suppress such thoughts, the warning from his college friends resonated in his ears: "Don't fall in love with a curmudgeon."

The caution of his close male friends would surely plague him later if they said as promised, "It's not as if we didn't warn you about Quakers. They're peculiar people."

In the weeks following the meal at Delmonico's, Edna didn't make any further critical comments after Wilmer explained: "Dinner is how business is done in New York." He shared with her the range of opportunities associated with traveling to work sites in the Philadelphia area. Granddaddy failed to mention a promotion defining him as management. If this subject had been raised, he was convinced Edna would have expressed her disapproval.

The story of Wilmer's dinner at Delmonico's was shared with Edna in passing. After all, they were "just friends." Granddaddy's future would be contingent on supporting the status quo rather than engaging in efforts to subvert or reform it. Wilmer told me that he held his breath about what might happen next. I had only a vague understanding of what this implied. I concluded that he accepted Mr. Corell's offer without fanfare. When I asked Granddaddy for specifics, he said: "I figured that I'd deal with telling thy grandmother Edna later. I'd explain it somehow."

My grandfather was convinced that Edna would find him a reliable and supportive husband if she decided on marriage. More fundamental were his reactions as to how Edna exhibited power over him, even though she might not be aware of the extent. Granddaddy then faced the unmentionable topic—the intense and powerful force within himself, an urge for personal liberation that informed his potential happiness, whatever this meant.

Granddaddy wasn't sure, he said, what contentment in marriage involved. Freedom slipped out of his grip in spite of his many attempts to isolate success, meditate, and pray over it. He could only rely on his instinct that he'd marry Edna eventually. My existence depended on this. But the stakes were even higher. Would my grandmother become a women's rights activist? And would I someday be able to tell the entire family story?

Chapter 14

Many Women, Many Views

*B*ess and Edna discussed the topic of marriage, especially the evening in 1903 when they attended a program in downtown Philadelphia about women's rights. Marriage was both a goal and a source of painful associations for young women. It also had an unsavory reputation among an increasing number of young women like Edna and Bess. The evening program featured an associate of activist Susan B. Anthony, as well as others participating in a panel at a lecture hall on North Broad Street. Volunteers gathered names at the entrance for a votes for women petition to present to the US Congress. Edna and Bess signed.

Granddaddy said Bess stood out in her long burgundy velvet dress with fabric-covered buttons, as if placed in bold relief against the audience background of dresses in ivory and muted colors. A painter might have relied on broad oil strokes and dotted detail to portray Bess. She couldn't hide an astonished expression when the speaker representing Susan B. Anthony appeared on stage wearing a red shawl and carrying an alligator purse, Anthony's signature trademarks. How did Granddaddy know this? He wasn't there, but Edna told him.

Bess uncrossed her arms and leaned forward to get an uninterrupted view of the stage of panelists filled with opinionated women, most of them like herself—dynamic and energetic. She considered herself a pessimist when compared with Edna, whose optimistic viewpoints bothered her. Edna was of the opinion that married and single women would both thrive once the ballot was secure. Bess and Edna remained friends over the years in spite of their differences in opinion. They'd grown up living next door to one another and had once attended school together. Bess realized that she'd never fit the conventional feminine profile, although when younger, she tried. Bess was of the opinion that marriage stunted a woman's health and welfare because, after a wedding ceremony, she became a man's property. Edna placed her faith in women winning the right to vote in order to shift the power equation.

I thought about Bess and Edna's long friendship the night I wore my best pair of rosebud pajamas to bed, sorting through what my grandfather told me. I should have realized the entire sky had cleared its throat and unloaded it on our neighborhood when a blast of wind rattled my bedroom's window frames. Many questions still had no answers, including: What was a woman's spirit anyway? How was a woman's spirit different from a man's? And where did this spirit reside? Near the waistline? In the brain?

"Spirit isn't separate from everything else," Granddaddy told me on one of our storytelling afternoons. "We have spirit within us all."

I closed my eyes tight to imagine the women's rights program on North Broad Street, relying on my grandfather's memories of what Edna told him. I enjoyed hearing from him about how Edna and Bess read the novel *Jane Eyre* to each other when young. Granddaddy said he imagined their giggling and uninhibited conversations, their outbursts of singing, and the evening they spent together hearing what the woman representing Susan B. Anthony had to say. Anthony died in 1906, at the age of eighty-six, of heart failure and pneumonia.

Granddaddy said American women loved their precious auntie, Susan B. Anthony, who didn't marry and supported the single life, suggesting that the "ideal" husband

Susan B. Anthony, circa 1870. Library of Congress.

shouldn't take advantage of the power the law conferred on him. Bess made a face at the speaker's claim that the turn of the twentieth century represented the first opportunity for American women to take control of their lives.

"A hopeless dream," Bess whispered to Edna.

"We can now identify the qualities of an ideal husband and then find the appropriate man for ourselves," the Anthony representative continued.

In 1896, with Edna in her early teens, May and Charles Buckman enrolled their daughter at Friends' Central School, a Hicksite Quaker secondary school in Center City, Philadelphia.[1] Bess lobbied her parents to register with Edna. Mr. Weiss agreed, but only after pressure from his wife. Even though Mr. Weiss considered it a waste of money to educate girls, Mrs. Weiss liked the idea of Bess being exposed to academic subjects. Mr. Weiss ended the experiment after one term. He couldn't contain his fury after Bess read the works of women writers that strengthened her arguments about the disadvantages of marriage.

I imagined Edna and Bess skipping along a Philadelphia sidewalk on their way to school. Friends' Central advertised itself as coeducational, even though staff members separated girls from boys in classes and assigned them separately to three tracks—literary, scientific, and classical. After Edna chose "literary," Bess signed up for it, too. She didn't mind mixing with boys in the schoolyard, at lunch, and fire drills, but not in classes. Friends' Central faculty assigned the second floor to girls, and the third floor to boys.

The teachers at Friends' Central recognized Edna's talent in creative expression, according to my mother. Edna's favorite Quaker teacher, Annie Shoemaker, supported equality in the larger culture and stressed the importance of educating girls. During Miss Shoemaker's tenure, drawing and Latin were added to the girls' school offerings. Her instruction in botany, geology, astronomy, physics, and chemistry was legendary. Stargazing nights for girls included identifying the constellations and associating them with lines from myth and poetry. If any female students needed advice or counseling, they could count on Annie Shoemaker.

Edna May Buckman's grades at the end of the 1898 school term reflected her strength in art, writing, literature, algebra, and rhetoric, according to records held by Friends' Central School. Her performance in physics, chemistry, French, and history, however, was less than acceptable to her parents. Even so, the average of Edna's grades qualified her to pass. Bess performed well in academic subjects, although the experiment of Bess attending school ended after Mr. Weiss realized that his daughter not only read the works of feminists, but in Quaker educational institutions, not only were girls and boys treated equally, but it wouldn't be long before both genders would sit side by side in classes.

"This goes against common sense and Christian tradition," Mr. Weiss complained. "In the Bible it spells out how women tempt men. Treating them too well only inflates their sense of power and results in types like my daughter Bess. Quakers like the Buckmans may believe boys and girls are the same, but I don't."

My stomach hurt. I relied on Granddaddy's stories about Mr. Weiss for building and fortifying my own inner compass. I dug deep for comforting thoughts but couldn't remember anything other than Wilmer telling me that Edna didn't view the eventual goal of women's activism to replace men in power positions. They would work together and "the chips," he said, would fall in unexpected directions.

Back in Snyder County where Granddaddy had been raised, young men met marriage-eligible women at church or through family connections. The girls and women of Wilmer's family were independent minded. Wilmer's mother and sisters may have considered women voting a legitimate goal for the future, but it wasn't at the top of their list of priorities. Work associated with survival was a priority.

"All of this support of romance is off the mark," Bess whispered to Edna as the evening lecture advanced toward a fifteen-minute break an hour into the program.

"The jury isn't in yet," Edna responded.

"That's so true," Bess countered. "Women aren't allowed to serve on juries."

"The husband of the twentieth century will support his wife's freedom," the speaker on stage continued after the break. "He will promise that marriage shall place on her no more limitations than it imposes on him. He will treat her as his equal, his companion, his closest friend. His personal life will be as pure and committed as hers. That's what our aunt Susan B. Anthony believed."

The women in the lecture hall broke into spontaneous applause when the speaker shared Anthony's opinion that more men than ever represented a "finer type" of manhood than the nation had ever known. The Anthony representative insisted that this new generation of men wouldn't be like their fathers and grandfathers who insisted that women should come to terms with their second-class status. Someone like Bess wouldn't entertain such a compromise. Flirtatious with men, Bess lured them into her nest and just as quickly kicked them out. Edna relied on instinct to respond to the divine in Bess, rather than focusing on their differences. And Edna questioned why Bess couldn't sit still and learn something, instead of responding in whispers to every controversial topic raised.

Edna had been anticipating Wilmer's next trip to Philadelphia when they planned to meet again. The women's rights movement needed men allies. Edna wondered if Wilmer would qualify as one of these candidates. And Edna had to respond to Bess in some way. She couldn't let her friend's remarks stand about the uselessness of men. Her comments were too provocative.

"Modern women believe the number of supportive men is increasing," Edna told Bess.

Bess shrugged and shook her head. Edna returned to listening to the speaker's view that the poverty of masses of American women was related to the hours they spent employed in factories, cooking, child rearing, and responding to their husbands' needs. She noted that Black women experienced even more discrimination than their white sisters. And before the Civil War, African American women suffered the horrors of slavery as well. For women of all backgrounds, the social hierarchy resulted in few free hours to carry out the demands and responsibilities associated with volunteering to win votes for women.

Granddaddy said Edna believed that many American women were reluctant to leave the family home to attend women's meetings and activism planning sessions. Women knew, only too well, about the majority of men's reactions. They were generally less than supportive, frequently abusive, verbally or otherwise. In households where men supported women's voting rights, often the wife felt called to complete her so-called womanly duties before leaving home to attend suffrage meetings and protest demonstrations.

Bess didn't oppose women organizing to win the right to vote. She just considered these advocates to be naïve. She supported a redefinition of power. Instead of power operating from the top down and exercised over others, Bess viewed personal power as functioning equally with others within a horizontal social structure. Labor strikes, economic depressions, and recessions pushed Bess to agree with Susan B. Anthony who had once said that marriage rarely resulted in women functioning as much more than a "doll" or a "drudge."[2]

"Good God," Bess murmured under her breath during the North Broad Street program. "Don't the fools here tonight realize it's stupid to expect equality with a loudmouth drunken father or husband taking up valuable space at home? Why should I put my confidence in a party political machine designed to repress or outright abolish women's freedom?"

As Bess folded her arms in front of her chest to demonstrate her willful opposition, Edna leaned forward in her seat to hear the speakers on stage more clearly. Edna was more familiar than Bess with the writings of social commentator and writer Margaret Fuller, who believed women and men were capable of a divine union and what she termed a "sacred marriage." Fuller's faith in humanity tottering on the cusp of a new age had been spelled out in her work, *Woman in the Nineteenth Century*. But as a new century dawned in 1900, Bess was convinced that American women were far from launching and completing a successful social revolution.

"I object to the word 'fools' applied to women. What should we do? Nothing? We have to start somewhere," Edna said as a response to her friend.

Edna shared with Granddaddy numerous complaints over the years that she'd heard from Bess about her father, Mr. Weiss. Bess claimed his eyes shifted to the left and then to the right in a way to suggest that his daughter wouldn't get the best of him in any argument about equality. Mr. Weiss smirked when something he said irritated his daughter and made her shoulders twitch. When he criticized Susan B. Anthony and other rights advocates, the bags under his eyes became dark. Granddaddy Wilmer seemed determined to warn me about all of the possibilities girls and women faced. Years later I could appreciate that such honesty required a fine line between pushing me in the direction of either subservience or protest. My grandfather made it clear that women's impatience was increasing, although at a very slow pace.

After Bess rejected the marriage proposal offered by her suitor, Philip, Mr. Weiss presented Bess with a deadline to move out of the family home. He demanded that she find another place to live in Philadelphia and support herself financially. He leaned on the handle of his black umbrella near the family's front door when announcing his intention to withdraw all financial support from his daughter. Dressed in his morning coat and top hat, Mr. Weiss insisted that his daughter pay the price of living as an unmarried woman. He had no patience for her view that females were generally forced into marriage, whether they agreed or not.

"Look around us," Bess whispered to Edna during the women's rights program. "Most everyone in this hall is in collusion with men one way or another. They depend on men's approval. Their mothers taught them how to make the best of it. Too much change and these princesses will lose their place in the pecking order."

I squirmed in the kitchen chair and imagined what Edna must have felt about her friend's cynicism. Edna didn't mention Wilmer Kearns to Bess. Unless the polarization between women and men was bridged, Edna couldn't imagine American women ever being able to lift themselves out of their wretched condition. Edna had once followed Bess's lead as a teenager and decided she wouldn't marry. But by 1903, still unknown to my grandfather, she hadn't ruled out Wilmer Kearns as a possible candidate for a romantic relationship. She worried about Wilmer living in New York and how this might undermine his woman-friendly views.

However well intentioned my goal of writing my family's stories, Granddaddy may have chosen the wrong grandchild on which to pin his hopes. I didn't have the proper writing skills. My grandfather dismissed my reservations and told me that Bess had been inspired by activist Emma Goldman, even if Bess didn't go so far as to define herself as an anarchist. Goldman made a valiant effort to connect her visionary ideals with her personal life.

When Emma Goldman marched onto stages across the US to speak, she presented her unconventional perspectives to a wide range of audiences. Goldman didn't act timid around shady characters lurking on the edges of café crowds to spy. Instead, she spoke openly about her controversial views everywhere she traveled.

Free love? Goldman supported it. Marriage? She was convinced it was a terrible idea. Birth control? Goldman stood one hundred percent behind limiting the number of children born. Capitalism? She hated it. War? She believed in nonviolence, except in certain circumstances. She was certain that some violence in the course of overturning a social and economic order was justified. She wasn't opposed to women 's suffrage, although she didn't consider voting a remedy for social ills as long as men directed traffic from the top of a social ladder. Reform? Emma Goldman supported a complete social and economic overturning of the status quo. When reporters asked her about the overall picture, she astonished the nation with her response: "If I can't dance, I don't want to be in your revolution."

"Do yourself a favor and attend one of Emma Goldman's lectures," Bess advised Edna.

"I'll think about it," Edna replied.

"Susan B. Anthony never tested her own advice about an ideal husband," Bess added.

"Those here tonight are excited about the new men of today," Edna responded.

"Really? I don't think so," Bess replied with more than a hint of sarcasm. "These women impostors will agree with the speaker for two minutes and then put up with the same old compromises at home. They smirk passively when men call them girls. They leap into the air for their treats like mutts. They take a baby step and don't notice how their brothers, fathers, uncles, boyfriends, and husbands push them back a mile."

"Many fine men are volunteering to be our allies," Edna offered.

"Don't hold your breath," her friend said with a sigh.

Edna didn't mention to Bess that she reserved emotional space for the possibility of romance and a long-term relationship with a strong, authentic, direct, and verbal partner. She had been exchanging letters with Wilmer since he moved to New York City. Based on what he wrote and said, Edna didn't find Wilmer Kearns patronizing or inconsistent with his support of women's rights. Even better, he shared with Edna his vision about a more equitable balance of power between women and men, much like he'd experienced when growing up in rural Central Pennsylvania.

This was more than Edna could say about some young men she met in Philadelphia. According to Granddaddy, many men close to Edna's age living in Germantown were more interested in her Quaker genealogy and the children she'd produce than in her plan of developing a spiritual "leading" as a woman's rights activist. At least that's what Edna told my grandfather, exactly the kind of remark she'd make to a friend rather than a beau or parent.

Granddaddy told me that Edna hid his letters in a locked box in her closet near her First Day shoes. This revelation suggested that anyone reading Wilmer's letters mailed from Manhattan would notice their developing intimacy. In 1903 Edna didn't mention to Bess the importance she placed on the letter exchange with Wilmer. The two women spoke at great length, however, about the books they read. Edna's bed stand displayed a pile of novels, including *Jane Eyre*.

Edna had read *Jane Eyre* twice. The book held a special significance because Papa had presented the work to his daughter for her birthday one Christmas. Edna was convinced that suffragist Susan B. Anthony kept a copy of *Jane Eyre* among her enormous collection of abolition, temperance, and women's rights literature. The work's protagonist, Jane Eyre, represented a free and independent young woman.

Edna and Bess dramatized *Jane Eyre* when reading it out loud. Bess was an especially fine reader—someone who raised and lowered her voice at exactly the right moments. She maintained the same inflections and tone for each character. So while English novelist Charlotte Brontë never directly stated that Jane was a Quaker, the character in the novel fit the profile in terms of dress and values. Brontë described Jane as Mr. Rochester's "plain, Quakerish governess," and there were references to Jane's Quaker-style beliefs and values throughout the work.

According to my grandfather, Jane Eyre lived from within and, fortunately for Miss Eyre, her inner beauty shone through. Edna's mother also lived from within, but the cultural landscape had changed. In an earlier generation, May's reliance on purity, temperance, prison reform, and upright values would have been considered heroic. Because social priorities had shifted, May's husband and son criticized her often for not having a sense of humor and worse. Occasionally even Edna found herself impatient with her mother, although in general she supported May. Edna had her own ideas. She left evidence behind summarizing her teenage view of independence, preserved on a slip of paper—twelve lines, written in groups of four lines over the course of a year in cursive handwriting, tucked into a scrapbook suggesting her changing perspective about young love.

April 1900

Lewis has his Lydia.
Harold his Edna fair.
But I have none thank goodness.
Who in the future will pull my hair.

September 1900

Lewis has had his Lydia.
He now has his Edna fair.
Harold's left out in the cold.
And I still hang on to my hair.

April 1901

Lewis has his Edna.
And Harold claims her too.
Boys you'll have to quit scrapping.
Let Edna decide for you.[3]

It wasn't great poetry, but Edna was experimenting when she set down in writing what it was like to have romantic interest from young men. Jane Eyre finally chose an intimate relationship with Mr. Rochester, who kept his former wife confined upstairs in his mansion in chains. Readers, of course, may have excused Mr. Rochester's decision because his wife was, after all, crazy. This was precisely the point Bess liked to make.

Wilmer may have wondered if Bess, not Edna, was correct about the consequences of unequal gender relationships. Edna's primary authority was Margaret Fuller, who died with her young husband and infant in a shipwreck off the coast of Long Island, New York, on her way back from Europe in 1850. He said that Margaret Fuller never fully tested her theory of a "sacred marriage."

Even if Edna didn't like Henry David Thoreau as a writer, I could identify with his philosophy. He wrote that if I couldn't keep pace with the other students at school, one reason could be that I heard the music of a "different drummer," however "measured or far away."

I wasn't sure how I felt about marriage. Perhaps it had changed since my grandparents' day. I never heard Granddaddy Wilmer speak against it. Marriage between women and men was in full force in most of the homes in my neighborhood in the Philadelphia area. Because marriage had a halo effect, I returned to the trail of finding out what happened to Edna's wedding dress. At my age, it was too soon to consider the pros and cons of marriage. I could only look away from the sun.

Chapter 15

Learning about Interviewing

I heard "Tommy loves Peggy" hollered in the schoolyard during recess at Montgomery Township Consolidated School. The shrill voices of my classmates carried across the playground—louder than the recess bell, louder than the recess sounds of dozens of children. Little Tommy Keenan entered elementary school in the middle of the year. He loved me. I was in sixth grade, and he was in fifth. Peggy loved Tommy, too, but she hated her nickname of Peggy and vowed to take back Marguerite, prominent on her birth certificate.

I wasn't sure that I'd marry Tommy Keenan. When I finished writing my first novel, I had only one copy, handwritten for school, set aside for the teacher who'd announced to our class that in 1920, American women were "given" the right to vote. I knew this wasn't true. Women won the right to vote after a long and difficult struggle. I was the only kid in the school aware of this. It seemed like no one cared about the truth, except me.

I could have titled my first book *A Girl from Lexington*, but didn't. I would get a good grade on my novel if my story was about a boy rather than a girl. I felt the wind stinging my thighs under a Scottish wool skirt held closed with a safety pin when racing across a nearby field. I sensed Tommy Keenan next to me. When we sat opposite on the playground merry-go-round, we dug a shallow trench with our feet by running in a circle. The spinning overcame the cumulative effect of memorizing multiplication tables.

Virginia Poe loved Edgar. Wilmer Kearns loved Edna. I loved Tommy, even as I both adored and was afraid of boys. If a boy were to step into my internal space, I pulled away to give myself pause long enough to figure out what to say next. Boys were mysteries.

I woke up at dawn one morning when the sharp light from the window split through the blinds. It was Saturday. I could sleep later than usual. I brushed my hair. I wasn't going anywhere special, other than spending hours polishing the final paragraphs of my novel, an extra credit assignment. I'd never written a book before or met a real writer, but wait a minute. My grandparents were writers—weren't they? Facts, sentences, and people talking to each other on paper seemed like magical elements emerging from a blank page.

Young Marguerite in love, circa 1953.

"I am a writer," I thought when examining the walls from one side of my bedroom to the other. I studied the open spaces from the closet to the windows to a shelf loaded with books. I wondered if a publisher in New York might discover my novel, *A Boy from Lexington*, and ask me for a copy. I divided my life into three parts—one for my regular school program, two for Granddaddy's version of his life as expressed through memories and stories, and finally, the separate dimension located in the past that I entered with my eyes closed.

When an adult asked me what I wanted to be when I "grew up," I replied: "Prima þallerina in a production of *The Firebird*." Twirling on toe shoes is what makes a powerful woman, I thought. No need to expose my fantasies to the entire school. To accomplish my goals, I'd have to work my way up in the Philadelphia Police Department as an intern by solving mysteries alongside a real detective. I'd watched enough mysteries on television to write my own script. I couldn't tell Wilmer and Edna's story without first learning how to conduct interviews.

I stared into the bathroom mirror at home and practiced: Ladies and Gentlemen—the story you are about to hear is true. The names have not been changed. Come along with me to find out as much as possible about my family. I'm at a standstill when searching for the real deal about my grandmother Edna. Granddaddy called my mother on the phone and told her about an appointment with his physician that afternoon. I was on my own. I couldn't advance the story of my grandparents' love affair unless I included myself in the story. I shivered. Granddaddy hadn't held Edna's hand or kissed her. Not yet.

I suspected Edna was falling in love with Wilmer, but I had to make sure they got together. Otherwise, I couldn't become the first child of their second daughter, Wilma Buckman Kearns, born on November 12, 1920. The month was significant. In early November of 1920, millions of US women voted for the first time after the ratification of the Nineteenth Amendment to the US Constitution. Not all women though. There was the constitutional amendment, and then its implementation, faulty and incomplete. Granddaddy said the voting rights reform was accomplished within an unbalanced social system.

"Shouldn't the women have wiped the slate clean first?" I asked my grandfather.

"They did the best they could under the circumstances," he said and added something about everyone being contaminated by this social hierarchy. "That's for thy generation to fix."

Did Granddaddy think I was a miracle worker? I lifted an imaginary knocker to history. Edna opened the door and told me she was busy ironing. I told her: "I don't mind if we talk until you're done."

"Would you like a cup of tea? I have a pot handy when figuring out what to do next."

"Is there a problem?"

"I'm in love with Wilmer Kearns, but I've been insisting on us being 'just friends.' "

"Why?"

"We aren't a match."

"How long has this has been going on?"

"For months."

Edna alerted me to another problem. "Wilmer has been acting strange," she added. I knew enough to keep my mouth shut. I'd never figure out what really happened with my grandparents unless I asked the proper questions.

"I picked up on something when Wilmer and I got together last at the Market Street teahouse. He kept checking his watch, like he had another appointment," Edna said before returning to her ironing. She hated ironing. She said that a respectable individual couldn't leave home with wrinkles in a skirt or blouse. Starch added to the rinse water complicated ironing. The garment had to be dried and moistened again before a hot iron could press out the wrinkles. Edna returned to ironing.

"I should take thee back to the beginning when the two of us met on Logan Circle after I dropped my art portfolio. Angel that he is, Wilmer helped me rescue the scattered papers."

"It's not necessary to tell me everything," I responded. "I know what happened."

"How?"

"I'm your granddaughter. Wilmer told me about your love affair."

"I don't know anything about a granddaughter. Did I have a child out of wedlock?"

"No."

"Then what's the story?"

"It's long. We'll get into it later. For now, tell me what has you so upset."

Edna told me about afternoon shadows merging with fading sunlight as she sat at a mahogany desk in her bedroom at Echo Dale. My grandmother positioned her diary on the desk. She tucked a sheet of paper underneath, a convenient location when writing a letter to Bess. I suspected Edna planned to hide the letter if her mother entered the room unannounced. Her brother Smythe called May a "busybody."

Edna's eyes squinted in the dim light. She stretched her cramped fingers. Downstairs, the standing grandfather clock chimed on the hour. The room's winter chill hadn't eased since Edna returned from the teahouse after sharing lunch with Wilmer. There had been an unspoken tension between the couple, a subject not mentioned—their fondness for each other.

Edna said that she pushed back her chair that grated against the bare bedroom floor when remembering how Wilmer had called her "Brave Heart," and she had tagged him as "Bold Billy." Granddaddy said Edna felt paralyzed for weeks, thinking about how to include him more fully into her life. Wilmer didn't pressure her. She hadn't refused any of his invitations to meet for tea when he traveled weekends from Manhattan to Philadelphia. She wrote in her diary about my grandfather's fine appearance, the confident way he held himself, his steady gaze when listening to her plans to become a women's rights activist. My grandmother realized that if she kept limiting Wilmer to friendship, he might lose interest in her. No guidebook existed for how to create equality in male-female and family relationships.

I stood next to the rocking chair in Granddaddy's kitchen and listened patiently. "The world needs to know about the US women's rights movement," he said. "They also have to hear about Bess and how, in her opinion, most unmarried young women are distracted and confused." Bess challenged Edna, asking how she could be sure that Wilmer didn't manipulate his audiences, including her, with his stories and promises. Edna stared out her bedroom window to calm her fidgeting. She straightened the folds of her ivory dress.

Edna added another sentence to the letter. Bess was right. She was convinced that most men expected girls and women to perform like trained seals. Wilmer didn't fit this pattern. He reassured Edna that partnerships between women and men could be genuine and loving as well as equal, rational, and practical. He understood Edna's position that romantic passion should be based in friendship. She had faith that honesty could contribute to a balanced and satisfying romantic relationship.

Their arms linked naturally at the Philadelphia train station when Wilmer left to return to New York City. Occasionally they remained silent when eating angel food cake and drinking tea at the teahouse where they bathed in the sunlight pouring from the floor-to-ceiling windows.

Without practicing what I'd learned about interviewing, I'd never be able to write a credible account of my grandparents' courtship. I needed to follow the advice of my favorite childhood television drama character, Sergeant Joe Friday, who in the program *Dragnet* kept audiences glued to the set with his "just the facts" style of interviewing.

"Stop wandering around in labyrinths and running off in tangents," Granddaddy cautioned me.

"Okay," I replied when pushing back my shoulders and standing straight. I cleared my throat. That's what adults did before making an announcement. I started with—Here is the city, Philadelphia, one of the largest in the United States. All right, maybe Philly is second to New York, but it sure is bigger than Trenton, New Jersey. I'm an intern assigned to a sergeant who works for the Philadelphia Police Department. On September 17th, my sergeant instructor was working the day shift out of the Twenty-Fourth and Christian Streets district office. His detective partner Fudge was sick. "Nerves," Fudge said. The phone rang. May Buckman was calling to speak to the sergeant on duty. She reported her daughter Edna missing. Apparently Edna left home after mentioning something about meeting her friend Bess at the Market Street teahouse. Mrs. Buckman sent her son Smythe to the teahouse to check. Edna wasn't there.

"She hasn't been here all day," the manager said, who added that Bess had been working the first shift as a baker of cinnamon rolls and crumpets. Mrs. Buckman made a special request of the sergeant to stop everything and find Edna. He agreed. As his assistant, I smiled and dialed. I asked questions, plenty of them, to anyone who answered the phone at Friends' Central and at Quaker schools and meeting houses all over Philadelphia. When asked about my progress, I answered, "I'm still checking." Mrs. Buckman was frantic.

"Someone must have seen my baby. She's wearing a Quaker bonnet and a gray dress. She couldn't have wandered away without someone noticing her."

"I don't think this is as tragic as it seems," the sergeant told her. "Try to relax if you can, Mrs. Buckman."

"It's dark outside."

"How old is your daughter?"

"Nineteen."

"Have you told your husband?"

"He's in Baltimore signing contracts for a hotel bed installation."

"Don't worry. We'll have three teams of detectives on duty. There's word that Edgar Allan Poe is missing too. We'll add Edna to the caseload."

"But Poe went missing in Baltimore in 1849."

"The case is still open."

"Please find Edna."

"We're doing everything possible."

The sergeant hung up the desk phone, but it rang again. He answered. I listened with my notebook open and my pen poised. I wanted to say that I'd tracked down the last individual who'd seen Edna alive—me. When I'd knocked on Edna's door, she'd been ironing. I didn't notice her mother or brother anywhere. What if Edna had followed me back to Granddaddy's kitchen?

The sergeant hopped into his squad car and headed to Fairmount Park to track down a lead from a source, a soda vendor, who suspected Edna Buckman may have run off with Wilmer Kearns. The Philadelphia police sergeant circulated Edna's picture among those waiting in line to buy lemonade.

"Have you seen this young woman?" he asked.

"Yup, that's her," the soda vendor said. "She was holding hands with a man."

"Can you describe this man, please?"

"I wasn't that close to them. But they acted like they were in love."

"Is there anything else?"

"The man was short. Taller than her, anyway. And he was strange."

"What do you mean?"

"He climbed up on a boulder and played a violin concerto with an invisible orchestra in the background. I'd never seen anything like it."

"And then what happened?"

"She stood on an opposite boulder and gave a speech about women's rights."

"Are you sure?"

"I know the difference between soup and nuts. She was soup, and he was nuts."

That's when the sergeant found the nearest public phone booth and contacted the mental health division of the Philadelphia Police Department. I hadn't said anything about my role in the investigation. By then, Charles Buckman had returned from his business trip to Baltimore. He left a phone message that the Baltimore police force had circulated an all-points alert for Edgar Allan Poe. The poet hadn't been found. The sergeant and I were on the right track. We returned to police headquarters and sorted through wanted posters for one of Wilmer Kearns.

The phone rang again at the police desk. Mrs. Buckman was on the line. "Edna has been found," she reported. So the sergeant and I took a ride down to City Hall in his Buick. Mrs. Buckman raced into the building with her husband Charles and introduced him to the sergeant.

"Wilmer Kearns is still on the loose. And he hasn't asked Edna to marry him," Mrs. Buckman added.

"Why should this matter?"

"American women still can't vote. If it's up to Edna, she won't rest until every single woman in the United States casts a ballot."

By my eleventh birthday, I'd learned about the drafting of basic interview questions. If I continued practicing my skills, I'd have a chance of writing about my grandparents and the early women's rights movement by the age of twenty-five. Granddaddy praised my potential. He believed in getting as much public exposure as possible for the cause of equality and women's rights. He was fond of saying: "All publicity is good publicity." Sooner or later, I'd figure out what he meant.

Chapter 16

"Is It Always Like This?"

*G*randdaddy told me that Edna accepted his invitations to visit the woodlands of Fairmount Park when he visited Philadelphia. The couple waded in creek waters and laid a blanket on the ground for picnics on open fields not far from the inner city's rush and clanging street noises. My grandparents carved out a retreat from the furious pace of downtown.

The city park offered serenity on meadows where Edna gathered bouquets of Queen Anne's lace. Wilmer chose a secluded spot to tell her about the open farm

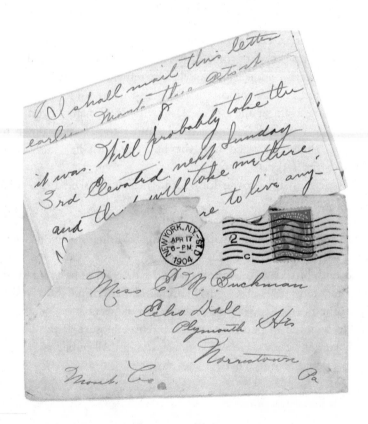

Letter and envelope from Wilmer to Edna, 1904.

fields of rural Pennsylvania. She liked hearing his descriptions of acres of stacked hay, the potent droppings of cattle and horses, and the composting of what the previous season's crops left behind. Through all of this, they avoided the topic so elusive and troubling—friendship and love.

Because of friendship, they had experienced the unknown with each other and opened the door to slow advances and depth. Because of friendship, they had delayed the first kiss, the rush to intimacy. When Granddaddy cupped Edna's chin to emphasize a point, he told me he hesitated long enough to admire her soft skin. If she reminded him of her decision to cultivate a friendship rather than a romance, it would spoil the mood. She didn't discourage his hand from reaching over to draw her face closer to his, if only for several seconds. His heart pounded and his breath slowed. The sensation of his fingers brushing her face must have scorched his skin.

"Is this usual?" he asked her.

"What?"

"Is it always like this between a man and a woman?"

"I don't know," she replied. "I've never been with a man like this. So close," she added, reaching to push one of her front curls to the side of her face.

"Nor I with a woman," Granddaddy said he replied.

Wilmer jumped to his feet. He pulled Edna to a standing position and then led her by the hand to return to the park's trail in perfect step. This action, he said, affirmed his instinct once more that they were meant for each other.

I decided my grandfather wasn't sure if Edna responded confidently after he asked if the feelings between them were "usual." My grandmother considered herself "practical," but she didn't have a close and intimate family role model other than her parents. This is what my mother explained to me years later. I understood then about Edna living in a transitional moment in history when all a young woman could count on was faith and trust in the future. Edna considered herself fortunate to have a father who paid the bills, a mother concerned about the quality of life for future generations, and herself enrolled in a school like Friends' Central. Edna had a friend in Wilmer Kearns who didn't expect her personal agenda to mirror his.

Listening to stories about my grandparents' hikes in Fairmount Park made me feel as if I might lose a grip on their future if I wasn't careful. I made up a new answer for adults when they asked what I wanted to be when I "grew up." I'd switched to becoming a choreographer and no longer a prima ballerina in *The Firebird*. Most adults didn't know about choreographers. I didn't want to tell the truth about my goal of becoming a writer in the event I didn't complete a book about my grandparents.

I considered writing about American women in general, who in Edna and Wilmer's day had no experience living in a social system other than one dominated by men. Whether they realized it or not, second-class citizenship required women giving up a part of themselves. I figured out that over the generations, prejudice and discrimination became institutionalized.

The women's rights movement, according to Granddaddy, had won some victories since 1848. Women in the nation's far west could vote, for example, but a national campaign, state by state, didn't inspire widespread enthusiasm and participation. Not as many women had faith in petitions. Committee hearings for votes for women campaigning didn't inspire the type of commitment that sustained activists like Susan B. Anthony, Elizabeth Cady Stanton, and others for decades.

Back at the Quaker boardinghouse room in New York City, Wilmer said he rearranged his books and dusted the furniture until it became clear that he should examine his feelings carefully before answering Edna's most recent letter. She was original, daring, and dynamic as a friend. Unless he took a risk, he might pass by an opportunity to ask her to marry him. Wilmer was approaching a decision to do this, even as the idea of his own independence appealed to him. He struggled with emotions that increased with each passing day as he mailed each letter to Edna and waited for her answer. He wrote:

215 East 15th Street
New York, New York

Dear Edna,

Thy long letter to hand. Read it three times. Please tell thy friend Emma Shepphard that New York is the Garden Spot of the World and that she never stayed here long enough to get acquainted with the city and its people. Tell her I said so . . .

The identity of Emma Shepphard was lost in the mists of time, other than that she was a Quaker and may have been Edna's cousin.

Wilmer introduced Edna to the city park near to where he lived in Manhattan, close enough to the Quaker boardinghouse for him to see naked winter trees outlined in the mornings as mist crept along East Fifteenth Street. Noise from the sidewalk outside the Penington made its way through the boardinghouse windows, determined to fill up open spaces inside.

In the letter, Wilmer wrote:

. . . I caught a slight cold. My room is not heated. Shall look for a letter from thee tomorrow, as I would feel even more lonely if I do not. Went to bed early last night and forgot to shave, so I had to saw my whiskers off this morning with an old razor. Had no breakfast. Will take a bath and stay in my room until eleven o'clock when I'll head out and find something quick to eat and then explore.

4:30. Returned from my ride. First, I walked down Broadway to the Brooklyn Bridge, back, and then took 6th Ave. El train north as far as the 155th Street terminal. I thought this would take me to the Bronx, but after consulting my map, found it to be Washington Heights. My reason to go to the Bronx Borough was to see what kind of residential district it has. Will probably take the 3rd Elevated there next Sunday . . .[1]

Manhattan wasn't one country, Granddaddy told Edna. On some walks, he passed through Greece, Italy, Ireland, the Balkans, and nations distant and unnamed. He described those in the streets he encountered as defending ideas that might have resulted in them getting kicked out of many communities in Europe, as well as small towns in Pennsylvania. Wilmer added vegetarians, vagabonds, socialists, garment workers, and artists in the city streets to his letters to my grandmother. He told her that his weekly expenses amounted to $11 and that he had saved "every penny" from his paycheck.

Although Wilmer shared many observable details with Edna, he said he only hinted of his tender feelings toward her in his letters. He couldn't face the possibility of rejection.

"Are you still stringing Wilmer along?" Bess asked Edna.

"I have more respect for Wilmer than that. He's a good man."

"Just because he's a good man doesn't mean you have to kneel at his feet."

"I can't devote myself to women's rights and support myself by licking stamps."

"Wilmer might drag you down."

"We'll see."

"You're so rosy eyed, Edna. But I should talk. I'm diving into water over my head by refusing to get married."

"Is thee planning, Bess, to race through life wearing bloomers and hats with feathers?"

"Yes. And I'll take as many lovers down with me as I please."

"Thee will never get anywhere."

"Even if I married Philip, I wouldn't go anywhere. I might as well be a single woman in style."

"Thee might fall on thy head and crack it open."

"At least I won't die of madness or boredom or overwork."

"Is thee suggesting I'll be doing this?"

"It's common for women to believe they're the rare exception."

"Bess, be careful."

"Why?"

"Thee could end up with no future after kicking Philip out of the picture."

"I'll have a future one way or another. What was Aesop's advice in one of his fables? That he'd rather be free than a fat slave?"

"Aesop should know. He was a Greek slave."

"And Mary Wollstonecraft wrote that we women are experts in bartering our freedom for a 'splendid slavery.'"

And so it went between the two women. They were friends, first and always. The same was true for Edna and Wilmer. He was aware of the necessity of becoming a Quaker if he were to marry her. He'd decided to take this step, even though he wasn't convinced that compassion and love had more power than physical force. The men at the Quaker boardinghouse lent Wilmer books questioning war and violence as effective ways to respond to human conflict. He read *The Kingdom of God Is Within You* by Leo Tolstoy, a classic work about nonviolence.

The Red Badge of Courage, a novel by Stephen Crane, made a deep impression on him. Wilmer read it twice as a way to feel closer to his grandfather, John Rhamstine, who was killed as a Union soldier during the Civil War at the siege of Petersburg, Virginia, in 1864. Crane's story offered insights rarely included in speeches on Decoration Day, or at veterans' parades and Fourth of July celebrations. As viewed through the eyes of Stephen Crane's main character—Henry Fleming—the novel established that war required following orders and wearing a mask to hide insecurity, shame, fear, and the suspicion there might not be any meaning to war at all.

After a day together in Fairmount Park, Wilmer and Edna took a trolley back to Center City. They stared out the window, hesitant to mention anything about the feelings washing over them. If he lacked experience with women, Granddaddy made up for it by preparing to reveal to Edna one of the most intimate subjects a young man could admit. He was preparing to commit himself to a romantic relationship with Edna. "I am thine," he longed to say, but he couldn't remember if such a declaration in Quaker plain speech was grammatically correct.

Granddaddy told me that his maternal grandmother, Jane Elizabeth Specht Rhamstine, told family stories to her children featuring ancestor Adam Specht Sr. He'd arrived from Germany during the 1700s and settled in Lancaster County, Pennsylvania. According to family history, the older Specht served as a private in the American Revolution during 1776 under Colonel Nicholas Hausger. Lieutenant Lewis Witner issued him an honorable discharge in 1779 after his participation in battles against the British at Trenton, Princeton, Brandywine, and Germantown.[2]

Adam's son—Adam Specht II—was born in 1784. The younger Adam moved his family in 1812 to Beavertown, then known as Swifttown, a remote village with little more than a scattering of houses located in Central Pennsylvania. Adam served as a corporal in Henry Miller's company of the Pennsylvania Militia in the War of 1812, a conflict involving more than 250,000 American soldiers determined to settle issues with the British unresolved from the war for independence. Adam married Catherine Smith, born March 8, 1788. The couple had two sons—Moses and Elias Specht—plus two daughters, Jane Elizabeth and Mary. Wilmer's maternal grandmother was Jane Elizabeth Specht.

Son Moses Specht operated a general store, tavern, and warehouse in Beavertown as an adult. His brother Elias Specht worked as a gunsmith. Daughter Mary Specht married John Kern and lived in Snyder County. The other child of the Specht family's third generation in America—Jane Elizabeth Specht—married John Rhamstine, who marched off for service in the Union Army during the Civil War. Henrietta Rhamstine, one of Jane and John Rhamstine's children—was my grandfather's mother. She married

John Preston Kearns, Granddaddy's father, who owned and operated a horse and buggy business in Beavertown.

Granddaddy told me that his old friends from business college in Philadelphia weren't shy about admitting that they sought a conventional woman as a life partner. They could absorb any number of personal and business risks, knowing in advance that many women would take advantage of any opportunity to marry a reliable man who could support them.

Wilmer told my mother once about how he'd obsessed over his good fortune in finding Edna because of her style and innocence. He stored her letters in an empty suitcase in his closet at the Penington, with the letters filed in the order they'd been received. He placed Edna's photograph on his bookshelf, the image taken when they visited a photography studio together, back in Philadelphia, the city he referred to as a place of brotherly and sisterly love.

I felt like a budding adult when listening to my grandfather's stories, even though I had a flat chest, brown oxford shoes, handmade dresses, winter wool leggings, and yellow galoshes. I'd never liked American history. When it involved my grandparents, however, learning about the past represented a door opening and a ladder straight into the unknown. I couldn't wait until one teacher or another in elementary school mentioned the accomplishments of US women. I'd feature Edna, the young activist in Battery Park, or perhaps Edna's friend Bess, who expressed herself about gender relationships. Bess didn't care if her best friend Edna agreed with her or not. Bess didn't want to get married, period.

"The truth is on my side," I reassured myself. My grandfather fell in love with Edna, and she with him. I pictured myself waiting until the moment when I'd raise my hand in school, stand before my classmates, and share one of the stories Granddaddy told me about Edna. I was shy. In this imagined moment, I'd bask in the spotlight and impress my teacher and the other students about how my family members had contributed to a pivotal part of US history. My moment of glory never arrived in elementary school. Why didn't more folks than my grandfather talk about the suffrage movement? Was it because my grandparents were crusaders who based their relationship on friendship? They refused to be prisoners to convention and placed their faith in equality and justice instead.

"Oh, well," I thought. "I still have junior high, high school, and college to catch up." I had no idea that over a hundred years later, US women would still be marching for their rights. I let out my breath, slowly, before I realized I'd been holding it in, tight, for years.

Chapter 17

"Will Thee Marry Me?"

My grandfather told me he couldn't have predicted that he'd propose marriage to Edna the same weekend anarchist Emma Goldman arrived in Philadelphia for a speaking engagement. She had a nationwide reputation as someone who could repulse, shock, as well as fascinate the US public.

City founder William Penn would have supported the right of free speech for an edgy activist like Goldman. Since Penn was no longer around, Goldman often had to confront the opposition head on. She had no hesitations when publicizing her controversial opinions about the equality of all humans, the inevitability of revolution, and the need for everyone to love without the state's sanction and control.

Edna's friend Bess could be counted on to portray Emma Goldman as a liberated woman, a complicated woman, and an outrageous woman. If my grandmother Edna were to place women into categories at the turn of the twentieth century, she might have found a place for Goldman among the small percentage of those who also insisted on freedom in their personal lives.

Wilmer suggested to Edna that they attend the Goldman lecture on North Broad Street. Edna agreed, although she did so to please my grandfather who'd missed hearing Goldman speak in Manhattan. Granddaddy told me he worried about the courage necessary to propose marriage if he were to take the initiative. Edna believed most women accepted the domination of men because they weren't educated and otherwise prepared for independent living. Granddaddy said she concluded that many women didn't have the confidence or resources, education or job skills to carve out free choices and lifestyles on their own. He wasn't sure if he could overcome Edna's limitation of "just friends." He thought about the Quaker expression, that the "way" would "open" at the appropriate moment.

When Emma Goldman lectured across the nation, she made it clear that in her opinion, vertical white male control of the social and political sphere couldn't be eliminated except by way of a social and economic revolution. Because the dominant culture suppressed the use of terms like "misogyny" and "patriarchy," many US women were in denial about why certain discriminatory patterns persisted. Emma Goldman was an example of someone who didn't edit her opinions, even when presenting her views to an unfriendly crowd.

Buckman family, circa 1904. Edna May Buckman is at the far left. Her brother, Thomas Smith Buckman, known as Smythe, is kneeling at center. Her parents, May Begley Buckman and Charles Harper Buckman, are to the far right.

Bess believed Emma Goldman to be a social critic of note because of the activist's conviction that love constituted the deepest level of human existence. After being twisted and manipulated within the institution of marriage, Goldman concluded that authentic love was rarely possible. She received widespread press coverage when elaborating on this topic. For this reason, Wilmer felt insecure about combining his marriage proposal with hearing Emma Goldman speak at the Odd Fellows Hall on North Broad Street. Wilmer had prepared himself for Edna's acceptance of his marriage proposal, as well as her refusal. If possible, he'd prefer to eliminate Emma Goldman's influence on Edna, not encourage it.

Goldman's points of view irritated many Americans because of the way she stood on stage with one hand on her hip as if to test the patience of critics. Philadelphia's fancy ladies weren't impressed with Goldman's mutton chop sleeves, her perspectives on marriage, equality and freedom, and her belief that working for women's voting rights amounted to a waste of time. Goldman didn't support an adjustment or reform of a social system. She was adamant about replacing it.

Goldman didn't oppose women's voting rights. But she didn't speak in favor of devoting one's life to bringing about a reform that didn't address the root causes of injustice. Goldman had a special talent for delivering her message of solidarity and

Emma Goldman, early 1900s. Courtesy of the Emma Goldman Papers Public History Project, Berkeley, California.

unity to working men and union members. Wilmer Kearns didn't agree with everything Goldman had to say, but he respected her intelligence and unique way of presenting unusual and controversial topics.

Wilmer crammed his final day of the weekend with activities, including a visit to South Philadelphia where Edna's maternal grandparents, the Begleys, once lived. Edna described them as committed and loyal Quakers, or "weighty Friends." After leaving Southwark, Edna and Wilmer passed restless crowds on street corners, as well as the usual families and couples running errands or taking walks. When the couple arrived at the Odd Fellows Hall on North Broad Street, they discovered that a contingent of Philadelphia police officers had moved into position to protect city residents from hearing Goldman's biting words.

The visit to Southwark gave Wilmer a chance to learn more about Edna's family background. Her maternal grandparents—Sarah Martin Begley and Thomas Begley—once lived in the neighborhood, south of City Hall, an area chosen by many established Philadelphia families for residency. On a weekend visit like this one, Wilmer heard more about Edna's relatives, including how Edna's parents, May and Charles, had been married in a Quaker ceremony in Southwark on December 22, 1880. Edna was born two years later on Christmas day.

Wilmer found out that the Begley side of the family regarded its Edgar Allan Poe associations as more than Philadelphia folklore. Stories circulated about how May's grandfather had picked Edgar Allan Poe up from "the gutter" in Northern Liberties during one of the writer's alcoholic blackouts. I heard from my mother the oral family history that Grandfather Begley had walked Poe home to find the family's kitchen pantry shelves empty.

When Wilmer and Edna passed by the Begley family's former home on Catherine Street, Edna described the structure from the outside as having absorbed the distinctive aroma of steamed cabbage with cream that Sarah Martin Begley prepared. She baked an Irish sweet bread often—Barmbrack—that Edna and her brother loved toasted for

Edna May Buckman as a child, circa 1880s.

a snack. Cabbage and bread reminded the family that Thomas Begley's father, Thomas Vantier Begley, had left Ireland around 1800 and settled in Virginia before moving to Philadelphia. By Edna's childhood, the Begleys' extended family members had put Ireland far behind them. Cabbage, potato, and bread recipes were stored in a box on the pantry shelf and consulted on fewer occasions with the passage of decades.

My mother Wilma told me that Edna's grandparents on the Begley branch loved leather books with intricate gold leaf designs on covers displayed on living room shelves. Friends and relatives at the Begley residence sat erect on parlor furniture with hard seats that reinforced formal visiting behavior. Most books on the shelves had the first page personalized. *The New Latin Tutor*, for example, published in 1836, featured Thomas Begley's signature at the top. Edna later wrote and dated the following message to my mother underneath:

> August 10, 1930. To Wilma. This was the property of thy grandfather Thomas Smith Begley, father of May Begley Buckman who was the mother of thy mother, Edna Buckman Kearns. Thy great grandfather was a Swedenborgian by faith but later joined Friends as his wife Sarah Martin Begley, daughter of Benjamin Martin, was a member of old Spruce Street Meeting.[1]

Inscriptions in books like these written by Edna and her mother May represented the method by which family genealogy was passed on to descendants over the generations.

Wilmer told me he felt confident with Edna, dressed as he was in a custom-made suit designed and sewn by his friend Aron, the Polish tailor. Granddaddy said he pulled in his stomach so Edna wouldn't notice his expanding layer of flab from the bread, butter, and beer he consumed at the German restaurant. I recognized lines of insecurity around Granddaddy's mouth with more than a hint of indecision in his shoulders.

A day of sunshine had opened to the warmth penetrating the streets of the inner city, enough to fill Granddaddy with optimism. If he could capture Edna's attention with his stories, he might convince her to marry him and move to New York. There, many residents could choose from the left to the right in their politics. Women activists dedicated themselves to freedom and women's rights issues. Yes, Manhattan would be a place where their differences wouldn't be as noticeable as they were in Philadelphia.

Wilmer didn't know what to say as they walked quickly toward the Philadelphia train terminal with his imminent departure back to New York the first order of priority. The moment of truth had arrived. Wilmer remained silent as they passed by theaters, grocery shops, and a bakery. Streets of brick rowhouses had balconies where silk flowers hung from baskets. Once inside the train terminal, they stumbled their way through dust, smoke, and dirt to locate Wilmer's train platform.

Edna reached for Wilmer's hand after she wiped away a thin layer of grime spread across her face. He checked his pocket watch and wondered whether he'd be able to ignore screeching brakes and train whistles. Would they exchange pecks on the cheek at the last minute, or share a lingering kiss? Would their parting amount to more than a hug and the usual reminder to stay in touch? Wilmer's shoulders sagged. He corrected his posture. He needed a ring to slip on her finger if she accepted his marriage proposal. He didn't have one.

Wilmer told me he reached into his pocket for the orange he'd saved for a snack on the train. With a pocketknife, he cut it into quarters and motioned for Edna to open her mouth so he could squeeze its sweet juices onto her tongue. Oranges were a special treat, best when purchased as Wilmer had, straight from boats arriving in Philadelphia's port from Florida. Wilmer presented Edna with a kiss tasting like orange honey cakes.

"I have a question I've been meaning to ask," Wilmer said after kissing Edna and doing his best to force more words out of his mouth.

"Does it have anything to do with me saying 'yes' even before the question is asked?" Edna responded demurely, opening the way to Wilmer's question.

"Will thee marry me—the Quaker man I am becoming?"

Edna's response was fast in coming.

"Yes."

The train platform racket faded into the background as Wilmer lifted Edna from her feet into his arms while sputtering words of endearment.

"I love her. She loves me. I'm a lucky man," Wilmer repeated to himself after the train doors slammed closed. Then the train left the station, heading north.

Chapter 18

Rumblings at the Dinner Table

"How are wedding plans coming along?" May Buckman asked Edna and Wilmer during Sunday dinner's first course at Echo Dale.

"Friend George at Quaker Meeting has been asking questions about Wilmer's job in the cigar industry," Edna replied. "He says it's a filthy business damaging to body and soul—unworthy of a future husband of mine."[1]

Wilmer spoke up. "Native peoples raised the tobacco they smoked as part of spiritual rituals. They planted tobacco as a gift to the Great Spirit."

No one remarked on Wilmer's defense of tobacco. Serving platters ended up in front of Charles Buckman so family members were forced to ask him for second helpings. Charles insisted that he supervise the sweet potatoes, cauliflower, sourdough bread, and fish stew prepared from striped bass caught from the Delaware River. Fresh fish was sold at the Reading Terminal Market in Center City.

Wilmer believed his invitation to the Buckman's dinner table was a major step forward. Edna told him the tension had been thick in the Buckman household after the engagement announcement. He could tell that Edna's mother wasn't enthusiastic about the news Edna delivered without warning. She resigned herself to providing Edna with support, even if her reaction had been subdued.

Wilmer Kearns wouldn't have been the choice of Edna's parents—not because of any fault of his own, but because Wilmer was a Lutheran. Or more fairly put, Wilmer wasn't a Quaker. "He will be," Edna assured her parents. Guiding him in the direction of becoming a Quaker seemed like a substantial investment in a young man who, in Charles and May's opinion, should have searched for more appropriate employment in New York City. Edna's brother, father, and several Buckman relatives weren't impressed with Wilmer's employment in the accounting office of a cigar manufacturing firm.

May Buckman suggested that Wilmer Kearns be invited to join family members for Sunday dinner as a way to acknowledge the couple's engagement. After Edna extended an invitation to Wilmer, her brother Smythe asked his father about including his friend Cecil in dinner plans.

"Why couldn't he join us some other evening?" Edna asked her father, who replied: "Because we treat boys and girls equally."

Edna didn't argue. She believed her father's excuse of equality between the genders to be inappropriate.

Edna decided not to challenge her father, who wasn't pleased about the news that she planned to marry Wilmer Kearns rather than a young man from an established Philadelphia Quaker family.

"Thee didn't ask my permission or consult with me," Papa Buckman complained. "I'm disappointed in thy choice."

"It's not required these days to ask a father first," Edna responded.

No one at the Sunday dinner table—not Edna, May, or Smythe—dared bring up Papa's continued late arrivals home from business trips to Harrisburg, Boston, and Baltimore. Smythe's acceptance to George School, the Hicksite Quaker secondary boarding school in Bucks County, wasn't mentioned either.

Edna's parents, Charles Harper Buckman and May Phipps Begley Buckman, no date.

Charles placed a serving of cauliflower onto his plate. Smythe set his elbows on the dining room table. This annoyed May, who at such transgressions, could be relied on to say: "If I told thee once, I've told thee a hundred times. Mind thy manners."

"Please pass the sourdough," Smythe said in a shrill tone. His reputation for indulging his impulsive nature received unspoken acceptance from Papa and a predictable frown from Mamma.

Wilmer walked with Edna in the family garden before dinner. They held hands. The prospect of five minutes together was less than ideal. After a respectable period of time as friends, holding hands as an engaged couple was, by comparison, thrilling to Wilmer and Edna. Granddaddy said he'd accomplished his goal of convincing Edna to marry him. He exhibited poise and composure for this reason. He told me that Edna was delighted with the news of their engagement. It affirmed their mutual love of books, their partnership, and their commitment to each other to "make history," a reminder Wilmer included in his letters to Edna.

As Sunday dinner moved toward a conclusion, Smythe announced plans with Cecil to attend a reading of Walt Whitman's poetry in downtown Philadelphia. Their desire to escape from the dinner table was barely disguised. Edna's brother had a reputation among friends and family members for being more interested in racing ponies or organizing cemetery treasure hunts than spending Sunday afternoons at home with

May Begley Buckman (*second row*) on one of her visits to George School, the Hicksite Quaker boarding school in Bucks County, Pennsylvania, circa 1905.

his parents and sister. Cecil asked Edna during dessert if she could introduce him to "some girls." As Edna prepared to answer, May broke into the conversation. Edna sensed a confrontation brewing over another instance of men calling women "girls," which May believed to be a condescending way of reinforcing the lopsided social equation.

"Does thee like playing with dolls and reading Louisa May Alcott?" May asked Cecil with a straight face.

"What are you getting at?" he replied.

"Girls love the book *Little Women* and playing with dolls. They are girls and little women for only a short while. Someone like Smythe's older sister Edna is an adult, someone engaged to be married."

"I like those types too."

"Does thee realize that many women don't like to be called girls?"

"Girls. Women. Young ladies. It's all the same to me. I don't get along with the selfish independent types," Cecil added. "They think only of themselves. And the men who love them are left out in the cold."

An increasing number of young women like Bess had assessed the social landscape and refused to accept the limited choices available to them. This raised the ire of Mr. Weiss who vented at every opportunity about young women who should be cured of their disobedience with black eyes. Mr. Weiss spoke so loud on occasion that he almost came to blows with Mr. Buckman. Mr. Weiss accused Mr. Buckman of suggesting to Bess that she not marry Philip, even though Bess had been frank with her parents about a marriage boycott. The Buckman family moved from Germantown in Philadelphia to Echo Dale, not far from Norristown in Montgomery County, because of the tension between the two households that culminated in a final clash.

"You're throwing your life away." Edna heard Mr. Weiss admonishing his daughter Bess from the porch of their home next door.

"Bess refuses to marry. And why? For no logical reason," Mr. Weiss shouted. "And Philip, such a refined man. Bess could have had him as a husband. I'm aggravated when my baby girl misbehaves. Young people these days don't respect their elders, and all their parents want is grandchildren. Now my daughter is spreading lies about me when I'm only doing something for her own good."

The discord between neighbors had been upsetting enough for Edna. And then Cecil's presence at Sunday dinner felt inappropriate to Edna. Since her relationship to Wilmer led to so much discord, she was tired enough to retire to bed. Her brother was acting up, and her mother tried unsuccessfully to keep the peace. Edna wanted to scream. To break the tension, Edna rose from her seat and stacked dirty dishes to carry into the kitchen. Wilmer left his chair to help. Once in the kitchen and out of sight of the rest of the family, they glanced left and right before dissolving into each other's arms. A rustle of taffeta from May's dress on her way back to the kitchen ended with Wilmer's ruffled hair and a stunned expression on Edna's face.

"If Edna would only bundle with me," Wilmer said he thought as May left the kitchen after leaving soiled dinner napkins behind. Wilmer was spending more weekends in Philadelphia, and he slept overnight at Echo Dale frequently. The couple shared little private time together. After dinner and a brief social visit, Wilmer would be expected to retire to his bedroom and Edna, to hers. For Wilmer, bundling wasn't a joke. A conversation about the subject had to wait until they were alone for him to introduce the topic. Bundling, the Pennsylvania Dutch custom of men and women sharing a bed with a board placed between them, might have relieved Wilmer's anxiety about birth control—a topic both city and country people avoided mentioning. The subject occupied the attention of most couples in love.

The federal Comstock Laws of 1873 made the distribution of birth control information illegal, an obstacle Edna handled by asking her women friends about the basics of reproduction. Wilmer's mother Henrietta Kearns had ushered eight children into the world; five survived. She'd spent most of her adult life caring for husband and offspring. Henrietta never recovered from the death of three children after a diphtheria epidemic passed through Beavertown during the early years of her marriage to John P. Kearns.

Wilmer longed for children. But how and when? And could youngsters be balanced with marriage and Edna's women's rights activism? Twentieth-century Pennsylvania Dutch men and women didn't bundle like other couples may have practiced the custom throughout the 1800s in rural ethnic communities. Wilmer could never be sure about traditions conducted behind closed doors. In novels both Edna and Bess read, passionate couples kissed until readers of these books had their minds split open by the sounds of bodices ripping. These couples usually searched for a bedroom, any room, where they closed the door and left readers of such books out in the hallway.

The custom of bundling, once an accepted custom in Pennsylvania, New England, and some traditional communities, offered a practical way for courting couples to sleep together without violating their chastity. By bundling, they were able to enjoy the intimacy of conversation by lying close and staying warm together. Many German parents approved of bundling. The custom featured the practice of keeping the couple apart by the use of a long separation in the bed's center, running from top to bottom. Occasionally a bolster was utilized or the man or woman, or both, wore body bags to keep the heat on, so the soup of passion didn't boil over. Numerous residents of Pennsylvania Dutch country tended to be practical about such matters. Country folk understood the importance of keeping the romantic coals glowing during courtship and marriage.

If the young people from German families in Snyder County bundled, they didn't discuss it outside of inner family circles. Wilmer's family members didn't practice this tradition, but Wilmer was curious nonetheless. He said that the Bible condoned bundling, as expressed in the story of Boaz and Ruth.

I heard about bundlers enjoying slow advances and retreats while they stayed awake for hours, conversing and prolonging their hugging and kissing. They figured out the extent to which they should feed the fire of passion and how not to extinguish it within a few minutes. Some of Pennsylvania's country people claimed that bundling couples reported marriages of harmony and contentment. They considered bundling common sense, in contrast to those who condemned it, like Edna's mother, who believed it was one step removed from inviting the devil into the household.

Wilmer and Edna discussed their reservations about conventional marriage roles and affirmed the importance of trust, companionship, freedom, and independence. Even if the issue of birth control could be resolved, Wilmer wondered how intimacy would be expressed in their own living space, evenings, after he'd spent the day toiling in the cigar accounting office. Wilmer suspected that by evening he'd be looking forward to a home-cooked meal and an hour or two with Edna to cuddle in bed.

After dinner at Echo Dale, Buckman family members adjourned to the downstairs parlor. Edna and Wilmer spent an hour with Edna's parents engaged in polite conversation before everyone excused themselves for bed. Wilmer packed his belongings to take on the train the following morning back to New York City. He didn't love Edna for being helpless, clueless, and incompetent. He was already aware that they were strong and powerful together.

The vision of them living together as a married couple, my mother said, thrilled my grandfather. He was in love and filled with anticipation about the future.

Chapter 19

"Happy New Year to Thee and All"

*E*dna stared out the bedroom window after Wilmer returned to New York. She rested in the same room where Wilmer slept. She liked curling up next to his scent on the pillowcases and sheets. My grandmother would have spent the rest of the afternoon reading with her head on Wilmer's pillow, but for an overwhelming weak feeling. She felt ill. Mamma, who usually held center stage for her poor health, asked Dr. Corson, the family's Quaker physician, to schedule a home visit.

When Edna wrote to Wilmer about not feeling well, I wondered if this admission was another way of communicating a sense of unease at the prospect of marriage. As a teenager, Edna had decided that while other young women her age would marry, she had other plans. This changed, and few of her family members understood why. Making a transition to a radically different lifestyle took all of her attention after realizing that Wilmer would provide her with the freedom to become a women's rights activist.

Edna had studied art in Center City until setting her sights on the Pennsylvania Academy of the Fine Arts, according my mother. She said Edna hadn't anticipated the rigorous discipline accompanying academy instruction and the stress of travel from Echo Dale to Center City by train. Edna didn't have the strength, and worse, a commercial talent for art. A teaching position in Manhattan was a possibility, but she'd need a portfolio and committed instructors to push her past barriers designed to keep women in their spheres. Edna would leave behind an unfinished art program when marrying Wilmer and then moving with him, as the couple had decided, to New York City.

In her upstairs bedroom at Echo Dale, Edna closed the chapbook, *Voices of Freedom*, published by Quaker poet John Greenleaf Whittier. When Whittier spoke of Quakers of old, he referred to a less complicated period of history when Quaker families like hers weren't struggling with a changing world and how their spiritual and political ground in Pennsylvania was shrinking.

If only Whittier had referred to the Quaker of the poem as "she," instead of "he." Edna was aware of this literary convention. She'd been raised to view the world consistent with the Quaker belief that girls and boys, women and men, and all humans were equal. In spite of this, Edna lived in a larger world constructed upside down from the Quaker perspective. Men had positions at the top, leaving women to figure out how they could navigate the stormy seas of life with few opportunities, a paucity of independent choices, plus a lack of legal precedents and civil rights protections.

Edna may have taken all of this into consideration when accepting Wilmer's proposal of marriage. I hoped so. And yet Granddaddy told me that Edna didn't tell her mother how she couldn't wait to move out of Echo Dale and be on her own in New York with Wilmer. Mamma spent hours and occasionally entire days with her bedroom door closed. Her foul mood had everything to do with Papa, the details of which everyone was aware of, although the subject was rarely discussed.

On his next visit to Echo Dale, Wilmer responded with attention. He doted over Edna, gifted her with flowers. He labored over letters written whenever he could, as the entries in Edna's diary revealed. Wilmer expressed his vulnerabilities to Edna. By agreeing to marry Wilmer, Edna experienced what it felt like to be naughty among Quakers and defy convention and social expectations by not marrying a Quaker man who'd been raised in Philadelphia. She'd never expected that the women's suffrage gatherings she'd attended in Center City would become opportunities to express buried rebellious feelings she'd harbored for years about authority figures and distorted gender relationships.

Edna liked to please, a trait that could be traced back to a childhood of being a good girl and acting according to her mother's wishes. And she couldn't and wouldn't please those who discriminated against others. It was difficult to be both rebellious and, on some levels, conventional. Edna found a balance by writing in her diary and keeping many of her opinions private. Because Wilmer promised to be an equal partner in marriage, Edna agreed to marry him.

The romance with Wilmer caught Edna by surprise precisely because of her former "just friends" stipulation. And now their engagement had not only been announced, but wedding planning was under way. The ceremony was scheduled for the Buckman family home, Echo Dale, just as her mother May's marriage to Charles Buckman had been at the home of her parents in Philadelphia in 1880.

Edna's birth two years later on Christmas day in 1882 had given May considerable delight in becoming a mother. Edna was an easy child to raise, with a few exceptions, such as the teahouse courtship with Wilmer Kearns. Once the date of June 8, 1904, had been set, May took charge. By doing so, she made certain that the family home would be filled with roses, palms, and ferns. The occasion would be simple, carefully orchestrated, and something for family members and friends to always remember.

May decided that the Begley side of the family, as well as Edna's Buckman cousins and Wilmer's family members would be present. The guests would include many friends, as well as a representative sampling of Quakers from Plymouth Meeting and the Green Street Meeting in Germantown. The bride planned to wear a satin and silk gown rather than Quaker gray linen. This caused May a twinge of anxiety when justifying the extravagance, but it was Edna's decision. The ceremony would be a Quaker wedding, or what was said to be "in the manner of Friends." This meant no minister, the bride and groom exchanging vows with each other "in the presence of God," and an overall atmosphere of simplicity.

Wilmer's employment remained an issue. In the minds of some members of the Religious Society of Friends, cigars were in the same category as saloons and red light districts. For others, cigar manufacture represented an expanding workforce of immigrants—many of them women—earning low salaries in nonunion jobs. May arranged for "weighty Quakers" to serve on the wedding oversight committee to counteract any more opposition to the engagement and marriage.

Hopefully Wilmer's position at T. J. Dunn would, over time, be minimized by critics and gossips. It was, after all, Wilmer's first paid position. Someone like Mary "May" Buckman, had to be realistic after so many rumors made the rounds in the Quaker community about Edna's earlier opposition to marriage. Edna had reversed her position about marriage for love based on expectant waiting in friendship.

Wilmer and Edna planned to leave Echo Dale by automobile and travel by train to the 1904 World's Fair in St. Louis for their honeymoon. On the way back to New York City, they'd visit Beavertown, followed by a brief stay with May and Charles at Echo Dale. They'd make do with a room at the Penington until they could rent an apartment within walking distance of the Quaker Meeting House at 15 Rutherford Place.

I glanced out my bedroom window and there she was—Edna as a silhouette against a starry sky. Bess wasn't with her. They kept in contact but continued arguing about the strategies linked to winning the voting rights of all American women. The backbone of their friendship was relegated to secrets that went to the grave with Bess and my grandparents, the type of private and shared thoughts that may have seemed significant in the moment but, like partisan politics, faded into the background of our family history.

My practice as a young person continued by asking questions. Why did Edna describe herself in her diary as a "naughty, jealous girl" on New Year's Day in 1904? Why did she reprimand my grandfather Wilmer in a tone she described as "cross"? What was the ailment troubling Edna's mother? I never found answers.

"Why" for me was like an aching tooth requiring a dentist's attention. More than a fundamental question, finding satisfying answers involved probing for the underlying spirit of my grandparents and our extended family. The missing teeth of truth explained my continuing restlessness. My upper arms itched until the scratch marks on my skin alerted my mother that the perpetual grin on my face could be better understood as a cover-up for frustration. I arrived at the gradual realization that the majority of the world didn't welcome the participation of most females, except under certain conditions.

From what Granddaddy told me, the suffrage petitions of women activists were ignored for decades. The idea of equality caused many men, and occasionally their women partners, to scoff at the idea of social standards shifting with the changing times. When I studied Edna's diary as an adult, some entries suggested the possibility that my grandmother may have been undecided about all of the possible responses to injustice. Without making the point overt, Edna's diary entries also confirmed a positive subtheme. Buckman family members accepted Wilmer as part of the family.

As a curious young person, I persisted in listening to Granddaddy's stories for a simple reason. I wanted to find out what happened next. Starting on January 1, 1904, most spaces in Edna's diary were filled through June 8th, her wedding day. This left enough room on blank pages for the honeymoon and the first six months of married life in Manhattan. Edna planned to tuck the diary into a leather traveling case destined for cushioning inside her luggage for the honeymoon. As the diary record confirms, Edna persisted in calling my grandfather Billy.

Friday, January 1, 1904

Dear Diary: *Happy New Year* to thee and all. I *am* happy. I begin this year engaged to the one man in all the world. What my future will be, we must leave to thee. Today I am very, very happy. We are all going over to John Conrad's. Mamma not so well, staying at Aunt Ada Yerkes.

Saturday, January 2

Went to Conrad's yesterday, Dear Diary. I am a naughty, jealous girl. I was cross to Billy—feel so sorry now. Grandmother Buckman came up for a visit. Billy and I are very happy today. My dear diary, I *am* a "lucky" girl.

Sunday, January 3

Had our New Year's today, Billy, Grandmother, Brother and I. Billy and I had such a happy day together. My dear, dear boy how I love thee.

Monday, January 4

Same old routine, went to Norristown to buy Lulu Kearns a dress, slippers, shoes, etc. for flower girl for Billy's cousin, Jim's wedding.

Tuesday, January 5

Norristown again for marketing, also to order Lulu's dress and send it. Brother left for George School today. Still busy. Coldest day ever known.

Wednesday, January 6

Very busy. Swept house and very tired. Lots of letters to write and M's [Mamma's] and P's [Papa's] affairs to attend to. Temperature 10 below zero.

Thursday, January 7

Jim's wedding day. Married Miss Blanche Rine of Beavertown. More snow. Now 2 ½ feet deep. Good sleighing.

Friday, January 8

Very busy—same old routine. Norristown again. Bought ice-cream spoons for Hattie Walker. Very difficult traveling. Caught cold. Warmer although more snow.

Saturday, January 9

Warmer & clearer. Grandmother went to town. Billy went to Logan to see Mamma, she is not any better. Wilmer missed his way, went to Olney, then walked in snow to Frankford car. Arrived here about 9 o'clock.

Sunday, January 10

Clear & nice, good sleighing. Wilmer and I went to Norristown meeting and First Day School—fine time. Then took trolley to Collegeville. A very happy day to me, my darling is playing [the violin] near me now and I feel thankful for him.[1]

Chapter 20

First Chance to Be Alone

*E*dna's trip to Manhattan to visit Wilmer came the closest to them spending a weekend alone during the spring before their June 1904 wedding. Granddaddy told me she rented a room at the Penington for three overnights. When navigating the city's street traffic, Edna held tight to Granddaddy's elbow. As they strolled, they came upon a street poster advertising a speech by social commentator Elbert Hubbard. Since Wilmer liked Hubbard's social and political writings, they stood in line to enter the lecture hall.

Edna didn't mention to Wilmer that the trip to Manhattan was her way of preparing for married life by becoming familiar with the people, sights, sounds, and events of the city. I didn't ask Granddaddy to tell me if he and Edna bundled during her visit. His ears turned red in his kitchen as he scoured the sink to avoid my penetrating gaze. I was mature enough not to press the point.

As he directed the storytelling in the direction of Elbert Hubbard, my grandfather mentioned that Edna complained of a sharp jab in the pit of her stomach. Her feet felt chilled. They weren't sure of the source of her discomfort. Wilmer said he told Edna about how the popular philosopher, Elbert Hubbard, practiced equality in romantic relationships and believed that conventional marriages resulted in the death of passion. He believed equality between partners left room for mystery and discovery.

Audiences across the nation found Hubbard's ideas provocative and memorable. As a speaker, he dressed and spoke well. His distinctive hat and bombastic style delighted and aggravated audiences. Lecture tickets sold out in communities as far apart as San Francisco and Boston whenever Hubbard arrived to speak.

Crowds roared at Elbert Hubbard's wit. When Wilmer heard him speak on prior occasions, he clapped and whistled at Hubbard's conclusion that exploitation, corruption, prejudice, and backroom deals should end immediately. Hubbard evoked a predictable response from a New York audience when describing simple pursuits such as returning to live on the land, communing with nature, and embracing the production of handmade objects for their beauty and spiritual significance. Women and men alike found Hubbard's speeches and writings irresistible, especially when he advocated social, economic, and political measures to control monopolies and what he identified as ruthless business interests.

Elbert Hubbard. Library of Congress, 1905.

At the lecture, Elbert Hubbard lifted his hands and arms high in the air when referring to the Upstate New York intentional community, Roycroft, that he founded near Buffalo in 1895. He shared his vision of creating a core of satisfied and productive craftspeople living and working there.

"They aren't caught up on factory assembly lines," Hubbard told the audience.

His confidence and dynamism fascinated audiences, especially when Hubbard referred to the ecstasy and contentment one could derive from engaging in handcrafted bookmaking, woodworking, and other utilitarian arts. An art colony similar to Roycroft named Byrdcliffe was established in Woodstock, New York, by Ralph and Jane Whitehead in 1902.

"Would living at Roycroft agree with thee?" Wilmer asked Edna during the lecture's intermission.

"As long as it doesn't interfere with my women's rights work," she replied. Wilmer told Edna about how Alice Moore, Hubbard's sweetheart and later wife, was a feminist active in votes for women campaigning. Elbert and Alice were able to model a comfortable balance of power in a domestic relationship, according to Granddaddy. Elbert Hubbard said that industrialization in the post-Civil War years had removed the heart and soul from men and women's lives. Hubbard told his audiences that factory assembly lines were nothing but emotional torture.

Edna and Wilmer agreed with Hubbard's fundamental principles—commune with the land, be productive with your hands, enjoy the good life, be creative, relax, read poetry and fine literature, and experience life to the fullest.

Hubbard predicted that a diverse range of women, men, and their families would live in utopian communities like Roycroft in the future. Tens of thousands of Hubbard's fans attended his lectures across the nation. Many subscribed to Hubbard's publications and supported Roycroft commercial enterprises.

My grandfather pointed out that whereas US president Theodore Roosevelt championed progressive reforms through government regulations, Elbert Hubbard

Woman worker engaged in bookbinding at Roycroft shops in East Aurora, New York, 1900. Library of Congress.

believed these proposals didn't go far enough. He told audiences that it was preferable, in his opinion, to prepare for life rather than death. He supported a nutritious diet, meaningful work and relaxation, music and study, as well as the drinking of golden grain beer. Wilmer said he attempted to exchange a knowing look with Edna, but she acted as if completely engaged in listening to the speech rather than agreeing or disagreeing with it in an exchange of whispers.

After the lecture, Wilmer led Edna to a bench in Battery Park where his left arm stretched around her shoulders. They shared a brief tender kiss because it wasn't Granddaddy's intention to express affection in public. They spoke of Elbert Hubbard as the light from the late afternoon sun faded. My grandfather said he was on edge when their shy glances lingered. The brushing of her chin with his fingers opened up another opportunity for an embrace or a kiss. I held my breath.

Since the announcement of their engagement, I gathered that Edna's head had been filled with a rush of anticipating freedom's possibilities in New York City. Wilmer told me he was tempted to suggest to Edna that they travel to Roycroft in Upstate New York and elope. However, reason prevailed.

Edna moved her face into position for a kiss, and then she turned away. Wilmer blinked when confronted with Edna's shy nature. Over the next few minutes she turned her head and his lips landed on target. Granddaddy admitted to me that he thought more kissing was inappropriate. It may have been an awkward gesture for him in public, but "for heaven's sake, we were engaged to be married," Granddaddy told me. I blushed.

Wilmer told Edna: "We should be heading back to the Penington. I must be at my office desk tomorrow morning with my sleeves rolled up." The next day was Monday. Edna planned to leave on an early train to Philadelphia. As they hiked through Battery Park after the Hubbard lecture, Edna told Wilmer about the importance of wage-earning women joining labor unions and winning the right to vote.

"This will improve working conditions in offices, factories, and sweatshops," she said. In Edna's opinion, voting rights would radically undermine the prevailing belief in women's inferiority. Wilmer barely listened. If he did well representing the cigar firm, he'd be in a better position to search for another job, something Edna would hopefully find more appropriate.

They paused when passing by the Ellis Island processing center in the distance. Ellis Island, the second-most important landmark after the Statue of Liberty, evoked pride and admiration for some city residents and sharp criticism from others. New York's newspapers regularly noted the thousands admitted into the United States in a single day. One newspaper article, Granddaddy said, referred to arrivals from abroad as "pauper hordes," frightened individuals who stood in long lines on Ellis Island to enter the country as steamships in New York's harbor lined up with more loads of passengers destined to be dumped at Miss Liberty's feet.

"Edna and I trusted in our ability to work things out," Granddaddy added, and he filled me in about their intention to establish an equal and collaborative relationship

Ellis Island, 1902. Library of Congress.

in marriage. Few role models existed other than the conventional husband breadwinner and the wife-mother as home manager. I had no life experience in this experiment. So I responded as I had done before when contemplating the future. I hoped my grandparents knew what they were doing.

Quaker families were different, but they were also like other people, working overtime to integrate love and equality into their lives. Most Quakers affirmed their trust in nonviolence and an end to war. Others gave up attempting to adhere to the spiritual testimonies, while others dug into their inner resources to do the best they could. I couldn't keep myself from searching for an answer to my long-standing question. What happened to Edna's wedding dress? Granddaddy didn't mention Edna's wedding dress after the ceremony. And I didn't ask again.

Granddaddy taught me about the importance of lifting accomplishments from the past and moving them forward. His advice was like my mother's when she spoke about greeting each day with a robust and hearty breakfast. The accomplishments ahead might not be obvious at first. Edna and her generation took serious risks. For Granddaddy and me, storytelling was like flying where the landscape was in color. The past lurked in the background, always in black and white.

Looking Back

The Wedding

Wilmer Kearns and Edna Buckman, at Echo Dale, June 8, 1904.

Friends' Intelligencer, Seventh Month 2, 1904

Marriages

Kearns-Buckman.—At the summer home of the bride's parents, Echo Dale, near Norristown, Pa., on Fourth-day, Sixth month 8th, 1904. Edna, daughter of Charles Harper and Mary Begley Buckman, and Wilmer R. Kearns of New York City, under the care of the monthly meeting of Friends held at Green Street, Philadelphia.

Wedding Notice, the *Herald*, Long Island

Kearns-Buckman

Philadelphia, Pa., June 9, 1904.

The wedding of Edna Buckman, daughter of Mr. and Mrs. Charles Harper Buckman, and Wilmer R. Kearns, of New York, was solemnized by Friends' ceremony at the home of the bride's parents, Echo Dale, near Norristown.

The bride was attired in a white liberty satin gown over white silk and carried a shower bouquet of bridal roses surrounded by orange blossoms.

The matron of honor, Mrs. Henry Ridgeway Knight, of Germantown, wore a white silk and lace gown over pale green silk with green chiffon girdle and carried a shower bouquet of green fern and white ribbon.

The bridesmaids, who were Miss Florence Sutter and Miss Clara Fling, of Germantown; Miss Marie Kearns of Beavertown, sister of the groom; and Miss Katherine Buckman of Phila., cousin of the bride; were all attired in pink organdie and lace and wore white lace hats trimmed with pink tulle and roses and carried a shower bouquet of maidenhair fern with pink ribbon.

The best man, T. Smythe Buckman, brother of the bride, was attired in the conventional frock coat. A. Scott Galbraith, of Easton, Pa., Ralph Radcliffe, of Frederick, Md., Russell and Roland Yerkes, of Logan Station, were ushers.

The little flower girl, Helen Kenderine, of Newtown, Bucks Co., was attired in white lace and carried a basket of pink sweet peas. Master Horace Yerkes, also cousin of the bride, acted as page and was attired in white satin.

The religious part took place on the lawn which was decorated with immense palms and ferns, after which the bridal party held the reception in the long drawing room, which was also elaborately decorated with palms and roses.

After the reception the bride and groom departed in an automobile for Phila., from whence they intend to take an extended trip in the far west. After their return, they will reside in New York City.

From Edna's Red Wanamaker Diary

June 2, 1904

Rainy. Mr. and Mrs. Savin, Will and Sally Smith, Cynthia Nyce, Mr. & Mrs. and Miss Rubican accept. Regrets from Grandmother Sally Gilliam. Grandmother sent me $3 and D.A.K. Preston sent oyster fork. Received a pamphlet from Joseph Wharton. Adele Hult sent me her veil. Papa went away. Made collars, spent all morning in Norristown, packed my trunks.

June 3, 1904

Clear. Glaziers came. Worked hard. Letter from Billy. Ironed and tried on wedding dress. Brother came for supper. Ironed in evening. Retired 10 o'clock. Roses out. One dozen cut glass tumblers from Parks.

June 4, 1904

Clear. Worked hard all morning. Three presents from Buckmans, book from Mr. Roland. Presents from Buckman girls, Mrs. Jost, Charles Jenkins. Brother, Papa, Marie and Wilmer came. The men went to Norristown, brought home ice-cream. Retired 10 o'clock.

June 5, 1904

Clear, lovely. Marie and Mamma went to Plymouth Meeting. Help came for kitchen. Yerkes boys and Katie B. stayed to dinner. Whole bridal party here, stayed to tea. Wilmer, Brother, Mamma, Papa, Marie and I saw them off, then walked to Plymouth Park.

June 6, 1904

Clear. Sick all day. Presents coming all day. Some regrets. Ann Tener accepted. Wilmer, Papa and Brother went to Norristown, brought gifts. Wilmer and Marie went to Philadelphia. Papa and Brother busy on the lawn. Wrote 20 letters of thanks this evening.

June 7, 1904

Busy all day. Tired to death at night. Lots of gifts. Marie, Mamma and I took bath. Wilmer's people in Norristown. Wilmer home at 11 o'clock. Returned 12:30.

June 8, 1904

Our Wedding Day. Everything beautifully done. No one nervous. Wilmer and I got away in an automobile to Chestnut Hill, thence to Philadelphia, thence to St. Louis. Had berth in sleeping car.

Part III

Chapter 21

Charles, Angela, and the Wedding Scandal

"*O*ur wedding was exquisite, although at moments, uncomfortable," was all Granddaddy would say about the wedding ceremony and reception at Echo Dale in June of 1904.

"Tell me more," I begged, but my grandfather made excuses. He was busy in the garden. He didn't have time to "stop everything" and respond to my requests.

"Why doesn't anybody tell me what happened?" I asked my mother Wilma. I persisted until she lowered her voice to answer me.

"Your great-grandfather Charles drank and fooled around when away on his business trips," she said.

"But the wedding?"

"Edna invited someone she wished she hadn't."

"Did something bad happen?"

"The woman caused a scene with Charles."

"What kind of scene?"

"I'll tell you when you're older."

If I didn't handle this matter properly, my mother and grandfather might clam up even more. I assumed the "other woman," who attracted attention at the wedding, must have been someone well known to Edna and the Buckman family. Because a scandal had to be a secret, trust any grandchild to investigate the family dirt. Granddaddy didn't want me to obsess over the wedding, so he warned me to step lightly when visiting the past.

"Thee could lose thy way as easily as getting lost walking home from school."

I thought about this. Once I'd walked home from school instead of taking the bus. My mother made it clear that such independence was forbidden. I was a bad girl, she said. Was Charles Harper Buckman a bad boy? And my grandfather? What if Granddaddy promised Edna equality in their relationship, but he wasn't ready to carry out his promises? What about the wedding scandal? Should I be concerned about my grandfather passing on a story that was best kept hidden? If I could only balance all the questions needing answering, I might be less troubled.

I wondered in the privacy of my bedroom at home if the entire Buckman family was linked to the mystery woman. It didn't matter if my free associations had a relationship to what actually took place on my grandparents' wedding day. My mother and grandfather confirmed the existence of a scandal. They were determined to cover up the details, while I was on high alert to figure out what really happened.

I longed to accompany my great-grandfather Charles into the void, but the wicker chair in the ordinary reality of Granddaddy's kitchen kept a tight hold on me. I was disoriented. My forehead throbbed. My instinct was to leave Granddaddy's house and follow Charles into the past. The inside of my eyelids went blank, as if someone had flipped a switch. I hadn't finished my homework, and my teacher wouldn't be able to check off that I'd turned in three pages of long division exercises. I stumbled out the kitchen door, chasing my great-grandfather Charles down the street, yelling—"Wait for me."

Charles couldn't hear anything. In my imagined next scene, I continued running in his direction. The sky lit up with lightning, and I tripped and tumbled onto the hard ground. When I returned to awareness, I was in a Philadelphia train terminal waiting area. Were these real train passengers? Had I lost touch with reality? Five minutes passed. Charles Buckman stood in front of a cashier's window covered with bars, buying a ticket. My great-grandfather wiped perspiration from his brow.

There was only fifteen minutes before he'd be on the train to Harrisburg, staring out the window, drowning in guilt for not having completed his Boll Brothers & Company vouchers. He hadn't spent an hour over the weekend preparing paperwork for his boss. Charles stared in the direction of a young woman in the train terminal. She stood too far away to get a whiff of the signature oil of lavender spread over her wrists and neck.

Charles was well acquainted with this young woman from social events with their friends, the Wharton family in Philadelphia. For years the young woman in the station had been like a baby sister to the Wharton daughters and cousins. With her mother bedridden, the young woman boarded with friends when she wasn't in Center City Philadelphia spending overnights with her aunt and uncle. But why should I think this imagined scene was any more authentic than the stories Granddaddy told me?

I was driven to dig into the mysteries of Wilmer and Edna's wedding. Both my mother and grandfather confirmed that something serious had taken place. It had been an event of such magnitude that awareness of the incident had been passed down to me, even if the details weren't. The rest was left up to me. I had to figure out more about the woman at the train terminal. Until informed otherwise, I called her Angela. I pictured her lips resembling a rose, and I couldn't help but notice a single pearl she wore on a gold chain. My version of what happened next represented one of an infinite number of possibilities.

The pearl necklace lured men's eyes down to the black lace covering the bodice of Angela's dress. Her soft purring voice tempted men of all ages, including older men like Charles Buckman, to move closer to her during afternoon teas. He invented questions to ask, even if he didn't care about her answers. Angela's solo wait at the train terminal set her apart from her uncle's usual hovering. It made sense that Charles would be anxious to rescue Angela at the train station and receive a hero's reception from her aunt and uncle.

Charles H. Buckman's business card, circa 1900.

Charles had little in hand but a round-trip train ticket to Harrisburg and a stack of business cards in his vest pocket identifying him as a company representative. Granddaddy told me that Boll Brothers advertising told potential customers that if they didn't already know about Boll's brass beds, one half of their life had been wasted. Some people, including Edna's mother May, liked brass beds with a simple design. Masculine tastes tended toward heavier, more solid enameled beds. Angela was the type to order an ornate enameled iron bed to accompany the firm's famous "snowflake curl cotton mattress."

What if Charles handed Angela his business card during a mad dash to the train? He had nothing else to give her. The card could be interpreted as a hurried act. Or it might hint of his hidden agenda. Charles had seen Angela last at an afternoon tea at the home of one of the Wharton relatives. "Of course, that's a clue," I reassured myself, although I had no evidence, only instinct to guide me.

In the course of planning for the June 1904 wedding, Edna recorded in her diary her request of Quaker businessman and industrialist Joseph Wharton to serve as a spiritual overseer for her wedding ceremony. Even though Wharton considered himself a busy individual with numerous business obligations and projects, he agreed. Edna's diary documented her informal conversations with him as a member of her wedding support committee.[1]

Although Buckman and Wharton family members couldn't identify a shared limb on a family tree, a long-term familial relationship was implied by the Buckman and Wharton social interactions. Deborah Fisher Wharton was a suffrage activist and mother of Joseph Wharton, who founded the business program known as the Wharton School at the University of Pennsylvania. Deborah Wharton could trace her Fisher family history back to the *Welcome* when her ancestors arrived in Pennsylvania with William Penn, the Buckman family, and other Quakers. Joseph Wharton represented the larger Wharton family group.

When writing about my ancestors someday, it would make sense, Granddaddy said, to rely on an outline. This list of topics and a timeline seemed like an ambitious project for someone like me. Granddaddy reminded me that I'd be on my own someday, responsible for securing the corners of tales entered into a documentary record of my family before my birth. The tale of the wedding scandal fit into this category. I didn't tell my mother or grandfather that I had my own version.

Granddaddy's phone rang. My mother wanted to know if I was ready to go home.

"In a few minutes," I said. She didn't need to know about the trouble brewing at the train terminal in Philadelphia.

The day Charles Harper Buckman ran into Angela, more hot and humid weather had moved in over Philadelphia. In his annual ritual, Charles shaved his mustache for the summer. After working in the garden, the sun transformed his face into a glow of brown accentuating his high cheekbones and prominent nose. When baked by the sun, Charles Buckman—an eighth-generation Pennsylvanian—could pass as a member of the Lenni Lenape tribe, from whom William Penn had purchased land for his Holy Experiment. Penn spoke the native Algonquin language fluently.

Charles Buckman's mother, Catherine Dedacker, wasn't a Quaker. And his father, Amos Buckman, didn't take his children regularly to Quaker worship. So Charles wasn't raised to consider himself an active Quaker, even though he married May Begley Buckman, a serious practitioner. Charles joined the Quakers as a member in 1895 when May transferred her own membership from Center City, Philadelphia, to Germantown. Perhaps because of his background. Charles generally made his own personal decisions, whether or not Quakers at the Green Street Meeting in Germantown or Plymouth Meeting approved. This included the habit of not wearing clothing in his own back yard.

Charles Buckman's full-body tanning occurred before he fully understood the history and aftermath of William Penn's 1701 treaty with native peoples to ensure peace and harmonious relations. It developed into an awareness of the sorry history following Penn's return to England, when he no longer personally supervised the affairs of Philadelphia and Pennsylvania. Penn handed over colonial decision making to several individuals he trusted. However, as the first governor discovered, the substitutes for Penn weren't in harmony with the founder's vision for a utopian community and a Holy Experiment.[2]

"William Penn meant well," Charles reassured his wife. The disappearance of all but remnants of native peoples in the Philadelphia area upset him. Granddaddy said that Charles slowly developed spiritual leadings to support the continent's original inhabitants. Lucretia Mott was among those Quakers with a spiritual commitment to work with the Seneca peoples, another branch of the Algonquins, over land rights. She was inspired by the native matriarchal social structure, a model for early colonial women and later women's rights activists who witnessed many native peoples practicing an advanced and equitable social structure.

"Imagine Penn naming a colony after himself," Charles told his wife May when discussing his agony over whether William Penn should have remained back in England. He could have responded to religious persecution there, Charles said, instead of collecting a debt from the royal court due his father, a well-known English admiral. William Penn insisted on turning a charter from the king into a refuge and homeland for those seeking asylum. He didn't expect to make money or become famous. In practice, the project forced him into serious personal debt.

Charles Buckman framed the issue by suggesting that if William Penn hadn't settled the land, someone else would have. Although this justification didn't ease his conscience, a plan to settle the land had been made long before Penn's decision. So Charles accepted the existence of Philadelphia and the larger territory of Pennsylvania. Quakers did well there. So did many others who fled Europe and elsewhere in the hope of freedom, a state of being they defined for themselves.

"Thee is as concerned about the Lenni Lenape as I am distressed about whiskey and rum," May told Charles when they spoke about shared issues of social concern.

Charles Buckman considered himself a Quaker with potential, but he couldn't reconcile his summer bronze with any advantages Buckman family members might have had over the generations because of their links to William Penn and the early Quaker migration. When Charles read the journal of Quaker John Woolman, he wondered if he'd ever had erotic thoughts like his own. Some referred to Woolman as a Quaker saint, even though the Religious Society of Friends didn't recognize saints. In his journal, Woolman mentioned "backsliding," as well as other conflicts posing distractions from keeping one's mind focused on the inner divine light.[3]

John Woolman didn't reveal the details of his own flights of fancy or document them in his journals. Woolman's passing reference to backsliding may have reduced the guilt Charles felt when observing Angela at the train terminal. Abolitionist advocacy by Woolman and others convinced many Quakers to free any slaves in their possession, resulting in a Quaker pre-Civil War cleanup of those forced into servitude. Woolman left a potent spiritual trail behind, as did Benjamin Lay, another New Jersey Quaker outspoken about the evils of slavery. Quakers denounced slavery in the Germantown section of Philadelphia as far back as 1688. The practice was abolished among US Quakers during the 1700s.

Granddaddy told me that John Woolman urged Quakers and others to respect the rights of native peoples and resist paying taxes to support the government's military forces. Woolman despised social injustice and cruelty to animals. This Quaker spiritual activist refused to draft wills for friends and associates in which an individual in bondage might be passed on to heirs. He wouldn't use silverware or drink from cups for which anyone had toiled against their will in mines to provide jewels and precious metals for the wealthy. John Woolman stood up to be counted. He was considered personally powerful and spiritually persuasive.

From my chair in Granddaddy's kitchen, I spent several afternoons hearing about John Woolman and then fantasizing about the drama of Charles Harper Buckman longing to stand close enough to Angela to feel her breath brush against his face. I pictured how my great-grandfather Charles ran his eyes like fingers down the lines of Angela's neck, past her single pearl on a chain.

I suspected Charles Harper Buckman considered other possibilities too, such as lifting Angela's chin in his direction for a kiss. Usually she attracted too much attention for Charles to compete with her many admirers at the Wharton family's afternoon teas. Angela was younger than Edna. A romantic relationship between Angela and Charles would have been considered a serious violation of community standards. I sensed that Charles couldn't risk a rejection from Angela at the train station that might be passed on as gossip to Wharton family members.

Sketch of John Woolman believed to have been made by Robert Smith III of Burlington, New Jersey, 1700s.

If there was that of the divine in Charles Buckman and all life forms, as Quakers believed, I wondered if my great-grandfather questioned what could be morally incorrect about admiring the wrists and fingers of a woman sitting across from him on a train traveling to Harrisburg. If Charles Buckman dared to even hint about the extent of romantic experimentation he would have preferred in his life, his wife May would have disapproved and pressured him to change. And why? So far, his plotting and scheming hadn't resulted in any inappropriate behavior.

Charles had tucked a copy of John Woolman's journal into his luggage to remind himself of the struggle with contradictions and spiritual challenges. If Woolman wasn't alone in experiencing physical desires, at least he overcame them to become an outspoken abolitionist in the towns and villages of New Jersey, up and down the East Coast, and abroad. Charles Buckman wondered if it would be acceptable to invite Angela to tea. When staring at himself at home in a mirror, he studied the reflection of someone who gave the impression of being a part-time native man and a part-time white playboy. He relied on a playboy persona when on the road for Boll Brothers. Banquets and sales dinners to entertain clients in the market for bed frames and mattresses didn't conclude after a meal. The job of a traveling man for Boll Brothers required a social life where wives and family members played little or no part.

According to my mother, Charles witnessed his son and daughter mature into adulthood from an emotional distance that seemed out of place to him. He found excuses not to attend Quaker worship on First Days, although he showed up occasionally. Especially upsetting was Charles's discomfort when he noticed no others with high cheekbones and tinted skin participating in his social circle. Native peoples had been driven west or killed in a series of massacres during an uprising of Ulster Presbyterians in Pennsylvania in 1763. Those settlers considered themselves justified in driving native peoples from fertile land.

Charles Buckman remembered what many others had forgotten, including the corrupt 1737 Walking Purchase overseen by William Penn's two sons, who turned their backs on their father's spiritual practice and withdrew from Quaker social and worship circles. Charles regretted the fall days each year when his skin paled and he faced long winter months with a mustache with curled ends for his role as playboy on the business trail with Boll Brothers.

Back at the Philadelphia train terminal, Charles Buckman obsessed over observing Angela from the distance of the ticket sales window. He felt like a hunter stalking prey—someone who moved in slow motion behind the high brush of the train station's benches, within view of flower and newspaper sellers. When other train travelers moved past him, Charles blended into the landscape. That's when Angela turned in his direction. He stared and wondered if she had ever made love, not that she would have told anyone.

My mother said that Charles remembered his wife May at her most innocent from an afternoon when she wore a respectable ivory dress sewn under her mother's supervision. May carried a cloth bag of ripe pears as they strolled along the Schuylkill

River's paths, pausing at small park enclaves with benches and statues lined with plaques and fountains. These monuments had been dedicated to the "dead" and the "fallen," the missing in action, as well as those anxious for recognition among the land of the living.

With the river in the background, Charles told May about the Germantown section of Philadelphia where he'd inspected a house on Rubicam Avenue they might consider purchasing. May noticed a culvert on a distant path, sloping down a bank where they sat and bit into the pears until syrup ran down their faces and stained May's dress.

Thoughts about women other than his wife May must have haunted Charles in the decades following their wedding and the birth of three children, including one named Harper, after him—who died as an infant before 1900. To complicate matters, Charles had noticed Angela's name on daughter Edna's list of wedding guests. The possibility that Angela might attend Edna's wedding both thrilled and terrified him. Charles felt guilty, even though nothing had happened, yet. He hadn't even exchanged a greeting with Angela. How long had Charles been staring at her in the terminal? Five minutes? Maybe ten?

The train to Harrisburg would leave shortly. Charles was overcome with urges he worried he might not be able to control, including blurting out to Angela everything he'd ever imagined about her. He dreaded exposing himself as an older man over the age of forty-five, with his mind on outcomes he had no business contemplating. He couldn't control an impulse to stand next to Angela, dive into the deep pools of her eyes and soothe her, even at the risk of missing his train.

I stood on my toes to see over and around train passengers from my position at the terminal, not far from where my great-grandfather remained standing, deep in his thoughts. Angela stood not far away, my first full view of her long hair drooping as she held tight to her luggage, distressed and nervous.

Charles wasn't greedy. I suspected he simply wanted to be with Angela for as little as a few minutes. He may have been convinced that remnants of her lavender oil would stay with him all the way to Harrisburg as he stared out the train window at open fields, thick forests, rivers, and streams enhanced by the fragrance of her words. Charles felt his legs propelling him forward in Angela's direction. He sensed a strong breeze rushing by. He came close to crashing into a woman carrying an infant. Charles stood next to Angela and dropped his suitcase on the terminal floor as he blurted: "What a surprise! Is thee all right?"

"Fine," Angela replied.

"Is thee coming or going?"

"I just arrived on the train from New York."

"And no one is here to greet thee?"

"Uncle promised, but he's not here."

"Thee must be tired. How about joining me for tea?"

My great-grandfather Charles couldn't have anticipated this. He could barely absorb the impact of Angela's affirmative answer as they strolled through the train terminal toward the street exit. She dragged a heavy satchel. He leaned over to add it to his burden as the hands of the clock high on the station wall passed over the moment for the train's departure to Harrisburg. Sitting at the kitchen table at my grandfather's, I imagined the delicate pearl Angela wore around her neck on a gold chain. I was convinced Charles thought about Angela and this pearl for the rest of his life.

Chapter 22

Honeymoon in St. Louis

oarding the train in Philadelphia headed to St. Louis, Missouri was a low point of June 8, 1904. Edna wobbled in train corridors, holding on to train railings while shifting from side to side on her way to the dining car with Wilmer. Edna rested her head on his shoulder. She choked from the dusty air and kept her eyes closed after staring at the streaking landscape outside the train window. Granddaddy told me that he smiled often during the journey.

The newly married couple gazed into each other's eyes, delighted to have finally ended up in one another's arms. Wilmer told me he made it his intention to love and respect women, especially his wife. To this he added a vision of being of service to humanity. Wilmer might not have had a high-profile job in New York City, but Edna considered him a catch. She had told her mother that Wilmer could be described as being more interested in his wife becoming all she could be, instead of encouraging her dependence on him.

"I've found my future with thee, Billy," she told Granddaddy.

When the couple shared a train dining car table with other travelers, questions surfaced such as, "Where are you from?" and, "Where is your hotel in St. Louis?" and, "How long do you plan to visit the World's Fair?" Wilmer spoke easily with strangers about the couple's reservations at the Hotel Epworth. Socializing with other passengers left few hours for Edna to reflect on the wedding ceremony and the gifts, as well as visiting with guests from Philadelphia and around the state. This included Kearns family members who'd arrived the day before the wedding. The ceremony had gone well, except for the troubling presence of Angela provoking gossip about her relationship with Charles.

"Is thee happy?" Edna asked Wilmer. She didn't mention Angela or her father Charles, although the situation must have continued to bother her. Wilmer's expression communicated his answer. He reflected the image of a happily married man. He wondered during these moments if Edna expected him to be a "pure" Hicksite Quaker, or a variation of the adaptations he'd observed in New York and Philadelphia. Few consciously watered down Quaker faith and practice, but Wilmer believed a pattern progressed through small decisions and then large actions that over years eroded the testimonies of integrity, peace, simplicity, and equality.

"Thee is a determined Quaker man," Edna reminded Wilmer.

Granddaddy told me he interpreted this as a compliment. Although the process of him becoming a Quaker hadn't been completed, the term "converted" didn't apply. Quakers were "convinced," not "converted." It was perhaps a semantic distinction, but one that Wilmer understood. According to Granddaddy, it wasn't a matter of adopting a spiritual ideology, a creed, or a set of principles and rituals. He had to be certain of his ability to personally connect to the divine, or the universal life force, as well as basic guidelines relative to the traditions of faith and practice. This Quaker content was new to him.

The American Revolution and other violent conflicts included examples of some Quaker men drifting away from a commitment to the peace testimony by marching off to war. Many of these "Fighting Quakers," more often than not, had been disowned or counseled by their worship communities. For some, the spiritual and moral instruction they received as children and youth evaporated when faced with the pressure of patriotism as defined in the context of war. Bess and Edna believed in a different type of patriotism, a version preferred by an earlier generation of social activists. They believed patriotism was a natural expression of and an extension of protest. It involved people on different ends of the social and political spectrum finding common ground. For them, patriotism required a serious examination of what needed changing, as well as a firm commitment to follow through in addressing root causes.

Pension records, military files, and oral history affirmed a familiar story about conventional patriotism. After family members greeted their loved ones returning from battlefields, they said, "He came home a different person," or "wasn't himself." Words and phrases like the "agonies of hell" and "wretched" didn't come close to describing the nightmares and memories survivors carried home with them to their families and communities after they returned from battlefields.

Edna Buckman Kearns, the newly married woman, was sure of one thing as the train continued its journey west. Her husband was a "good man." Granddaddy's eyes lit up when he told me this. If anyone were to describe the second Kearns boy, also known as Wilmer or Will or Billy or Blinker, family members would have characterized him as adventuresome. His curiosity spread to a variety of people and places. Edna found this appealing in Wilmer and wasn't surprised when he engaged train travelers in conversations in the dining car, the observation deck, and train passageways during their journey to the 1904 World's Fair. Wilmer welcomed social interactions in the aisles of the passenger coach. It didn't matter what others talked about. Wilmer expressed interest.

Edna entertained herself with memory reruns of the June wedding during the trip west. She recalled that John P. Kearns, Wilmer's father, dressed in a dark suit. Henrietta R. Kearns towered over him in height and exceeded him in weight. This provoked the elder Mr. Kearns to repeat a phrase frequently mentioned in Pennsylvania Dutch country: "A plump wife and a big barn never did any man harm." Kearns family members had been briefed about Quakers in advance, Granddaddy said, especially that

Quaker weddings didn't require a minister. The bride and groom exchanged vows with each other "in the presence of God," their friends, and family members.

My grandmother Edna opened her handbag to review letters from family and friends delivered the day of the wedding. Joseph Wharton sent a custom-made version of a nickel coin with his face as the likeness, made from a mineral he'd mined, made a fortune with, and delivered to Edna accompanied with a personal note.[1] Quaker historian, professor, and theologian Rufus M. Jones, a distant cousin, sent an apology that he couldn't attend the ceremony. George, the Quaker Meeting overseer with reservations about Wilmer's employment in a cigar firm, sent a letter. He assured Edna that his opinion about Wilmer's employment shouldn't be considered a judgment of him personally. George and his wife sent a wedding gift of a large dark blue plate. A gift from Bess of a silver pitcher included a card expressing her wish to see Edna when she visited Echo Dale in the future.

Edna was aware of her new position as a married woman throughout the train journey. Her rest was unsettled, disturbed by the train's whistle, and later the sounds of those in nearby compartments stumbling out of bed for breakfast in the dining car. Wilmer and Edna held each other, kissed, and postponed other intimacy until they unpacked at the St. Louis hotel. They had enough to do adjusting to confinement in a compartment as the train rolled over tracks and spanned hundreds of miles in between stations.

Edna sat upright as a conductor moved through the passenger cars and announced in a loud voice, "St. Louis, Missouri—next stop." She prepared to leave the train.

The 1904 World's Fair in Missouri had been advertised as an example of how the twentieth century would become a turning point in human history. Granddaddy told me he couldn't wait to discover what the fair organizers had in mind, especially what many called a "Ferris wheel," a large rotating wheel with passenger buckets. Edna favorably recalled previous fairs in which women were involved in planning and in exhibitions, even though the main organization didn't take a formal position on social issues.

Edna and Wilmer held hands on the train whenever possible. How did I know this? By my usual method of weaving together impressions, asking my grandfather questions, and integrating family oral history into the overall drama. I noticed how Granddaddy's memories weren't as fresh and fluid as they once were. Occasionally his words sounded distant, brittle, and grainy. I noticed how vintage photos of Edna in his bedroom had faded with the passage of decades.

I stared at the image of Edna in her Quaker bonnet displayed on my grandfather's bedroom side table as I made my way to and from the bathroom. When I did this, Edna stirred into being. Her eyes followed me. I heard her reminding Granddaddy to carry his cape and not pack it in the luggage. No, I wouldn't skimp on the details of their honeymoon involving the train trip from Philadelphia to St. Louis. I memorized this entire story. And as soon as I wrote it down so I could remember, I'd be ready

(17) Biggest wheel on earth (240 ft. diam.) with heaviest axle ever forged (56 tons), World's Fair, St. Louis, U.S.A. Copyright 1904 by Underwood & Underwood.

Ferris wheel, 1904 World's Fair. Library of Congress.

to tell it again. As I lay in bed at home, I heard Edna's whispering voice in my head. Or was it Granddaddy? I wasn't sure.

"Thee is paying attention. Not everyone likes so many facts, but persist in listening. Thee will be glad someday." This advice must have originated with my grandfather. He was determined that I receive an inspired torch from his generation.

Chapter 23

"I Am a Writer"

*E*dna Buckman Kearns waited for the Hotel Epworth office to open the next day to find out if a telegram had arrived from her mother. She had sent a message to May at Echo Dale when the train stopped at a station along the way. Disappointed after hearing that no telegram waited, Edna sank into a large hotel lobby chair to read the next chapter of *Herland*. She'd tucked the novel by suffrage activist Charlotte Perkins Gilman into her traveling bag about two men travelers discovering a remote utopian country ruled and inhabited only by women. Edna loved the story. She laughed at the novel's humor.

The book distracted Edna, Granddaddy told me, from something they hadn't expected—the World's Fair as representing not only "progress" but the ever-present and rapid pace of change. Attenders at the fair gasped at the displays of electricity, the music of Scott Joplin celebrating the miracle of water, and exhibits of native peoples from around the world.

"It was as if we walked in a cloud. The World's Fair pushed us up against something we'd been avoiding."

"What do you mean?" I asked Granddaddy from his kitchen typing table where I sat in front of his unfinished manuscript typing.

"Both Edna and I felt minuscule compared to the hundreds of exhibits and people rushing their way into the future."

"I am a writer, just like Charlotte Perkins Gilman," Granddaddy said Edna repeated to herself, firmly and simply, without apology, even though she felt awkward about having no personal publishing record other than her daily diary notations. Someone like Edna who'd received excellent grades in English at Friends' Central School pinched herself when repeating the statement: "I am a writer."

Writing could be a defense, a way to protect my grandmother from the broader landscape of steam engines, telegrams, and electricity illuminating every World's Fair building and booth. Bands and their music added to the overstimulation, which is how my grandfather said he experienced the fair.

It was one thing to hear about progress and yet another to witness its rhetoric and symbolism plastered over the more than one thousand acres of the 1904 World's Fair, said to be the largest event of its type in history. According to my grandfather,

Edna found enough emotional strength to relate to the World's Fair by thinking of the implications for women's rights. The next century would open doors for women. She was convinced of this, and told Wilmer so. Wilmer had replaced Bess as Edna's closest friend, although she and Bess would stay in touch.

Bess persisted in the stubborn pursuit of believing that someday she'd own and operate a women's teahouse, as well as writing and publishing novels like George Sand. Bess accepted a job at the Market Street teahouse as a cook with the intention of finding a financial partner committed to collaborating on a woman-owned business. The project stalled when she couldn't find bank funding because single women weren't considered reliable financial risks. The possibility of writing novels, like George Sand, even for Bess was still possible.

Edna understood that becoming a writer involved craft, talent, as well as a pen and paper. Some female writers blazed trails in the cultural wilderness far beyond what others accomplished. Authors like this included Louisa May Alcott, Jane Austin, Charlotte Brontë, George Eliot, Mary Wollstonecraft, Phillis Wheatley, Margaret Fuller, and many others. A handful wrote under men's names. Others published poetry or expressed themselves through limited literary channels. They produced chapbooks when condescending publishers avoided them. Edna decided to strengthen her creative instincts by writing the phrase "I am a writer" on scraps of paper until the notion finally stuck.

"Is thee hungry?" Wilmer asked Edna in the Hotel Epworth lobby after meeting with the hotel manager about a bill overcharge.

Edna told Wilmer she wasn't interested in breakfast. She stowed *Herland* in a day bag, but didn't mention to Wilmer that she considered the novel an example of how literature could change hearts and minds when logic and reason weren't effective enough.

May hadn't been forthcoming about informing her daughter Edna about becoming a woman back in 1895 prior to her first menstrual period. Her track record was also less than adequate, according to my mother, when it came to telling Edna about what was expected of a bride on her honeymoon. Even though May shared with her daughter the general requirements of marriage, Edna didn't understand the frequency that intimacy involved. My mother said my grandmother was under the impression of the sex act being an expression reserved for conceiving children rather than a routine part of married life. Edna worried about becoming pregnant on her honeymoon. What a setback that would be, a concern interfering with her honeymoon expectations when she should be feeling light, carefree, open, and appreciative.

Edna suspected her mother's return telegram would confirm her instinct that a honeymoon wasn't a vacation as much as a crash course in marriage. Edna may have had a vision of her future as a writer. But she was convinced that no one would pay attention to her if the only venue where she'd been published had been on diary pages in her own cursive handwriting. Her diary postings appeared opposite line drawings of the John Wanamaker department store's advertising of fashionable gowns and slippers.

As they strolled the streets of the World's Fair, arm in arm, Wilmer listened carefully when Edna told him of her ambition of writing columns about women's rights. He questioned how her interest in reporting would complement her interest in other social issues. At the World's Fair, Edna and Wilmer were but two among millions enjoying what had been advertised as a preview of technological advances of the upcoming century—in particular, timesaving machines and the spread of electricity.

Most visitors viewed the 1904 World's Fair as a fairyland with its palaces, sunken gardens, and waterfalls. Edna had never seen anything like it. She longed to be in New York City to begin married life. Wilmer would respect and encourage her. It was in her best interest, Granddaddy told me, for Edna to consider herself a liberated woman who stood firm and confident on the ground. Edna couldn't come up with anything to counter her insecurity and mood swings other than to repeat to herself, "I am a writer."

1904 World's Fair, St. Louis. Library of Congress.

After the first night when the couple slept together at the Hotel Epworth, Edna felt stiff and sore the following day, according to my mother. Edna hoped the telegram from May with motherly advice would be reassuring. The telegram didn't arrive until late during the second day of their stay in St. Louis. The message was cryptic. Only Edna was aware of what she had written to elicit such an answer. Edna's concerns about the wedding night had been urgent, and May sent a reply: "Thee is a married woman now. Thee will get used to it. Love, Mamma."

Edna set the telegram aside. Earlier in the day they had met two strangers, Isabel and Stanley, in the hotel lobby. They planned to reinforce their meeting by knocking on the couple's hotel door.

"Come and see the Apache—Geronimo—with us," Wilmer and Edna called to them from the hallway.

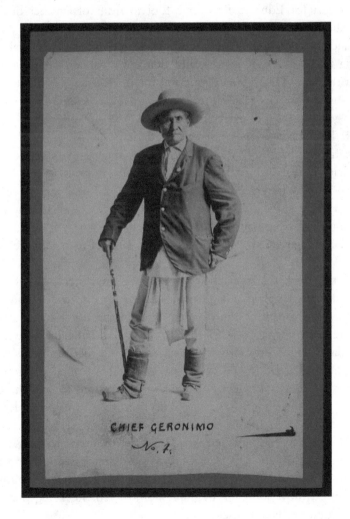

Geronimo, 1904 World's Fair. Library of Congress.

Geronimo, a captive from the federal government's Native American wars, was put on exhibit at the fair as an example of a warrior who had resisted colonization. While well-guarded, Geronimo sold portraits of himself and signed autographs for pennies within the confines of a display promoting the conquest of the American West's native peoples. Isabel wanted to leave immediately to see Geronimo. Stanley preferred a substantial breakfast of oatmeal, maple syrup, and milk in the hotel dining room first. The two couples visited the hotel dining room before leaving for the fairgrounds.

After leaving the fair, Wilmer and Edna would be on their way next to visit with the Kearns and Rhamstine families in Beavertown. In his pinstriped suit, Wilmer would seem like a stranger to his parents. He planned to tell them about the unusual exhibits at the fair such as Geronimo. He'd stress the real and imaginary, the offensive and strange, branded onto acres of buildings designed to last little more than a year. It took extra effort for Edna to force one foot in front of another during their stay in St. Louis. She held tight on to Wilmer's elbow the afternoon of the second day. Granddaddy said she rested on a bench while he visited exhibits with Isabel and Stanley.

Henrietta and John P. Kearns would demand as much detail as possible from Wilmer about the fair. He wouldn't disappoint them. He'd tell them about drinking Dr. Pepper sodas and eating ice cream cones—enough sugar, according to my grandfather, to keep him "going until we arrive in New York." Many years later he told me this, including how he'd made friends not only with Isabel and Stanley from Denver, but others on the fairgrounds. According to Wilmer, Stanley and Isabel acted like distant cousins who hadn't seen Wilmer since the last family funeral.

The two couples purchased tickets to ride on the moving wheel designed by George Ferris. Edna resisted riding but was finally convinced to give it a try. The idea terrified her, especially the way the wheel operators packed fair visitors into buckets until many on board clung to each other or the railings in a mixture of excitement and fear.

Edna's silence masked a stomach-curdling sensation of being swept up and around while Isabel and Stanley sighed and groaned. Wilmer bit his lower lip. Edna wasn't sure what was worse—the ascent or the descent. Later in the day, Edna described the ride as uplifting when writing a postcard to her parents and mailing it with a one-cent stamp. There wasn't enough room on the postcard to add that the Ferris wheel elevated her high enough, Granddaddy said, to view her possible future. She imagined herself in Manhattan as a writer specializing in women's campaigns to win the right to vote.

The Ferris wheel stripped Edna of connections to the material plane. The newly married woman soared high above the fair to a dimension where time and space were fluid. She left her body and couldn't hold on to memories or facts—little but the recurring question of how to transition into a married woman and a writer. She suspected that staring out at the Missouri countryside from the summit of the big wheel came close to how someone might respond when observing the totality of the planet from a cloud or heaven itself.

That's when Edna realized that her writing would have to feature an awareness of so-called progress that didn't move in a straight line. A telephone wasn't a burden, but a tool. An electrical lamp would allow her to work from midnight to dawn. She could avoid anything that might diminish or undermine her determination. And Wilmer Kearns, her friend, her lover, and her husband, supported her goals.

"Edgar Allan Poe wrote about this," Wilmer said, reminding Edna that occasionally Poe wrote about the human soul separating itself from its local and specific identities to be able to reflect on a larger journey through the cosmos. On the train from Philadelphia to St. Louis, Wilmer had read to Edna selections from "A Chapter of Suggestions," an 1845 essay where Poe had written: "These people awake from their musings with a start, and an air of bewilderment . . ."

The poet suggested that few humans had the ability to view their lives objectively and only later in life would they realize how they'd lived too fast and missed valuable life experience along the way. A honeymoon to the World's Fair might be later defined as a major historical event if Wilmer and Edna chose to see it this way, my mother told me. A few observations couldn't be challenged. Wilmer and Edna loved each other. They were meant to be together, a relationship grounded in friendship with the potential to expand in innumerable directions.

Some women's rights activists were discovering how to express themselves as writers. Edna needed to keep score and circulate as much information as possible about the voting rights movement. When writing, Granddaddy said Edna felt most alive. Quakers called women like Edna and those at the women's convention at Seneca Falls a complimentary term: "witnesses for change."

Stanley and Isabel shook hands with Edna and Wilmer and wished them a safe and pleasant journey ahead. In spite of their promises to stay in touch, my grandparents never saw or heard from them again. This can happen with chance meetings. Wilmer always remembered the couple from Denver, and Edna viewed the experience as a way to come to terms with the fact that detours and wrong turns would also be in their future.

My grandparents carried their luggage down to the Hotel Epworth's lobby to leave on the train to Beavertown. Edna gripped her stomach, still unsettled and close to a gurgling mass remembering that she'd have to get off the train in Snyder County with Wilmer and establish a kissing and hugging relationship with his parents and siblings. "Lovely people," he called them, especially Henrietta Kearns, who couldn't hide gray hair strands juggling for exposure and attention.

"We'll always be honest with each other, from now on," Wilmer reminded Edna.

"Definitely," she replied when realizing that her initial reaction to the World's Fair had been predictable. She noticed many details of the exhibitions and the reactions expressed by a sampling of the tourists traveling there from all over the nation and world. Many took advantage of special packages and discount rates offered by railroads and hotels. It occurred to me that the visit to the World's Fair for my grandparents also represented a new way of defining themselves together—lifelong partners engaged in a social and political struggle to expand civil rights.

"Someday I'll think of the World's Fair and a flash memory will surface. I'll look at thee over toast and eggs, and we'll grin, just the two of us. I'll set down the morning paper when I say how much I love thee," Wilmer said to Edna as they shared another meal in the dining car when heading by train to Beavertown, Pennsylvania. They'd visit with Kearns relatives there and then continue on to the Philadelphia area to be with May and Charles for an overnight. Then my grandparents would travel to New York City where a new phase of their life waited.

"We'll be together years from today, still sharing breakfast," Edna said.

"Count on it," he assured her.

I balanced on the chair in Granddaddy's kitchen. I couldn't visualize myself in a world where I wouldn't hear stories like this. When all else disappeared, including the houses where my grandparents lived, the flowers they grew, the clothing they wore—all of these stories would still find a way of circulating in the air, close enough for me to reach out and touch them.

Chapter 24

Civil War Orphan School

*H*enrietta Kearns was constantly in motion as she moved from rolling crust for cherry pie to stirring a simmering soup in preparation for the dinner planned for her son Wilmer and his bride Edna in the summer of 1904. Husband John Kearns was on his way to pick up the couple at Beavertown's nearby train station while Henrietta cooked.

Soup at the Kearns household consisted of a thin broth, hot or cold, made from fruit, meat, and vegetables, or prepared as thick as stew. Ginger seasoned a variety of dishes, including pot roast, gingerbread, ginger cake, and ginger snaps. This represented the Pennsylvania Dutch style of cooking. Lou, also known as Lulu, the youngest Kearns child, set out apple butter, cold cider, and the ingredients for coleslaw. Helping her mother, she chopped cabbage, steamed it until tender, and prepared a dressing of vinegar, butter, milk, sugar, flour, and mustard.

Granddaddy told me once that comfort food healed the wounds of the Civil War. If bowls of Pepper Pot soup were rumored to have been responsible for success in the American Revolution, many of Snyder County's residents insisted that homemade scrapple and dandelion salad made German farmers healthy. The thought of pickled beets, glazed doughnuts, and sticky buns had people's mouths watering in every community throughout Central Pennsylvania. Children fantasized over hard pretzels and mustard, or waffles and maple syrup. Egg noodle chicken soup had the power to cure whatever Pennsylvania Dutch folklore healing practices couldn't.

Henrietta attended her son Wilmer's June 1904 wedding with reservations, according to Granddaddy. Henrietta excused herself by blaming it on her physician, who advised against strenuous journeys due to her persistent headaches. Her worries also included feeling insecure about conversations with the bride's parents. Henrietta wanted to be liked and was concerned that May and Charles Buckman would be too cosmopolitan to relate to. When on a trip outside of Beavertown, she felt on edge. It was difficult, but Wilmer convinced his mother to attend the wedding, a day's journey from home.

It had been upsetting for Henrietta Kearns when Wilmer moved more than a hundred miles away to Philadelphia to study at a business college. Then he fell in love with a Quaker woman and accepted an office position in Manhattan. Henrietta had little interest in visiting either New York or Philadelphia after she'd heard about train wrecks there.

Country life, by comparison, was tight-knit and personal. Even though Wilmer had promised to take the initiative to visit his parents back home after the wedding, Henrietta and John P. Kearns would have to adjust. It wasn't unusual for younger generations to move to large cities for employment and rarely return to live in the rural landscape where they'd been raised. Henrietta still worried. She could think of only one solution—to make a recipe book as a wedding gift for her daughter-in-law Edna so Wilmer would have his favorite foods to remind him of his family even while he was so far away.

Some of Beavertown's residents were Lutherans like Henrietta Kearns. The communities of those broadly referred to as Pennsylvania Dutch included the Amish, Germans, Moravians, Brethren, Schwenkfelders, Dunkers, Anabaptists, and others. Concepts such as the separation of church and state, freedom of conscience, a love of independence, and disdain for tyranny were familiar to Wilmer Kearns from his childhood living in Pennsylvania Dutch country. Wherever Henrietta went, her German Bible wasn't far behind. She preserved her Specht and Rhamstine genealogies on empty front and back Bible pages so everyone on the family tree would be accounted for and remembered.

Henrietta was technically an orphan of the Civil War. Her mother, Jane Elizabeth Specht Rhamstine, simply had to provide proof to the Commonwealth of Pennsylvania

Henrietta Rhamstine Kearns, Beavertown, Pennsylvania, circa 1900.

that she was a war widow who couldn't financially support her children. Admission to a state boarding school involved petitioning the state to enroll Jane's children in a special system of institutions created after the Civil War to educate the fatherless children of "fallen comrades." Jane Rhamstine decided to send her three daughters to an orphan school.

Pennsylvania governor Andrew Gregg Curtin carved out a secure political future by designating himself as "the soldiers' friend." He made headlines and a reputation for the state by following through on its obligation to care for war widows and orphans. One story making the rounds featured Governor Curtin's awakening to the war veterans' plight. The impact of two soldiers' orphans begging for bread at the door of the state's Executive Mansion in Harrisburg on Thanksgiving morning in 1863 haunted him.

Governor Curtin succeeded in establishing a network of state-sponsored Civil War orphan schools. The Union Army reported about 340,000 Pennsylvanians in its fighting force. Of these, thirty-three thousand died in service, or they were killed on a battlefield. Thousands more suffered serious physical, emotional, and mental damage. After legislation passed in Pennsylvania to establish more than forty Civil War orphan schools, their doors opened for applications from war widows like Jane Rhamstine. The orphan schools were segregated so the offspring of African American soldiers were enrolled in separate boarding schools.

Henrietta Rhamstine (*top row, far right, marked with* X) while a student at McAlisterville Soldiers' Orphan School, circa 1868.

Not all Civil War widows sent their children to orphan boarding schools. Many living in Pennsylvania's ethnic communities suspected the state might expose their offspring to strange and possibly subversive ideas. School administrators promised to establish and maintain curriculum records, as well as respect the backgrounds of their charges.[1]

School employees documented the type of religious instruction provided, details about school uniforms, and the routines of orphan school life. Boys learned practical skills and marched in military drills. At the McAlisterville Soldiers' Orphan School, girls excelled in sewing. Both boys and girls from Pennsylvania's orphan schools did their part by traveling to the state capital in Harrisburg to sing for the legislators and appeal for additional funding. The McAlisterville students well known for their pleasant singing voices, reportedly moved many state legislators to tears. In the process, elected officials opened the state's coffers for more dollars to continue the institutional programming. Granddaddy said the words the young people sang to elected officials went something like this:

"The Orphan's Prayer"

O'er my father's grave,
O'er my father's grave,
Through that bending willow
O'er my father's grave . . .

McAlisterville Academy, in Juniata County, was turned into a boarding school for children whose fathers died serving in the Union Army from Pennsylvania, circa 1860s. From James Laughery Paul, *Pennsylvania's Soldiers' Orphan Schools* (1876).

McAlisterville school officials accepted the application of young Henrietta Rhamstine, as well as her two sisters, Mary and Melissa. Henrietta entered the orphan school program on December 18, 1865, a little over a year after her father John Rhamstine, a Union Army soldier, died at the siege of Petersburg in Virginia. Henrietta was discharged from the school five years later on March 14, 1870, at the age of fifteen. Young Henrietta's school records included her progress in learning penmanship; the technical skills she demonstrated on Finkle and Lyon, as well as Singer sewing machines; an outstanding rating in "promptness, obedience, and truthfulness"; the completion of a sixth grade education; and an expectation that Henrietta would return home to live with her mother in Beavertown, one of many Pennsylvania communities stripped of male residents during the Civil War.

The final report card written by McAlisterville's principal was handed down to Kearns descendants over the generations:

This certifies that Henrietta Rhamstine, a pupil in the McAlisterville Soldiers' Orphan School, is now discharged on age. While we regret her loss as a pupil, we feel pleased to know that she will be a credit to the institution wherever she may go. We take great pleasure in recommending her to the public as an honest, industrious, and energetic girl . . . Her good behavior in every department entitles her to the affectionate and long remembrance of all her instructors.

The orphan school remained in operation until 1899. After leaving the program at McAlisterville, Henrietta Rhamstine returned home and married carriage and wagon builder John Preston Kearns from Beavertown on April 24, 1873.

After birthing two girls and a boy, who died within three weeks of each other at ages four, two, and eight months, respectively, Henrietta buried them in the local cemetery after a diphtheria epidemic passed through Snyder County. Granddaddy was one of the next five Kearns children. He claimed that relief from Henrietta's underlying depression over the deaths of the first three Kearns children could be traced to the kitchen where his mother prepared dried beef gravy, apple crumble, and ham and bean soup.

At age eleven, Lou Kearns was familiar with her mother's stories about the years at McAlisterville. Henrietta indulged her daughter by saying that the state boarding school for Civil War orphans fulfilled its mission of sending back to the community young people with more than a reasonable chance of recovering from the loss of a parent.

Fluting her piecrust's edges and rolling out the remaining pastry into a circle meant continuing dinner preparations for Wilmer and Edna. This was one of her favorite kitchen tasks—slicing the pastry into half-inch strips and weaving them across the top of cherry pie. She beat an egg and brushed it over the pie's top and sides.

"Will you teach Edna how to cook Pennsylvania Dutch?" Lou wondered.

"If she asks. I won't insult her by suggesting she doesn't know how to take care of our Blinker," Henrietta said.

Lou knew Blinker was Wilmer, given the nickname and teased by friends and family members for his bouts of frequent blinking as a youngster.

"Before you jump to conclusions, will you listen to me, Mama?"

"Of course, Lou."

"Give Edna a chance."

"I will, dear."

Henrietta smiled at the thought of two wedding gifts from the Kearns side of the family. One, presented at the wedding, had been the chinaberry set husband John purchased in Harrisburg as a wedding gift. A desk and tablecloth had been added to the offerings from the Kearns side of the family. The chinaberry dish set would have been enough, but Henrietta, also called Etta, labored over the handmade recipe book with a cover, hand-decorated with angels and fanciful birds.[2]

My great-grandmother Henrietta would present the handmade cookbook to the couple before they left on the train to return to the East Coast. It included Wilmer's favorite recipes such as pfeffernüsse cookies, honey bars, and dried beef gravy on toast that Henrietta served for weekday suppers. If Edna asked for a cooking demonstration, Henrietta would show her how to prepare the beef gravy. She'd start with a quarter pound of dried beef, to which she added butter, flour, and milk. Wilmer always asked for second helpings.

"Melt a chunk of butter in the iron frying pan," she wrote in the cookbook directions for the dish. "Brown the beef lightly. Stir in a palm full of flour. After the flour has dissolved in butter, slowly add the milk until thick. Serve on toast."

Although storytelling was an essential part of my grandparents' relationship, young Wilmer still hadn't mentioned anything about his maternal grandfather, John Rhamstine, to Edna by the couple's third meeting at the Market Street teahouse. Since Henrietta had been educated in a Civil War orphan school, her past couldn't be mentioned without noting in some way how the war between the states radically changed life in Pennsylvania. Few families in Beavertown—including the Rhamstines, Kearns, and Spechts—had stories to ease the painful news of their loved ones' death on a battlefield. Granddaddy wasn't sure how Edna would react to such a narrative.

Some tragic news traveled home with another soldier. Or it was passed on by way of letters delivered to parents, wives, and family members from a public agency. Many on Civil War battlefields died instantly and escaped wounds, amputations, disease, or being taken prisoner. Civil War prisons had dreadful reputations. Those who survived prison overcrowding, starvation, toxic water, and disease also faced mental illness and possible suicide resulting from the physical and psychological damage of being taken prisoner. Few personal stories arrived home intact. Of those that did, most reports of a soldier's experiences or final moments were forgotten, sanitized, romanticized, or fictionalized.

Civil War trenches near Petersburg, Virginia. *Harper's Weekly*, September 24, 1864. Shortly thereafter, Henrietta's father, John Rhamstine, was killed when serving on the Union Army picket line near Petersburg.

A few, like those in the extended Kearns, Specht, and Rhamstine families of Beavertown, had stories delivered to them directly from the battlefield by a messenger raised in their hometown. These accounts were then told and retold and passed down to descendants over the generations. The stark account of the death of my great-great-grandfather John Rhamstine on a Civil War battlefield in 1864 rang of truth. But it also may have been spread for the purpose of lessening the pain of those who didn't rejoice at the conflict's end.

A deathly silence resulted whenever the names of the Civil War dead were read in public on Decoration Day, later renamed Memorial Day. John Rhamstine's death stood out from the narratives of many other soldiers, many of whom were dumped into mass graves without a hint of how they'd met their end. As the family story went, another Beavertown young man, Private Sam Wetzel, had been crouching next to John in the trenches of the Petersburg picket line. Sam warned, "Keep your head down, John." As he said this, a Confederate sharpshooter behind a chimney was reportedly responsible for making my great-great-grandfather John Rhamstine a Civil War statistic.

At a Memorial Day ceremony years ago in Beavertown, I listened to the traditional speeches and readings of veterans' names who'd died during the Civil War. The skin on my arms tightened when John Rhamstine's name was read. No photo existed of John. None of the belongings he left behind survived, only a tombstone at Poplar Grove National Cemetery in Virginia with his name.

Faint information filtered down to me over the generations about John Rhamstine from family stories and official records. He'd been a volunteer in the Union Army, age thirty-five at the time of his enlistment, five feet eleven, fair complexion, an ore miner by occupation. One set of papers had his hair color as black, and another as light brown. His eyes were blue in one document and sandy in another. He received an enlistment bounty of $100, and he died in the fall of 1864. John Rhamstine was a private in Pennsylvania's 184th Volunteer Infantry Regiment, Company 1, organized in Harrisburg. It was John's second enlistment.[3]

Few questioned the merits of the Union Army digging in so close to the Virginia capital of Richmond with the goal of breaking the Confederacy close to the end of the Civil War. Survivors of the siege at Petersburg described the war as "hell itself." Daily life consisted of digging trenches, strengthening fortifications with logs and other materials, sleeping, shooting, and ducking mortar fire. During one six-week period, the heat had been brutal. No rain fell. Then it rained so hard, the men wished for heat again for relief from sickness and battle fatigue.

Deaths like John Rhamstine's at Petersburg resulted from manning a line in advance of the army's main encampment. Privates served with several commanding officers on picket lines. These soldiers were constantly on the watch for enemy advances or retreats. By nature of their vulnerable positions, soldiers on picket lines were the most likely to be wounded, killed, or taken prisoner. Before the siege was over, Union Private Rhamstine died. He left behind a widow, Jane, and five children. John's daughter Henrietta, Wilmer's mother, passed on the stories of grief about her father to Wilmer and, by way of him, to my mother, me, and the extended family.

Most of my grandfather's ancestors led conventional lives. Their birth and death dates were recorded on genealogical charts and confirmed by certificates issued by government agencies. Books, national cemetery brochures, and photographs documented the grim Petersburg battlefield. Records highlighted that most of the dead could be accounted for. For others, there would never be a confirmation of the details. Stark archival images featured tidy rows of bodies wrapped in fabric waiting to be transported to graveyards. Many written accounts avoided detailed descriptions of the horror, misery, and tragic outcomes of one military confrontation after another.

When attending the wedding at Echo Dale in June of 1904, Henrietta Kearns didn't have an opportunity to speak more than a few sentences to Edna. She looked forward to having private time with her daughter-in-law in Beavertown after their World's Fair honeymoon. Quiet moments were best to ask questions or tell the story of John Rhamstine to be passed down to members of the family who hadn't heard it before. If Wilmer or Edna raised the issue of John Rhamstine at Petersburg, Henrietta answered. Otherwise, she focused on completing the recipe book.

Henrietta Kearns rushed to finish copying the last of the recipes. She couldn't imagine how her precious Blinker could be satisfied with living and working in New York City. She lifted two cherry pies out of the oven. Then, with Lou's help, she set the dining room table. A family recipe collection with Wilmer's favorite dishes brought together comfort food with the cutting of his mother's apron strings.

Decades later, I learned how to prepare and serve dried beef gravy on toast after my mother passed on the recipe to me. Edna had shared the recipe with her. The recipe book was lost over the years, but the gift persisted in family memory. A plate of dried beef gravy on toast was more than regular family fare. It reflected a woman's commitment to her family and the love of millions of American women. They had agreed to set aside their passion for personal freedom and voting rights with the assurance that after the Civil War, women would be rewarded for their contributions and sacrifices. This never happened.

When young men marched off to the Civil War, many didn't return home. Communities were emptied of a generation of young men, even though their names were later read on holidays, carved onto stone monuments, and their families presented with metals and ribbons. Hope was included in the thousands of pies, pots of soups, platters of dried beef gravy on toast, and the tradition of mothers passing on handwritten recipe books to family members and descendants.

As Granddaddy told the story to me, home-cooked food was a way to heal the wounds of the Civil War. Beavertown women, like Henrietta Rhamstine Kearns, prepared dishes that led to second and third helpings. Favorites included cherry pie, egg noodle chicken soup, and rhubarb wine, recipes that accompanied the ongoing process of collective forgetting and remembering.

Chapter 25

Sinking Spells

*A*fter the *General Slocum* passenger steamship sunk in the East River on June 15, 1904, Wilmer went to Little Germany. More than a thousand German women and children from the Lower East Side of New York drowned. Edna noted this in her diary, writing that the Quaker community in Manhattan rallied to assist the surviving families. Almost everyone on board the ship that day lived in Little Germany where Wilmer had once patronized a local restaurant and beer garden.

Few survived the *General Slocum*'s sinking. Many men in families that were wiped out had been at work when friends and family members left the city docks to sail away for a day's excursion to a Long Island picnic site. A week after the tragedy,

General Slocum passenger steamship, circa 1891.

crowds gathered in the city streets to sob and wail. Many thoroughfares were closed to traffic, except for hearses.

Granddaddy told me he merged into the thick of the grieving masses. After the boat sank, metropolitan papers filled special editions with editorials blaming the incident on runaway free enterprise, inadequate safety regulations, and a corrupt system of inspections. My grandfather said pickpockets and gravediggers turned out in force after the news made headlines. Police officers broke down weeping while directing traffic.

Strangers and family members gathered on street corners to toss flowers in front of hearses as the names of the departed were announced. Relatives of the drowned attached ribbons to the front doors of residences to indicate the number of victims. Reporters described how makeshift morgues turned into mob scenes. Granddaddy said the front door of his favorite German restaurant on the Lower East Side was locked and the shutters fastened.

In Granddaddy's kitchen I opened a box with Edna's diary. In it, she described Manhattan after their return from the 1904 World's Fair. My grandfather told me he wondered how long it would take for Edna to get used to a noisy location like New York City. They rented a room at the Penington while waiting for an apartment

East Side, New York City, circa 1905. Library of Congress.

to open up in the vicinity of the Quaker Meeting House on Rutherford Place. At school, I memorized facts associated with US presidents and their wars. Women were rarely mentioned.

The years passed quickly for me, from junior high to my graduation from George School, and from there to college, my first lover and marriage, all of it in the Philadelphia area. Occasionally my grandfather visited Edna's trunk in his garage to find documents or photos to show me. The family archival collection stored in my grandfather's garage contained papers from Edna's women's rights work, overflow that didn't fit into Aunt Serena's upstairs closets. During his retirement years, Granddaddy worked on preserving Edna's horse-drawn suffrage wagon. He also had his own interests as a peace activist.

After carving out my own life path during my early twenties, I moved to Colorado after the end of a four-year marriage. I returned to the Hudson Valley following the 1969 Woodstock Festival on the East Coast. I was only a few hours' drive to the Philadelphia area where I visited my parents, grandfather, and aunt regularly. Aunt Serena drove up to Woodstock, New York, to bring me Edna's trunk of suffrage movement documents. In 1972 I left public school teaching to transition to a reporting and editorial position at Woodstock's weekly newspaper. This led to me acquiring the discipline and skills necessary for completing the work about my grandparents.

A general lack of awareness about the early women's social movement put me into a category with few allies. If I used the word "suffrage," few understood what I meant. Even among the informed, the early women's rights activists were often dismissed as "boring" or irrelevant. Literary agents tended not to be interested, claiming books on the topic of women's voting rights didn't sell. Even a women's voting rights warhorse like Susan B. Anthony rarely merited more than a photo and caption in US history books. Some women activists of the 1960s honored earlier activists who prioritized women's rights, but my impression was that most Americans took women's voting rights for granted.

The time had finally arrived to write about my grandparents. When Granddaddy and I continued with the storytelling after I moved to Woodstock, New York, he told me about the racket of Manhattan's streetcars, police whistles, and the tramping of thousands of commuters' feet. The noise overwhelmed Edna as she unpacked luggage from their 1904 honeymoon. The unrelenting flow of humanity arriving at Ellis Island persisted. In cafés and lecture halls, patrons argued about women's voting rights, labor, and immigration issues. New Yorkers spoke faster than what Edna was used to in Philadelphia. The conduct of city business relied as much on the telephone as face-to-face interactions.

Family dynamics also shifted. On Monday, July 11, 1904, Edna wrote in her diary, "Cleaned room again. Clear all day. Rained 6 o'clock. Papa came. (he and I cried). Billy home 6:30. Papa took dinner with us, and then in evening took us to 17th and Broadway and treated us to ice-cream soda. Retired 10 o'clock." I never found out why Charles Harper Buckman wept with his daughter Edna about a month and a

May Begley Buckman, Edna's mother, 1900s.

half after her wedding. I suspected that this emotional vulnerability and sharing was associated with the family's wedding scandal.

On July 11, 1904, in Pennsylvania, May Buckman retreated to her bedroom on the second floor of Echo Dale. She locked herself in. Her husband Charles was off on another of his business trips, visiting Boston and New York City. Edna's brother Smythe broke through May's bedroom door and discovered her under the covers—pale and incoherent.

Smythe sent word to Edna in New York about the urgency of his sister's immediate travel home. The appeal also included Wilmer and Charles. The three caught the train south to Philadelphia. Edna wrote in her diary:

Saturday, July 16, 1904

Clear. Busy all morning, getting ready to go away. Went to Wanamakers and Lord and Taylor with Miss Brown. Afternoon—Papa, Wilmer and I started for Trevose, arrived 7 o'clock. Found Mamma very low, almost despaired for her life. Sent for doctors.

Dr. Corson, the family physician, and Ada Buckman Yerkes, Charles Buckman's sister, hurried to Echo Dale to consult with family members about May's condition. If May inhaled at all, shallow breaths barely provided enough oxygen for her to stay alive. Pale and moaning, she wept. She didn't care about fresh clothes or a bath. Even Smythe stayed at home instead of his usual afternoon disappearances to play cricket with friends.

Granddaddy told me that after arriving at the Penington following the honeymoon, Edna had told him more about her concerns about her parents' peace of mind. Without Edna and Wilmer's wedding to plan for, May had little incentive to live. Edna believed this precipitated her July emotional collapse. Edna felt guilty about not being more supportive of her mother after the 1904 wedding, according to my grandfather. By mid-July, Edna told Wilmer with relief that she'd made it through another month without becoming pregnant.

Because Dr. Corson was in a position to make a medical diagnosis, he suspected that May Begley Buckman suffered from the emotional impact of her husband's infidelity. Granddaddy said that Dr. Corson expressed a cutting-edge view that the cause of May's "hysteria" could be traced to gender double standards. May suffered from fainting spells, an emotional collapse, or what had not yet been classified as a nervous breakdown. So-called hysteria among women had a lengthy history of documentation based on the belief that women were fragile and not believed to be as capable as men when responding to personal and social conditions. Women could be committed to institutions with only the recommendations of their husbands or fathers, some of whom claimed that females were imbalanced and even worse, insane. Rest cures and isolation were common recommended treatments.

After Edna, Wilmer, and Charles arrived in the Philadelphia area to respond to May's crisis, they unpacked, prepared a quick meal, and gathered in the downstairs tearoom to rest on the Edgar Allan Poe chairs. The family gathering included Aunt Ada Buckman Yerkes, Mary Ann Brooke Buckman, and Smythe. They assembled in a circle, with May wearing her rumpled robe after being coaxed downstairs to join the family's silent worship.

Wilmer admitted to me that for everyone present but himself, spiritual reflections spoken and shared might include either scolding or forgiving Charles, who was perhaps the most ruthless in condemning himself, even if his routines remained unchanged. In the quiet of Echo Dale's first floor, Wilmer said he felt the closest to Mary Ann Brooke Buckman because of her family history.

Mary Ann's participation in the family gathering stood as a reminder to Granddaddy that she'd spent a lifetime reconciling her military ancestors with those on her Quaker nonviolent family branch. Mary Ann and Edna both rejoiced when after the honeymoon, Wilmer secured a part-time paid position in New York City preparing correspondence for the Universal Peace Congress that met in Boston in 1904. It was the thirteenth such gathering in a series of over thirty international peace congresses held between 1889 and 1939.

May Begley Buckman, circa 1904.

Wilmer said he surprised himself with the contentment he experienced sitting on the Poe chairs with Edna's family members. By all appearances, May had resigned from family life. Their job was to convince May not to surrender to chronic depression. The facts were clear. She'd almost suffocated in her sorrow. May needed her family's support and compassion. Charles Buckman checked his watch. Granddaddy told me this in order to prepare me for my great-grandfather's decision to remain at Echo Dale for a day, fuss over May, and then leave for a short business trip.

Edna remained at Echo Dale with her mother. Wilmer returned to New York to complete the audit of T. J. Dunn's accounts and show up at his new part-time job, evenings, at the office of the peace congress. Of all the ways he could demonstrate his commitment to Edna about nonviolence and peace, the peace congress position led to his full acceptance by the Buckman family. My grandfather was friendly and agreeable. Edna mentioned Wilmer's job at the peace congress to as many people as possible at the Quaker Meeting in New York City.

I visualized my grandfather at a peace office desk writing letter after letter, wondering as he did this how the planet could become war-free if delegates to the

Universal Peace Congress of 1904 couldn't agree on effective strategies for creating an ongoing peace. It was relatively simple to identify the dangers of war, he told me. It wasn't as easy to agree on methods to address the root causes of violence that included greed and power politics.

Granddaddy said his part-time job included the production of peace congress bulletins and generating correspondence with public figures, including Theodore Roosevelt, who was campaigning for his second presidential term. Antiwar advocates like Wilmer Kearns solicited Roosevelt's assistance in bolstering the strength of peace organizations and their influence. The replies to his letters included praise and bureaucratic language revealing little.

If rough and ready Theodore Roosevelt could lean in the direction of support for international peace, Wilmer said he hoped his own ancestors would forgive him for working on behalf of a world where war might someday be considered unnecessary, inappropriate, and outdated. If there had been disappointing news about May, the good news involved Wilmer's employment with the peace congress. This delighted Edna, but her enthusiasm was undermined by May's emotional crisis.

As Buckman family members decided where to sit for silent worship, Wilmer asked himself if he had the confidence to speak from the Spirit during the silence and provide inspiration and guidance relative to May's emotional breakdown. If so, what would he say? If nations seemed incapable of solving problems without machine guns and explosives, what could anyone expect of an imperfect Quaker family when working through a crisis? Granddaddy told me he settled into silent worship. After an hour, he arose refreshed. May and Charles left the downstairs to climb the staircase to the second floor, holding hands. Edna wrote:

Sunday, July 17, 1904

Clear and bright. I stayed up all Saturday night with Mamma. Mamma had sinking spells all day. I stayed with her and Wilmer did housework. Brother a most excellent nurse. Aunt Ada here helping all the time. Better in evening. Papa and Wilmer left for New York at 11 o'clock.

Edna expressed herself freely during her brief sojourn at Echo Dale. She didn't hide the fact that she felt homesick in Manhattan, according to my grandfather. While Wilmer spent weekdays at the New York accounting office, on her return Edna tested her resolve to make the best of Manhattan, even in the humid summer heat. She experienced the city's busy streets and the incessant hammering of machines at construction sites. This resulted in more delays in working for the women's rights movement.

Wilmer remained calm. He was, as usual, eager to be supportive. And he avoided stepping into the center of a family controversy. So he kept the peace at home, as well as at the cigar and peace congress offices. Edna and her Buckman family members appreciated Wilmer for his easy-going personal style. He assisted Edna with daily life duties and was supportive of the occasional visits Bess made to New York. Granddaddy said he thought about asserting his authority in their marriage, but he didn't. He'd accomplished his goal of marrying Edna. It wouldn't be appropriate to rub it in.

Chapter 26

Holly, Mistletoe, and Evergreens

Sunday, December 25, 1904

Christmas Day. Clear, cold, no sun. All went to Meeting. Had a grand dinner. P.M., Brother, Wilmer, and I went up to Grant's Tomb and down Riverside Drive to 113th Street, took subway to 14th Street. Evening, had ice cream, cake. Papa and Brother took walk. Retired late. Wilmer and Brother went to St. George's Church.

*C*ity residents marveled at how snow brought Manhattan to a standstill on Christmas morning in 1904. Granddaddy told me of the sights and sounds of the city and that an unusual silence spread through some neighborhoods, keeping many residents inside to eat iced cookies resembling crystals falling from a hazy sky. Youngsters raced outside to build snow creatures. The storm encouraged sleeping late in order to avoid slipping on sidewalks. Holly, mistletoe, and evergreens decorated even the humblest of apartment windows. Long waits were predicted on subway and elevated platforms.

Edna and Wilmer had spent Sunday afternoons since Thanksgiving at a Fourteenth Street theater preparing for a reading from Charles Dickens's *A Christmas Carol*. Wilmer played Ebenezer Scrooge's exuberant nephew. Edna accepted the role of the Ghost of Christmas Past. She insisted on this due to a lifetime of celebrating her birthday on December 25th. The cast relied on a single narrator while the roles of Scrooge, Jacob Marley, Cratchit, and others were interpreted by performers. They relied on basic costumes and accessories such as hats, scarves, and a replica of Marley's chains.

Wilmer delighted in watching Edna prepare fruitcakes before the holiday. Her diary noted a purchase of sugar and nuts on December 5, 1904. On December 12th she prepared fruitcakes moistened with orange juice for storage. This was followed by a purchase of figs, dates, and raisins for another round of baking two days later. She'd forgotten to set aside a cake for Bess to share with coworkers at the Market Street teahouse. Edna's diary documented that she spent forty-five cents for a turkey baking pan. On December 8, 1904, Edna wrote that she'd been married to Wilmer Kearns for six months.

Fifth Avenue, New York City, after a snowstorm, circa 1905. Library of Congress.

"Seems like ages," she wrote, adding, "We are and have been very happy."

Over meals Wilmer and Edna spoke of "the baby" and little else. They lounged in bed weekends, occasionally until noon. Wilmer made a stop in the kitchen and returned with mugs of hot tea and cinnamon rolls.

"How perky Edna looked," Granddaddy told me. By then I realized that pregnant women were likely to glow from the new life within. Some conversations between Wilmer and Edna concerned the lack of space for an infant in their small apartment.

Edna and Wilmer invited family members and friends to visit from out of town to greet the New Year on Times Square with extravagant fireworks displayed from the roof of the *New York Times* office building. The Beavertown branch of the family was expected in Manhattan by December 29th. Reports about gifts purchased or handmade filled empty spaces on Edna's diary pages.

After announcing Edna's pregnancy, Wilmer's prior resolve to apply for another full-time job fell to an even lower position on a list of tasks to complete. When I heard about the holiday season of 1904, I questioned if Granddaddy was as ambitious as he promised. He was content with preparing for the new infant and didn't mention to me any downside to his employment with T. J. Dunn. Edna was disappointed about the delay in participating in the women's rights movement. She purchased a crib for their baby. Granddaddy said he was "thrilled" about the changes under way. His part-time job with the peace congress ended after several months. The prospect of searching for and training for another full-time position wasn't a priority. Only the baby was.

"All the better to serve thee, my dear," Wilmer told Edna as she thanked him for delivering her breakfast in bed the morning of December 24th. After a cup of tea and a muffin, Edna placed an apron over her holiday dress and headed to the kitchen for what she called "domestic duties." She needed to prepare more food before they took a cab to meet Charles, May, and Smythe, who'd traveled from Philadelphia to New York City by train.

Edna buttered tube and loaf pans, lined them with paper, and sifted dry ingredients while Bess, who arrived for a visit several days before, participated in the holiday preparations. Bess was critical, as always. Her expression after hearing about May's nervous breakdown was predictable, she said, reinforcing her long-standing opinion of marriage as a way that men controlled women and children.

Wilmer creamed sugar and butter until fluffy and light. He told me he did his best to be cheerful with Bess. In the kitchen, he cracked eggs for the fruitcakes, followed by the addition of flour, spices, molasses, walnuts, and candied fruit for a thick batter. He inhaled the heavenly aroma of nutmeg, cloves, allspice, and mace. He marinated a turkey to roast and serve with sage and chestnut dressing. Bess and Wilmer managed the kitchen when Edna left to meet Charles, May, and Smythe.

The aroma of fresh spruce, pine, and cedar filled the outside chilly air when May and Charles arrived in New York carrying packages. They carried a yule log cake, ripe pears, and oranges. Edna whispered instructions to the cab driver to choose a modified route to protect her mother from observing the city's brothels, saloons, and cheap thrills. Although May's state of mind had improved since the summer crisis, Edna took no chances.

After a meal of oyster chowder, eggnog, and fruitcake on Christmas Eve, Granddaddy told me that his baritone voice filled the apartment while he played the violin. He lit red and green holiday candles. A subzero wind chill outside sent everyone to bed early. Bess and Edna's family members from out of town stayed at the Quaker boardinghouse on East Fifteenth Street, as did Bess. On Christmas morning, an explosion of church bells and shouts in the street accompanied celebrants outside shoveling snow. Granddaddy said the city retained the atmosphere of celebration on the 26th as well. Bess took off on her own to attend a Greenwich Village lecture about free love. Edna summarized other activities in her diary.

Monday, December 26, 1904

Snowed, but cleared later. Brother, Wilmer and I went on top of bus up 5th Avenue. Got so cold, got off at 59th Street and walked to the Metropolitan Museum. Went all through it. Walked to 3rd Avenue, took elevated to South

Ferry, visited Aquarium, then home at 2 o'clock, turkey dinner. Evening, brother, Wilmer and I attended Shakespearean recital of "Hamlet."

Wilmer told me that Edna looked forward to Bess's visits to New York when she stayed overnight at the Penington. The two women set aside afternoons to spend together at establishments like the St. Regis, which Edna believed was the best hotel and teahouse in Manhattan. They devoted several days to shopping before Christmas. This annoyed Wilmer. Where was the Quaker lass he'd married? The one concerned about eroding Quaker values and lifestyles? When he posed this question to Edna, she justified the money spent on new clothes.

"The old dresses don't fit me anymore," she said.

Wilmer wasn't satisfied. He'd heard from Bess that Edna searched through Lord and Taylor's dress racks to indulge herself by feeling the luxurious textures of satins and silks between her fingers. The two women scheduled cultural events on some evenings. They didn't always include Wilmer. Granddaddy said he was uncomfortable when Edna shopped with Bess. None of his salary had been budgeted for hats with feathers and fancy shoes.

"A couple of dresses make sense," Wilmer told Edna. "But does thee really need two wool coats and three pairs of silk gloves?"

"People dress differently in New York," Edna replied. Wilmer said he noticed how much she liked new outfits for lectures and dinner with friends. My grandfather told me he felt as if his wife's interest in shopping had a higher priority than her spiritual and intellectual development. And who was he, but a Quaker in training? I tried not to judge Edna's shopping excursions. This is why Granddaddy suspected I might be on my way to becoming a reporter—someone paying close attention to the external dimension and less focused on my ever-changing internal emotions.

Wilmer and Edna chose a name for a baby girl, but no decision was reached about a boy. Edna's delicate physical condition set in motion plans to travel back to Echo Dale so the infant could be born in Norristown during August of 1905. Edna had been so sure the child would be a girl that everyone, when teasing, referred to the new member of the Kearns family as Serena, the girl's name the couple selected.

Wilmer and Edna spent as many weekends as possible preparing for Serena. Occasionally my grandfather would choose city events to attend. He checked books out of the public library so he could read to Edna when she rested in bed. He saved money to purchase a custom-made Martin guitar. Edna's goal of women's rights activism seemed too far into the future to even mention. The baby's anticipated birth required the couple's total attention. Wilmer's friends and family members contemplated gifting cigars to the new father. When they asked for his preferences, Granddaddy said he replied without hesitation: "Cuban cigars."

T. J. Dunn's cigar management officials offered flexibility to Wilmer when he requested leave from the office to accompany Edna to doctors' appointments or to address other family matters, including a search for larger living quarters. If he hadn't assumed a position of management with T. J. Dunn, his employers might not have been so flexible.

During 1904, cigar manufacturing executives Theodore Werner and Benjamin Corell agreed that Wilmer's talents could best be utilized by initiating a limited working relationship with the cigar workers' union and, in particular, Samuel Gompers. This labor leader had grown up at his father's knees learning the craft of rolling handmade cigars. Wilmer was impressed by Gompers's service as an official of Cigar Makers' International Union Local 144 before moving up in the labor ranks to head the American Federation of Labor.

When Granddaddy told me about Philip being a smooth-talking rascal and Bess a soured spinster, I bit my tongue. I hated hearing him talk this way. Then my grandfather told me about how T. J. Dunn officials had assigned him to a mission of finding a way to work with the cigar makers' union on "something—anything."

Samuel Gompers, American labor leader, circa 1902. Library of Congress.

Wilmer doubted he would be able to perform a miracle until he discovered Samuel Gompers had supported and participated in the 1904 international peace conference.

Because of Wilmer's part-time employment at the peace gathering, this opened the door to their informal conversations. Unfortunately, the outreach to and interaction with Gompers satisfied neither Wilmer nor his employers. Wilmer not being a cigar roller might have kept them from a resolution bringing the cigar bosses and the labor union together. Or perhaps it had been an unrealistic project from the start. Gompers cooperated to some extent, but the idea of finding common ground with the cigar rollers evaporated.

"Thy grandmother Edna didn't stop criticizing me for working for T. J. Dunn," Wilmer said. He told me that many veteran cigar makers were still resentful of women workers who could be paid lower wages for cigar manufacture. These women, particularly immigrant single women, widows, and married individuals whose wages were essential for the support of their families, had ventured outside the home to compete with men for nonunion jobs. Wilmer told me he was relieved not to have to walk a fragile line between his wife, his mother-in-law, and his work supervisors. By then, May and Edna were more involved with anticipating baby Serena than caring about the politics of Wilmer's job.

Echo Dale, Wed. Eve

July 1905

Dearest Billyboy,

Mamma received a note from Papa today saying he was coming home with Thee. I hope Bro is too as it would be so nice for all to be together . . .

Oh! Dearie, I wish I could tell Thee my worries about my family because Thee and I are *one* and I can trust thee and I also can depend on Thee, for which I am thankful to my Heavenly Father. I am blessed indeed in my husband as few women are, simply because Thee and I can consult each other and do not do anything without the other's consent. Oh! I do hope it isn't only for this year or next or the year after but always to the end. What an ideal life. Could we do it? Would it be possible for me to have a husband who wouldn't deceive me in anything ever?

There are few such men in the world. Even Uncle B. says, "Oh, wait until you're married a few years. All men are that way the first years of married life." Mamma says, "Well, I think this is lovely for Thee, but dearie, so was thy father and so are all men and then in a few years they change . . ."

Dearie, it would break my heart if I thought Thee would ever be different toward me, even in telling me of Thy business affairs. I think we should always tell each other all our joys, all our cares, sorrows and troubles. Then we are of a more *one* . . .

Dear, I want to talk to Thee. My brain is so full and I worry so I go away by myself and cry and dear, I am helpless. I can't do anything. I can hardly wait to unburden myself to my own sweetheart and lover. I suppose Thee knows it won't do for us to sleep together as even a caress might bring the baby before its time. However if we do, Thee must not even caress me. Mamma was much alarmed about Thy coming and said she felt she must speak plainly to me and told me to tell Thee that Thee had better not come, but I told her Thee was sensible and also loved me enough to take care of me.

"Well," said Mamma. "He must certainly be different . . ."[1]

Chapter 27

"It Is Awful. Awful."

The first Kearns child, Serena, was born on August 5, 1905, at Riverview Hospital in Norristown, not far from Echo Dale. Edna highlighted Serena's infancy in a baby book added to the family's archival collection. Edna and Wilmer named the baby Serena after Serena Minard, a Canadian Quaker and recorded minister whose reputation for theological discernment spread among those living in the larger East Coast Quaker community.

By naming the infant after Serena Minard, Edna hoped that the elder Quaker's insights and accomplishments would be passed on to the infant. This included a well-known speaking tour where Minard shared the platform with Susan B. Anthony, Anna Howard Shaw, Phoebe Wright, Lucy Stone, and Emily Howland.

Many Quakers in New York considered Serena Minard and her friend, Phebe Anna Thorne, to be visible members of one of the last generations of Quaker ministers who valued plain dress and speech. Phebe, who grew up under the care of the Nine Partners Meeting in Upstate New York, was as outspoken as Serena Minard about social issues. This included public education, gender equality, the abolition of slavery, an end to genocidal Native American government policies, public health, prison reform, temperance, and equal rights for all.

Edna took advantage of any opportunity, Granddaddy said, to explain to friends about the importance of honoring women as mothers, as contributors, as creators, and as a source of personal power. My grandmother, as before, challenged the prevailing view of women as weak and dependent creatures, limited in education and opportunities, and burdened by the social and economic hierarchy. Even though Edna and her mother May supported Phebe's social witness and use of plain speech, the Buckman family's gray Quaker outfits and bonnets were stored for special occasions and gradually replaced with factory-made items.

"Serena is such a doll," elders from New York's Quaker community told Wilmer and Edna. They spread word of the child's plump rosy cheeks and the way she became the center of attention wherever she went. This was the public persona of little Serena Kearns. Wilmer and Edna knew better. Behind the scenes, family members struggled to keep a smile on their faces.

Serena Kearns, age two. Edna B. Kearns's handwriting, 1907.

When Serena Minard arrived at the Kearns's East Fifteenth Street apartment to visit her namesake at age two, the occasion was noted in Edna's ongoing record. In one baby book account, Edna featured Serena Minard, in Quaker dress, walking with toddler Serena, who wore pink and blue ribbons in her hair as they made the social rounds of First Day worshippers at the meeting house on Rutherford Place. The image of the two Serenas, hand in hand, became one of the highlights described by Edna during the two years she added faithfully to her daughter's baby record. At home, Edna and Wilmer spent their free time reacting to the child's unpredictable outbursts.

Charles Sprague Smith, the founder of the People's Institute in New York, interrupted a public reception in 1906 to lift baby Serena high in the air for dramatic effect, according to Edna's account in the baby book. The event marked yet another page turned in Serena's perceived rise to public recognition and her eventual role as a suffrage movement poster child in New York City and on Long Island. Smith, a Columbia University professor who organized lectures and forums, attracted as many as a thousand people to his New York City events. Serena could also fascinate a sizable crowd. While some might have called her spoiled, others have pointed to possible explanations for her challenging nature, including a potential milk allergy, inexperienced parents, learning disabilities, or even an intolerance for the noise and business associated with city living.

New York City turned out to be everything Edna and Wilmer hoped it would be—a source of intellectual stimulation, a place to meet like-minded people, and a way to network with the Quaker community of the East Coast. Granddaddy said that whenever possible, he and Edna attended lectures and special events held at Cooper Union in the East Village. They loved visiting Greenwich Village where they ate ethnic food in neighborhood restaurants and engaged in lively conversations with social reformers and dissidents. By then, my grandmother Edna loved New York.

Edna and Wilmer attended most of the lectures and events sponsored by the People's Institute. They served on committees at the Fifteenth Street Monthly Meeting and enrolled in classes there on Quaker faith and practice. Edna practiced writing and journalism when serving on the Yearly Meeting's press committee prior to 1910. On one occasion, Edna and Wilmer attended a lecture about art and social critic John Ruskin. His views included a return to the land, guarantees of meaningful employment for all, plus creative and spiritual expression through an intimate relationship with nature.

Ruskin, unfortunately, wasn't sympathetic to women and their issues. According to what Edna read of John Ruskin, he preferred traditional women in his personal life. Granddaddy added that even though Edna wasn't yet participating in the women's rights movement, the stimulation of New York was perfect for meeting others and hearing speakers from all over the world on a wide range of political and social issues.

John Ruskin, for example, influenced Elbert Hubbard, the social commentator both Wilmer and Edna liked, as well as the founders of the 1902 art colony in Woodstock in the Hudson Valley—Ralph Whitehead, Bolton Brown, and Hervey White. Manhattan's atmosphere was dynamic and immediate. It offered numerous outlets for Edna and Wilmer to pursue their own interests, even if baby Serena demanded most of her parents' attention. My grandparents mixed into the city scene as much as possible while focusing on home life, especially when May Buckman or other relatives visited. Edna documented Serena's rollercoaster moods in the baby book. My mother told me that Wilmer and Edna felt overextended. Serena was a handful.

"Remember baby's first year forever," had been the message Edna responded to when she purchased Serena's baby book. As the new mother filled in the blanks and documented the weight, height, and burps of her first infant, the daily entries also featured Edna's frustrations. During Serena's first year, the journal featured the infant's first rocking horse; what she ate and how often; the number of toys, rattles, and dolls she broke; each new word she used; the results of various cough medicines; the frequency of Serena's bowel movements; and how she systematically tore the family's living space apart. The baby book postings included one day in Rockville Centre when Serena ran outside and down the street while Edna hung laundry. My grandmother mentioned little about herself other than her usual disappointment, such as, "I had a nervous crying spell. Serena is very self willed. Because she is as wild as a hawk, someone has to watch her all the time."

The baby book mentioned in passing the Kearns family's move from 318 East Fifteenth Street to a home of their own in Rockville Centre, Long Island, purchased with financial assistance from May and Charles, as they had promised. They moved there on September 1, 1906.

Edna's documentation summarized Serena in her many entries as "fretty and cross" and that she had "a terrific temper." Edna documented most incidents of colic and constipation, a problem she associated with Serena's transition from breast milk to cows' milk. She noted when the "screaming spells" accelerated. On November 22, 1905, she wrote: "She seems to be very good one day and terribly naughty the next, sometimes screaming all day long."

By January of 1906, the increased level of frustration prompted Edna to write: "Serena, for the last four or five days, has been screaming at the top of her lungs day and night. She has had severe coughs, sometimes almost choking and changing color. The more we try and pacify her, the more she cries or rather screams. It is awful. Awful."

When Wilmer took Serena to the accounting office, T. J. Dunn cigar officials assumed the role of uncles. The firm's management and floor employees set aside business and took turns holding Serena and encouraging her to laugh and dance. Serena complied.

Edna's friend Bess cultivated a sense of humor about Serena. When Bess was able to sense that friends and acquaintances had grown tired of her opinionated gender tirades, she'd tell a joke or make fun of herself, or mention George Sand, her favorite writer. Bess liked little Serena. A welcome addition to the Kearns family bookshelf had been Bess's gift of a collection of O. Henry's short stories she presented to Edna for her birthday on Christmas in 1906, the year of Serena's second birthday. When Edna read O. Henry, Wilmer said he could hear his wife's laughter in the bedroom—a sign of resilience and recovery in his opinion.

Wilmer waited to read "The Ransom of Red Chief" by O. Henry, the tale about the red-haired freckle-faced boy kidnapped and held for ransom by "two desperate men," what might have been a tragic tale transformed into an O. Henry hilarious classic. The kidnapped child, Red Chief, assumed the upper hand over the kidnappers, demanding a ransom. By the story's end, the kidnappers delivered the young demon back to his family for a price. The kidnappers paid out of their own pockets. Wilmer told me he didn't smirk when reading the tale, but instead he groaned after concluding that Serena was his and Edna's own creation—a version of Red Chief.

Even though Wilmer arrived home from the office at the dinner hour in need of rest, he rocked Serena, bounced her on his knee, and entertained her with stories. During warm weather, they visited the neighborhood in a go-cart that Serena later destroyed. She engaged adults outside their home with displays of song and dance, similar to what defined child performer Shirley Temple decades later. Throughout this period, Edna didn't attend women's rights meetings and events. From what Granddaddy told me, Edna barely had enough energy during the day to pin up her hair.

"Everyone makes a fuss over Serena," Edna added to the baby book. "People call her 'bright and observing,' and she wants us to notice her and praise her for her dancing black eyes." Serena begged to accompany Wilmer on trips around Manhattan. Along the way, Serena kissed cats and dogs. She adored visiting Coney Island, strolling through Central Park, catching trolley rides, drinking two quarts of milk a day with lady fingers, and choosing starch and sugar over vegetables and fruit. Lists of gifts the child received during holidays and birthdays consumed large portions of the baby book record.

During the first few years of Serena's life, Edna's words "I'm exhausted" appeared frequently in the baby book. Wilmer and Edna's progress relative to establishing equality in marriage, as well as Edna's delayed hope of fulfilling her ambition of becoming a votes-for-women activist, remained on the back burner.

Granddaddy told me he found relief when traveling home from the office to purchase tasty treats of cinnamon sticky buns at the bakery around the corner from their apartment. Edna met Wilmer at the front door when he arrived home daily

Lulu Kearns (Wilmer's sister), Serena, and Edna, at the seashore near Long Island, circa 1913.

from T. J. Dunn. He'd have a piece of wisdom stored up to share with her, a story or gossip about his job.

"Pain helps in building courage," Edna noted when thanking Wilmer for his support. He emphasized that her responsibility was to clear her mind and rid her heart of fear. Serena wouldn't always deliver pain to her parents, my grandfather predicted. And no situation was permanent. My grandmother Edna would find a way to engage in women's rights organizing. Wilmer was convinced of this. And conveniently, Serena was most content when she was the center of attention and in the position of serving as a suffrage poster child for the women's movement.

Edna, Wilmer, and Serena Kearns, circa 1913.

Part IV

Chapter 28

"Trust Me"

"Could you bring Edna's photos on your next visit? We could label them," I suggested to my mother Wilma on the phone.

Silence.

Weeks had passed since I'd asked her about moving ahead on the study of our family history. Minutes can feel like hours on the phone, but most likely it was a minute or two until my mother started to sob. She admitted that looking at her mother's photos brought back the unresolved pain of Edna's death in 1934. This explained why none of Edna's photos were displayed in our house during my childhood. My mother told me she wasn't sure if she could open the boxes of family memorabilia in storage without bursting into tears.

My jaw dropped. My chin trembled. Sound roared in my ears. Edna, Wilmer, and Serena Kearns left New York State in 1920 and moved back to Pennsylvania where they lived at Echo Dale, the Buckman family home, and established a flower nursery, Echo Dale Gardens. My mother Wilma was born in early November of 1920 when millions of American women voted for the first time after the Nineteenth Amendment to the US Constitution.

Wilma was in her early teens from 1933 to 1934 when she missed a year of school to stay home and care for Edna during her last stage of breast cancer. Edna insisted that Wilma repeat back to her the surnames of the women on their family tree. The bank foreclosed on Echo Dale not long after Edna's passing, a result of the Great Depression when the sales of flowers and ornamental plants hit bottom.

With the help of a scholarship, Granddaddy enrolled my mother at George School, the same Quaker school in Bucks County that her sister Serena had graduated from and her uncle, Smythe, attended. Wilma dropped out of George School after a year or so and graduated from Springfield High School when she met my father, Joel or "Bud," as his family and friends called him. They married in 1941. My mother added my father's family name, Culp, to the Buckman and Kearns family identifiers following her first and middle name. In many instances during my childhood, she used her birth name, Wilma Buckman Kearns. She would proudly sign her name in practiced, ornate cursive letters.

Wilma Buckman Kearns (Culp) and Joel Winfield Culp, in Lansdale, Pennsylvania, 1984. Photo by Marguerite Kearns.

It took extra effort to explain to my mother that stirring the pot of the past represented an act of love—a demonstration of affection that could also heal descendants. My mother and I worked together during the 1980s sorting through images and documents. Eventually she couldn't tell me enough about both sides of the family, especially Edna. This led to research trips and a decade-long collaboration. My mother no longer wept when holding Edna's photos.

Wilma told me stories I'd never heard before, from both sides of the family. We shared intimate insights about what her own life had been like—a rare and precious exchange between mother and daughter. I filled dozens of journals with notes, anecdotes, and memories. We visited libraries, Quaker Meeting Houses, historical societies, conferences, courthouses, archives, plus any and all communities where family members and ancestors once lived. I couldn't reach my Woodstock kitchen without passing walls of cardboard boxes stuffed with books and papers. I inched sideways to the bathroom past containers filled with primary and secondary documents.

"Hopefully I'll become a storyteller someday like my father and grandfather," I told Wilma when pointing out each box numbered with a black marker identifying "FAMILY HISTORY" on labels securely attached with packing tape.

"Your take on family history is exactly what I'm afraid of," she responded. "We're no different than other folks with some skeletons in our closet."

Although it didn't feel natural, I called my mother Wilma by her first name to give her the recognition she deserved as an individual separate from her role as a wife and parent. Our research project shifted toward a healing phase of our relationship. I added to the effort by saying: "Don't bring me any more towels or blenders. I'm finding out why I am the way I am by digging into the record and family legends."

During one of her visits I asked: "Why do you tell me so many family stories and then expect me to keep most of it under my belt?"

"I assume you'll pass on a few sensitive things, but not anything else," she replied.

"Trust me," I replied in my own defense.

As the words left my mouth, I realized that I'd followed some of her editorial direction and then exercised my own. My mother would choke if she discovered that I'd found the drama of Edna's first menstrual period in 1895 relevant. I'd be in worse shape if I broadcast the secret of my great-grandmother May sorting through her husband's wallet while he soaked in the tub. Serena's baby book highlighting her as a brat might also be a source of disagreement.

The scandal revealed at my grandparents' wedding wouldn't win me any awards. My confession about eavesdropping on my mother while she smoked cigarettes and gossiped on the telephone party line guaranteed that I wouldn't hear about any other family intimacy. I'd be in deep trouble if I included in any manuscript May's nervous breakdown as a response to my great-grandfather Charles Buckman's extramarital affair from 1903 to 1904.

"Don't make our family look flawed. And God forbid, don't paint me out to be an irresponsible mother for telling you so many secrets," my mother reminded me.

"I'm doing the best I can" was the only response I could muster.

"I regret telling you anything," Wilma added during another visit she made to see me in Woodstock, New York. "And I hold my breath when thinking about what you'll write next."

"You'll like the family history when it's done," I assured her when holding in my hands numerous family documents and photos I'd never seen before. The evidence had been locked in my aunt Serena's closet for decades, "for safety," Wilma emphasized, away from the prying eyes of family members and curiosity seekers.

The heavy security wasn't necessary. After 1920, the Nineteenth Amendment to the US Constitution and the drama of the uphill campaigning toward ratification receded into the background. Women's suffrage was taken for granted by Americans with little or no recognition or understanding of the sacrifices and effort invested by tens of thousands of citizens. Why? My grandfather once told me that in the larger culture women remained second-class citizens. So the enormous accomplishment of the Nineteenth Amendment to the US Constitution was marginalized and regarded as unimportant and boring.

Although the constitutional amendment guaranteeing women's voting rights applied to all American women, regional and political resistance blocked its overall application. Women of color were barred from voting booths in the South. Native Americans were denied national voting rights unless individual states took action. More decades passed until individual states addressed the issues festering from the passage and ratification of the Nineteenth Amendment. From listening to my grandfather's accounts, I concluded that in spite of the opening of the doors to voting booths, the vertical social and economic structure hadn't changed significantly. It wasn't until the 1960s and 1970s when female pushback and resistance in the US surfaced again.

My grandmother's Spirit of 1776 suffrage wagon and her activist collection of documents remained stored in Granddaddy's garage and Aunt Serena's upstairs closets. Then the wagon was placed on loan to a small historical site in the Philadelphia area for several years. My mother set aside boxes of news articles Edna wrote during the height of the two New York State votes for women campaigns in 1915 and 1917. When my parents arrived monthly for visits with me in Woodstock, they transported boxes of this material stacked in the family station wagon's back seat. I interviewed my mother about her peace work during the 1950s and 1960s as an example of intergenerational activism.

My mother, Wilma Buckman Kearns, was born on November 12, 1920, a little over a week after millions of women across the US voted for the first time. She was part of the first generation of US women who exercised the right to vote their entire adult lives. This placed me in the second generation of women voters, a direct gift from Edna, Serena, and Wilmer and tens of thousands of others.

Before the working collaboration with my mother gelled, I'd reached my limit as to how many pot and pan gift sets from her that I could store on my kitchen shelves. Because my parents' generation had lived through the Great Depression, they were aware, firsthand, of the necessity of Americans helping each other. Because they were in a position to help me, my mom insisted that I spend my paycheck on items other than household necessities. I didn't buy myself new kitchen items until I was in my midthirties. The ethic of save and share from the Great Depression era was constantly reinforced with me and my siblings.

"Hitler doesn't smile when we save miles," my mother said when referring to one of many Second World War slogans. She epitomized a life based on survival thinking and this meant they never ran out of clothing or food, or family stories. They traded, made due with less, and appreciated treats such as a cup of sugar or a package of fresh Earl Grey tea.

Extracting facts about family history was reminiscent of an archeological dig. Since Granddaddy was in his eighties, and I had no way of knowing how much time he had left, I was impatient with the stacks of crumbled paper from my draft manuscript piling up on tables and floors. I had to learn more, and quickly. Little did I know it would be decades until I finished my book, years after my mother and grandfather died.

I was certain that mother and daughter working together to study family history would be simple, but it wasn't. We survived contentious discussions, and needed breaks from the project. On one of Wilma's visits, she showed off the most recent trimming of her short blunt-cut hairstyle—anything to vary our interactions and keep our collaboration fresh and fluid.

My mother wore sensible brown walking shoes and carried a stack of used paperback books about US history in a shopping bag, ready to skim the pages during free moments. She liked wearing thrift-shop specials, except when attending a genealogy conference or volunteering for the Montgomery Township Historical Society. For special events, she set aside a Harris Tweed skirt, cashmere sweater, and matching pumps purchased at either Strawbridge & Clothier's or John Wanamaker's department store in downtown Philadelphia.

The matching skirts and sweaters merited a prominent place in my mother's bedroom closet, neatly covered with a dry cleaner's plastic bag and a note pinned to the hanger, "RESEARCH CLOTHES," to distinguish between the outfits she wore for investigating ancestors and the outfits she relied on for psychic readings. Wilma followed her instincts when tracking down a variety of subjects, ranging from family history, to homeopathy and Reiki, to works written by those channeling angels and spirit guides.

My mother flitted from one branch of the family tree to another. Like a glowing red beetle, she raced through neighborhoods in the vicinity of Lansdale, Pennsylvania. She either fascinated friends when sharing her research adventures or left them scratching their heads. Her research included her role as descendant of veterans of the American Revolution—Thomas Kern(s), William Frampton, and Adam Specht—all from Granddaddy's side of the family. Because Wilma opposed war and nuclear stockpiles, she made it a priority to look her best in public when advocating for world peace. In my kitchen, she wore a polo shirt and a pair of discount-store slacks.

I never told her about my longing during elementary school to have parents like the other kids. Those moms and dads let their offspring eat baloney sandwiches on squishy Wonder bread, drink Coca-Cola, and devour bags of salty potato chips. When playing outside weekends or during the summer, the neighborhood kids munched on frosted sugar cookies. My mother sent us children off to play softball and Simon Says with raw green peppers and cucumber slices wrapped in wax paper.

Carrying on the tradition of activism modeled by her parents, Wilma was the only mother at my public elementary school who phoned into local radio talk shows and presented her views about the US government testing nuclear weapons in the Nevada desert. As a youngster in elementary school, I wasn't sure how to react when I heard my mother's voice on the airwaves lecturing about radioactive fallout landing on meadows.

"Cows eat the grass," she said during radio broadcasts. "And radioactive strontium 90 from above-ground nuclear tests contaminates the milk that mothers pour into their children's cereal." My mom and thousands of other women across the nation participated in the "Pure Milk, Not Poison" campaign during the 1950s and early 1960s. This initiative stressed how the US government's above-ground nuclear testing compromised water supplies and the food chain.

These women activists poured out into the streets with picket signs. They lobbied Congress, chained themselves to the White House fence, and inconvenienced Pentagon employees with their protests and lie-ins. They wore masks and overalls and sponsored house meetings, town hall sessions, vigils, information gatherings, and conferences. They visited women conducting similar protests around the world and described themselves as representing all races, creeds, and political persuasions.

Picketing women protesting at the United Nations, New York, 1962. Library of Congress.

My mother and many others supported shifting from a war economy to a peaceful society. They faced public pushback when demonstrating concern over the Bay of Pigs showdown in Cuba, the building of the Berlin Wall, and the Soviet Union's shooting down of a United States U-2 spy plane. Breakfast at home featured my mother's remarks about Polaris missile submarines, Strategic Air Command bombers, and International Ballistic Missiles. The House Un-American Activities Committee ordered representatives from Women Strike for Peace to appear at Washington, DC, hearings and answer charges of foreign influences on their organization and activities.

A generation of American women tilted at nuclear windmills, above and underground testing. Peace activists like my mother didn't hesitate to claim that the CIA, the FBI, State Department, and all the branches of the military had Women Strike for Peace members and supporters on their radar. And in spite of the protests, the number of nuclear arsenals around the world increased.

When it came to my brother Joel, who'd enlisted in the marines for a stint in Vietnam, Wilma made it clear: "I stand by my son," and "the best thing for our boys is to bring them home." My mother was no Pennsylvania wallflower. When dinner was ready and my younger brothers and sister were charging around the neighborhood on stilts, Wilma called us home by ringing an antique cowbell. When dinner was ready and my brothers Joel and Robert and my sister Winnie were charging around the neighborhood on stilts, Wilma called them home with an antique cow bell. She wore orthopedic inserts in practical shoes while other mothers tottered around in shiny nylon stockings and spike heels. My mom read *I.F. Stone's Weekly* and subscribed to the newsletter *A Minority of One*.

"What's next for you here in Woodstock?" Wilma asked in my kitchen years later as I plopped a New York garlic bagel into the toaster. "You've made a good life for yourself here. I couldn't have predicted you'd find your grandparents Edna and Wilmer interesting enough to write about."

I didn't mention to her that committing myself to documenting the lives of my grandparents brought me closer to figuring out myself. There had to be a good reason why my mother gave me the middle name of Buckman. My brother Tom also had Buckman as his middle name. My mother and aunt's middle names were Buckman as well. The family's history and activism was branded into our names and genetic codes.

With my mother at my side over the course of a decade, we collected family artifacts and genealogical material. I'd danced around at age ten wearing Edna's old suffrage parade dresses before wrecking them sliding in mud during a thunderstorm. I documented the drama about my grandmother Edna through her different stages of life, starting when she met Wilmer Kearns in 1902. I couldn't help but notice how my mother Wilma followed in the footsteps of her mother Edna, whose peace activism during the First World War had been, for her, a spiritual leading. My grandmother Edna was active in the Woman's Peace Party, and she served on the executive board of Women's International League for Peace and Freedom, an organization founded in 1915 by Jane Addams and others.

Even before the decade-long research collaboration with my mother, I felt Edna pulling strings in the background as I stumbled through high school and college. I hung framed diplomas on my bedroom walls and made an effort to combine romance with activism. I wasn't as fortunate as my grandparents in making this work. In the fresh dew of my own activism and love affairs, the history of my grandparents' generation frequently took second place to my own adventures and wanderings. I heard myself saying more often, "I'll deal with Edna and Wilmer later." Someday I'd express gratitude by telling their story.

Chapter 29

The Wagon in Woodstock

Dearest Granddaddy—

My Studebaker is in the shop so I'm on the train bound for Grand Central Station in New York. The passenger car where I'm riding isn't the interstate kind with a dining car and plush seats. On this stretch from Poughkeepsie south to the city, I can stare out the window on the Hudson River side through a clearing in glass surrounded with crud.

When we're together next, I'll have more questions about the old wagon. I hope to get down there before Labor Day after my Studebaker is fixed because I have a story to tell you about Woodstock . . .[1]

*J*ane Van De Bogart raced into Woodstock town board meetings with her nose pointing in the direction of her council seat. She balanced stacks of books, maps, and reports under each arm. The monthly session would have the usual budget line items to discuss, a zoning report to review, and one more town employee to advise about New York's Freedom of Information legislation.[2]

Jane stopped, laid down her burden, and yanked a steno pad from the stack to check off another task completed. She added three more items. Jane Van De Bogart modeled multitasking before the rest of us ever heard the term. The town of Woodstock in the Hudson Valley teemed with vocal and visible individuals like her, those determined to "change the world" during the 1970s. Many local residents were convinced the town of Woodstock should remain as it had always been—a laid-back retreat and art colony stirring only from Memorial to Labor Day.

In the years after the music festival in 1969, Woodstock residents reluctantly came to terms with the transition from a part-time to a year-round town. Did the community need a conventional or a custom solution to take care of the disposal of municipal sewage? Town board members considered additions to a community master plan and circulated progress reports on the town's projected growth. Council members like Jane Van De Bogart immersed themselves in detail. I survived hours of public

Wilmer Kearns, at home on Beechwood Drive, circa 1971. Photo by Marguerite Kearns.

Woodstock town board member Jane Van De Bogart, 1970s. Photo courtesy of Historical Society of Woodstock.

deliberations by taking copious notes and then heading to the newspaper office to file my articles before the Tuesday deadline. Reporting for *Woodstock Times*, I believed, had to be one of the best jobs in town.

"What drives you to serve on the town board?" I asked Jane Van De Bogart.

"Among other things—my great-aunt Elisabeth Freeman and what I heard about her pounding the pavements for the women's suffrage movement," she replied. "I owe my ability to represent the people of Woodstock to my great-aunt, Elisabeth."

"My grandmother Edna organized for votes for women too," I told her.

We weren't aware then that Jane's great-aunt, Elisabeth Freeman (1876–1942), not only knew Edna but they had worked together for what they called "The Cause." Both were wagon women, on-the-ground organizers who drove horse-drawn wagons

Marguerite at *Woodstock Times*, 1980s. Photo by Michael Weisbrot, with permission.

Elisabeth Freeman and her suffrage campaign wagon, 1913. Bain Collection, Library of Congress.

to mobilize support for women's voting rights. New York's men, as voters, were in the position of approving these rights. But would they?

Novel organizing techniques such as horse-drawn wagons took the women activists to locations in rural areas where they might not otherwise have canvassed. Advocates on both sides of the voting issue flooded the state, from top to bottom, during the 1915 referendum campaign that failed and then again in 1917 when New York's women celebrated a statewide voting victory. Elisabeth Freeman and Edna Kearns were in the forefront of these on-the-ground efforts.

Edna Kearns drove the Spirit of 1776 vehicle in New York City and on Long Island. Elisabeth Freeman and Rosalie Jones traveled in another wagon within Long Island and around New York State. They also drove to Massachusetts, Ohio, and Washington, DC. Rosalie Jones was from an old Long Island family that identified as Tories during the American Revolution. Generations later, her family members were sympathetic to the "antis," those who opposed women voting.

Wagons on the suffrage campaign trail were popular attention-getters. A woman driving one with freedom messages might not sound like a cutting-edge organizing tactic today. But at the turn of the twentieth century, the vehicles attracted publicity, and best of all, crowds. Wagons required skill in driving. Occasionally the women managed the wagons themselves. Frequently they hired someone to handle the horse so they could concentrate on public speaking. Wagons provided instant speakers' platforms. Pedestrians and others responded to the suffragists' impromptu demonstrations and rallies with curiosity, support, and heightened emotion. Jones, Kearns, and Freeman wrote articles for publication, agreed to interviews, and served as press agents for votes for women issues on the local, state, and national levels. They took advantage of the emerging presence of weekly and daily newspapers in the New York City metropolitan area and other population centers at the turn of the twentieth century.

Jane Van De Bogart and I worked out a partnership with the Floating Foundation of Photography in High Falls, New York, for a 1986 exhibit in Ulster County featuring Edna and Elisabeth.[3] The exhibit justified moving the Spirit of 1776 campaign wagon from Granddaddy's Philadelphia-area garage and placing it on exhibit for the first time in New York State. Large format archival prints and wagon collages designed by Jone Miller guaranteed that, after the exhibition, the wagon would take on a life of its own.

Suffrage activist Rosalie Jones (*front row, third from right*) assembles "hikers" in New York City to march to Albany, January 1914. Also in the photo are Wilmer Kearns (*back and far right*), Serena Kearns (*front row, second from right*), Edna Kearns, and Elisabeth Freeman (*second row, far right*). Bain Collection, Library of Congress.

Over the decades, the Spirit of 1776 wagon became recognized as a prime artifact of women's struggle for the franchise, and as a symbol of patriotic protest themes embedded in this and other twentieth-century American nonviolent social movements. After the wagon's inaugural Hudson Valley exhibition in 1986, the importance of building a support infrastructure prior to the 2020 centennial celebration of the ratification of the Nineteenth Amendment to the US Constitution became clear to me.

Edna was well known for her community organizing and public speaking. Elisabeth, an organizer and lecturer, emphasized the anticipated benefits of voting rights with working women in cities. Elisabeth supported peace efforts, women's trade unions, equal rights for African Americans, and Irish independence. She also conducted a lecture tour to raise money for the NAACP antilynching fund. She traveled to Washington, DC, in 1913 with Rosalie Jones and others on the "Pilgrim's Hike" to join the suffrage parade organized by Alice Paul and Lucy Burns under the auspices of the National American Woman Suffrage Association. This was the same suffrage parade that Edna, Wilmer, and Serena marched in. The following year, in 1914, Elisabeth Freeman was arrested with writer Upton Sinclair for protesting the treatment of striking Colorado miners.

Researching Elisabeth and Edna uncovered several collaborations. Jane's great-aunt, my grandparents, and my mother's older sister Serena showed up in New York City in early January of 1914 to join a march to Albany to speak to the governor. The appointment of poll watchers for the 1915 suffrage referendum was considered essential to prevent election fraud. Another purpose of the march, which some referred to as a "hike," was to educate citizens on the way north. Not every participant completed the over-150-mile trek from New York to Albany on foot. The Kearns family didn't. They returned home. Elisabeth Freeman persisted though, in addition to hike organizer Rosalie Jones and several others.

After the weary group reached the Mid-Hudson Valley, they slept overnight at the Mansion House near the Rondout Creek in Kingston, then a popular hotel, before continuing on to the state capital. Shortly thereafter, the *Daily Freeman* in Kingston published an editorial criticizing the women for attempting to push themselves into inappropriate spheres of action for women.

The suffrage marchers might not have won over the majority of male voters of the Hudson Valley, but the goal of the march was accomplished when New York governor Martin Henry Glynn approved poll watchers for the 1915 suffrage referendum. The men of Ulster County and statewide voted down women's voting rights in 1915, but New York women finally won in 1917. New York City's 104,000 affirmative votes carried the state. When New York women won, it was considered a major victory tipping the balance of women's voting rights support across the nation.

Jane Van De Bogart and I continued sharing family suffrage tales with others long after the 1986 exhibit about Elisabeth and Edna closed in Ulster County.

"Elisabeth Freeman was my mother's aunt, a daring and dramatic single woman who dazzled my mother when she was a young child with a flamboyant green velvet dress, titian red hair, and wild stories," Jane Van De Bogart told a college audience at SUNY New Paltz. "I never met my great-aunt. She died when I was six months old, but I know my mother and her sisters liked and admired her."

I presented several voting rights programs with Jane at the state university in New Paltz, from 1986 to 1990. Our respective mothers, Jeanette Wittman and Wilma Kearns Culp, participated. This contributed human interest to the programs. Jane and I dug even deeper into the past to uncover what both women believed about militant versus more conventional suffrage tactics and strategies. The Pankhurst family of suffragettes in England had trained Elisabeth. She served time in an English prison for voting rights activism and referred to herself as a "militant suffragist." In an article explaining her position, Freeman wrote: "Six years of battle on English soil and two terms in the hideous Holloway jail have convinced me that militancy is the only way to suffrage for women in England."

"But what about suffrage militancy in the United States? Is it justified?" Edna Kearns asked in an undated copy of a speech I found buried in my grandmother's archive. In it, she wrote:

> I feel that Miss Freeman has taught me a great lesson in regard to passing judgment on others. For I had judged the militant women when I heard that they attacked the property of private merchants. I said, "They can break all the government windows they want to, but when they attack the property of private merchants, I am afraid I cannot sympathize with them." And then, being a believer in justice, and with the knowledge that had I lived in the time previous to the Revolutionary War, I too, regardless of the fact of whether it was lady-like or not, I too would have done anything in my power to help free my country from the tyranny of England. And because of this sense of justice, I am in sympathy with our brave English sisters . . .[4]

Edna Kearns and her suffrage movement associates dressed in colonial costumes in July 1913 and hung banners on the Spirit of 1776 wagon. With the pending approval of a federal income tax that year, they protested "taxation without representation." This reinforced a pattern of returning to the nation's founding principles to define and support dissent as an essential part of American history.

Frederick Douglass's speeches and writings also relied on arguments of patriotic protest to justify the abolition of slavery and the extension of freedom to those long denied. Dr. Martin Luther King Jr. grounded many of his arguments for equality and social justice in patriotic protest. Examining the speeches and journals of many US women's suffrage leaders and organizers during the decades following the 1848 women's convention in Seneca Falls uncovers examples of patriotic protest arguments in literature, protest art, speeches, and poetry.[5]

Three artists, Clifford K. Berryman, Robert Satterfield, and J. H. Donahey, published these patriotic protest cartoons in 1913, suggesting parallel sentiments expressed by suffrage activist Rosalie Jones and General George Washington. Library of Congress.

Not until I reached age thirty and lived in Woodstock did I fully grasp the contributions of a generation of activists, many of them like my grandparents. Their spirit, vision, and impatience led to committed action. They understood the difficulty of organizing in their own communities and continued in the unflinching awareness of a tradition of patriotic protest. They never considered retreating from a social commitment. It became their duty, their mission, and reflected the burning fire in their hearts.

Chapter 30

Uproar in Huntington

*F*lies landed on Edna Kearns as she stood on the Manhattan sidewalk. Wilmer Kearns braced himself to not react when nine-year-old Serena stepped into a pile of horse manure. His short fuse ignited when his daughter's hair bow drooped in the humid air. With a wet rag, he cleaned Serena's shoes. Edna had dressed in an American Revolution costume for her ride in the Spirit of 1776 wagon, a blue coat with yellow facings and a three-cornered hat. Serena accompanied her in a red, white, and blue revolutionary-style outfit.

Sitting in the horse-drawn wagon as it made its way across Manhattan was the last thing Edna wanted to do on July 1, 1913. It was a typical city summer day—hot, humid, and miserable, especially when wearing heavy garments. Kearns family members were on their way to the wagon's dedication ceremony after spending the night in their room at the Penington. They'd continued renting the room after the family's move to Long Island in order to maintain a presence in Manhattan.

Granddaddy hailed a cab. Edna felt sweat dripping down her body, and remembered the argument with Wilmer over breakfast about his responsibilities for the Kearns Motor Car Company. He reduced his hours at the cigar company and opened an office in New York City at 1779 Broadway from where he promoted the Kearns Motor Car, manufactured by the family business back in Beavertown, Pennsylvania. He served as the company treasurer.[1]

"Don't bother thyself with the Kearns family business affairs any more than thee has to," Edna told Wilmer. "More customers are needed, other than Germany. Thy brother Max procrastinates, and he won't listen. And all along, there's talk of war in Europe."

Edna disagreed with Wilmer's proposal to buy oranges for the women's rights organizing journey from Manhattan to Long Island in the campaign wagon.

"Why bring up oranges at the last minute?" she asked. "No use stopping the cab on the way to Madison Avenue. We're already late."

Edna, Serena, and activist Irene Davison served as stars of day, at an event reporters from the *New York Times*, *New York Tribune*, and other metropolitan newspapers were assigned to write about. The Kearns family members arrived at the wagon's dedication ceremony on Madison Avenue with a half hour to spare.

Letterhead from the New York City office of the Kearns Motor Car Company, 1900s.

Kearns motor car in front of the Kearns family residence in Beavertown, 1900s.

The finishing touches of preparing for the wagon ceremony turned into a blur, Wilmer told me. Andrew Wilson, president of the I. S. Remson Company in Brooklyn, rewrote a paragraph of his speech at the last minute to incorporate Wilmer's suggestions. The dedication program featured the wagon as an American Revolution relic that could be traced to Long Island patriot Ebenezer Conklin in 1776. The president of the Brooklyn wagon firm relied on unsubstantiated ownership claims when company founder I. S. Remson purchased the Spirit of 1776 sleigh and wagon before 1900.

Whether the story of the wagon's revolutionary origins was true didn't matter to A. F. Wilson. News reporters featured his speech as if they'd personally confirmed the relevant facts. Then the wagon and its passengers headed to Long Island with messages of "no taxation without representation" attached to banners and featured in leaflets. The horse trotted across the Queensboro Bridge toward Richmond Hills and Edna tried to keep from fainting in the heat as the caravan generated the anticipated interest.[2]

"If taxation without representation was tyranny in 1776, why not in 1913?" was the slogan of the wagon's ceremony and related newspaper coverage. Pedestrians stared at the horse-drawn wagon as it passed in the streets. A caravan of brightly decorated automobiles emblazoned with votes for women banners followed. Some passersby on the street waved and cheered. Others shook their fists in anger. Voting rights for women was a sensitive and volatile issue, opposed by the liquor industry, many business

Edna Kearns (*left*) in the Spirit of 1776 wagon wearing a costume of the American Revolution. Serena Kearns is at far right in the wagon. Long Beach, New York, July 1913. From the collection of Rose Gschwendtner, with permission.

interests, and millions of American men. Some women, known as "antisuffragists," held firm to the concept of separate spheres for the genders. This didn't include voting for women. The "antis" insisted that politics was a dirty business, and women shouldn't soil their hands or reputations.

Organizations with different philosophies and tactical approaches to winning the vote competed for credit. Harriet May Mills, president of the New York State Woman Suffrage Association, had a long history of supporting the "taxation without representation" rationale for women voting. With her retirement from the state suffrage association pending, promoting the wagon's journey with a taxation angle became a priority for her.

According to Granddaddy, Harriet May Mills recognized the potential leadership ability of someone like Edna Kearns. Harriet's middle name was May, coincidentally Edna's mother's name. Reverend Samuel Joseph May, a well-known supporter of abolition and women's rights, was the actual source of Harriet's name. Her family members claimed the minister's spirit had been passed on to her, the type of committed activist who rarely rested, even on holidays.[3]

Mills worked around the clock, full-time, for women's rights. She refused to compromise in her pursuit of equality. A graduate of Cornell University after it opened its doors to women, Mills gathered around herself the support and friendship of prominent individuals, including a close friendship years later with Franklin and Eleanor Roosevelt. Her parents, well-known abolitionists in Upstate New York, operated a station of the Underground Railroad from their home before the Civil War.

Harriet May Mills (*right*) and Alfred H. Brown (*left*) representing the Men's League for Woman Suffrage, 1913, outside the headquarters of the New York State Woman Suffrage Association at 180 Madison Avenue in New York City. Library of Congress.

After graduation, Harriet May Mills taught school and then devoted the rest of her life to social causes—most visibly to women's rights. She spoke before local suffrage organizations, state and national conventions, open-air, and indoor mass meetings. She wrote articles and was a strong strategic and tactical campaign planner, reaching out to working women, the labor movement, and men's organizations. Mills published suffrage news, promoted citizenship classes for women, and offered trainings for speakers and organizers. She wrote thousands of personal and organizational letters. Mills established a suffrage booth at the New York State Fair and relied on her Underwood typewriter for copies of speeches to take with her around the state and nation.

Mills kept an ample supply of membership enrollment cards on hand. She stored supplies for the purpose of fundraising, drafts of notes for writing, votes for women leaflets, and suffrage souvenirs. She had a reputation as a speaker for attracting large crowds. Edna Kearns worked closely with Harriet May Mills to promote woman's suffrage in New York City and on Long Island after 1910. Mills became well known as someone who wasn't distracted by political side issues.

Granddaddy said that when Serena Kearns came of school age, Edna took an active role in the campaign for women's voting rights. She volunteered as a campaign worker in support of working women organized by Harriot Stanton Blatch in 1910. She continued her outreach to include the campaign wagon in suffrage organizing.[4] Edna held key positions in Long Island suffrage clubs. She worked with newspaper editors and reporters, in addition to participating in statewide organizing for the 1915 and 1917 statewide suffrage initiatives. During the 1915 campaigning organized statewide by Carrie Chapman Catt, Edna Kearns assumed a visible advocacy and media role. During the national campaign for an amendment to the US Constitution, she worked closely with Alice Paul, a New Jersey Quaker and founder of the National Woman's Party.[5]

In a 1913 letter to Edna, Harriet May Mills noted the competition between suffrage organizations to take credit for organizing Long Island. She believed it essential for the New York State Woman Suffrage Association to gain recognition. Mills made sure that Edna had a thorough grounding in advocating at the community level. My grandmother collected letters, articles, photographs, and memorabilia documenting her own voting rights work on Long Island and in New York City. She spoke to local clubs and organizations and brought local organizations together, planned rallies, attended county fairs, and participated in marches, protests, and more. My grandmother didn't miss an opportunity to speak to the grocer or train conductor about the importance of women voting. Wilmer advocated for woman suffrage with his work colleagues as well as Kearns family members. His sister Lou Kearns collaborated with Edna on the Spirit of 1776 wagon tour on Long Island during 1913, and Chester Rhamstine from Beavertown, a relative of Wilmer's mother Henrietta Rhamstine, marched in suffrage parades holding little Serena's hand.

Edna faced an unexpected challenge when the wagon joined a parade in Huntington on Long Island's north shore before traveling around the island for the purpose of community organizing the summer of 1913. The suffragists weren't prepared for when vehement "anti" Mary Elizabeth Jones, also known as Mrs. Oliver Livingston Jones, placed herself in the middle of the downtown street where the parade was held. She refused to move.[6]

After Jones raised her hand high to halt the parade, drivers of suffrage-decorated automobiles slammed on their brakes. Musicians in the fife and drum band from the local fire department stopped in the middle of a melody. A silence settled over the hundreds of local residents lining Huntington's main street as they observed the confrontation.

"No longer will this old wagon be put to such a base use!" Mrs. Jones bellowed. She claimed the old wagon had been stolen from her relatives' care and sold to I. S. Remson, the Brooklyn carriage company president. Mary Elizabeth Jones announced her plans to file a lawsuit. This was no idle threat. She hailed from one of the wealthiest aristocratic families on Long Island. Exacerbating the tension of the showdown in Huntington was the fact that Jones's own daughter, Rosalie Jones, had developed a reputation as a high-profile votes for women activist. Many of Rosalie's and Edna's friends were parade participants. Mary Jones didn't hesitate to find fault with the wagon's alleged link to American revolutionaries as the suffragists claimed publicly that Long Island patriot Ebenezer Conklin had built the wagon.

"Not true!" Mrs. Jones argued in a tone of voice that an unidentified *Brooklyn Daily Eagle* reporter described as "belligerent." Mary Jones claimed the wagon had been in the hands of the Hewlett family (her relatives) as far back as anyone could remember. And she added that the extended Jones and Hewlett families on Long Island couldn't be traced to revolutionaries—quite the contrary. Family members were sympathetic to King George III since before the war for independence, Mary Jones claimed. She pointed out that family descendants were proud of their loyalty to England. From her perspective, the "patriots" had been traitors to the English crown, unsavory individuals who, in her opinion, threw temper tantrums over tea and tax.

Mary Jones's disdain for the independence cause reflected tensions existing between Loyalists and Patriots on Long Island after the British captured New York City in 1776. But it wasn't only the American Revolution that upset her. Mary Jones and another daughter, Louise, were loyal members of the New York State Association Opposed to Woman Suffrage. The Huntington incident wasn't the only example of when they'd spoken out in public about their opposition to women voting.

The first time Rosalie Jones "hiked" to Albany to meet with the governor to discuss votes for women in 1912, her mother Mary Jones drove north by motor car to demand that her daughter Rosalie return home immediately. Rosalie didn't. At the March 1913 suffrage parade in Washington, Mary greeted her daughter Rosalie and the other marchers as they reached the city by commenting to reporters that suffrage activist tactics were, in her view, "ridiculous" and "foolish." Then Mary Jones issued "anti" statements to the press and headed off to attend an "anti" convention.

The uproar over the ownership of the Spirit of 1776 wagon dissolved into a whisper after Mary's husband and Rosalie's father, Dr. Oliver Livingston Jones, committed suicide in August of 1913 at the family's residence in New York City. The suffrage wagon may have been key to Mary Jones and her pride in her family's past Tory associations on Long Island. But it apparently wasn't high on her list of priorities when compared to her family's reputation.

The *New York Times* article announcing Dr. Jones's death identified him in the headline as the father of women's suffrage activist Rosalie Jones. The family claimed the fatal incident was an accident during the cleaning of a gun. City officials, however, ruled it as a suicide. Mary Jones must have been shaking inside and clenching her hands in an attempt to appear calm. But she never filed a court case disputing the claims of the suffrage activists. So my mother wasn't alone in claiming that more folks than our family had secrets in their closets.

Chapter 31

One Woman per Century

"*I*f it hadn't been for Charlotte Perkins Gilman, Woodstock and its art colony might not be what it is today," town historian Alf Evers told me one afternoon when I visited his vintage cabin in Shady, not far from Bearsville Post Office, during the 1970s and 1980s. I consulted with Alf as part of my beat with the Woodstock weekly.[1]

"Who was Charlotte Perkins Gilman?" I asked. For the next hour, he gave me an earful. Gilman had her fingers in many pies by 1900 as a novelist, poet, nonfiction writer, feminist thinker, controversial social commentator, and women's suffrage activist. She also had a close connection with the town of Woodstock in the Hudson Valley.

Alf Evers, author and former Woodstock town historian, 1980s. Photo courtesy of Historical Society of Woodstock.

She traveled widely, booked speaking tours, and stirred up critics after making a name for herself challenging conventional gender expectations. Gilman raised the ire of audiences most everywhere she went and also made friends with artists and activists of many types and backgrounds. Her writing included support for the production of handmade arts and crafts, as well as a more direct relationship with the earth. These interests mirrored the views of generations of cultural creatives who had lived and worked in Woodstock since the art colony's founding in 1902. Gilman's 1915 satiric novel *Herland* attracted a widespread readership due to its theme of fantasy and feminist idealism.

Without Charlotte Perkins Gilman, the art colony of Woodstock might not have taken off as it did at the turn of the twentieth century, Alf told me. I asked many questions as I sat on an overstuffed old chair on the fringe of his kitchen. What about those who founded the art colony in Woodstock? How did they make a lasting contribution to the community? What if artist and gadabout Hervey White and solid, respectable Ralph Whitehead hadn't met each other? What if the vision of establishing an art colony in Woodstock had developed into a road not taken? What if Gilman hadn't acted on her instinct to bring together two close friends, artist and gadabout Hervey White and solid, respectable Ralph Whitehead?

What if she had instead interacted with Hervey and Ralph separately? Would the art colony and community of Woodstock have evolved in a significantly different way? Would it have evolved at all? Or would the collaboration between White and Whitehead have morphed into another form relative to the arts and crafts movement sweeping the nation? I listened to Alf's anecdotes involving Ralph Whitehead, blue blood to his core, interacting with Hervey White, the zany and gifted artist, writer, and innovative thinker. Hervey White loved dreaming up projects involving performance, theater, music, art, and publishing, Alf said, as he rolled out story after story for me.

When Hervey White established his own artists' colony called the Maverick in 1905 following his break with Byrdcliffe (the original Woodstock artists' colony), others joined him to participate in a creative community not considered as stiff and formal as Byrdcliffe, the pet project of Ralph and Jane Whitehead. The Maverick splinter arts colony, located several miles from Woodstock, developed a reputation for fresh artistic perspectives. Hervey White was said to be energetic, lusty, inclusive, and supportive of the creative expression of others.

Art colonies and related utopian communities had the potential to nourish innovative living situations involving many, whether in Byrdcliffe, the Maverick, or the Roycroft arts and crafts community established upstate near Buffalo by Elbert Hubbard. Because of their interest in Roycroft, my grandparents Edna and Wilmer Kearns became friendly with Elbert Hubbard and his wife Alice, a high-profile votes for women activist.

Hubbard endorsed the Kearns motor car produced by Maxwell Kearns, Wilmer's brother, in the family business operating back in Beavertown, Pennsylvania, because of its worker benefits. Sadly, Elbert and Alice died when the liner *RMS Lusitania* was

Vintage photo postcard of Hervey White at the Maverick concert hall near Woodstock, New York, 1919.

torpedoed and sunk by a German submarine in the ocean not far from the coast of Ireland in May of 1915. The sinking of the *Lusitania* was an impetus leading to the US entry into World War I. The Hubbard and Kearns families might have otherwise remained friends up to and beyond the ratification of the Nineteenth Amendment to the US Constitution in 1920.

The Kearns motor vehicles had a large market in Germany that dwindled rapidly as hostilities associated with the First World War progressed. National public opinion in the United States turned against Germans in the US and abroad. The Kearns family vehicle business headed toward financial failure by 1929. To compound the problem, anti-German public sentiment across the US lumped those of German descent into a category of potential spies in spite of how many generations they'd lived in the United States. This worried my grandfather Wilmer who never expected to be forced into defending his family's multigenerational US citizenship.

Edna's mother May snapped out of her depression through her involvement in the movement to win votes for women. Her support for temperance was replaced by the quest for women's rights and that had her climbing onto soapboxes in Center City Philadelphia and speaking to passers-by. May made it clear that she didn't know of any social revolution throughout history that didn't encounter obstacles and resistance.

"We're making progress. I can feel it," May insisted.

Bess and Edna made sure their friendship continued after the 1904 wedding. My mother told me of the interests the two women shared in spite of their different beliefs about women's voting rights activism. Both set a priority on individual freedom and manifesting it, one in marriage and the other by remaining single. While Bess agreed that voting rights represented a tool to increase women's power, she was convinced that the impact was limited. Newspaper social columns in Long Island documented Bess visiting Edna, Wilmer, and Serena in Rockville Centre. My mother Wilma remained a source for me about Bess during the family history research phase.

Like her daughter, May was an optimist who believed that social change was possible within the fragile structure of the existing social order. Edna and May agreed that voting would, in the long run, have an influence on what many referred to as the "old boy" network. Bess, however, thought women's voting rights were a reform that didn't change the hierarchy of men at the top and the rest of the population in social positions below.

Charlotte Perkins Gilman spread a controversial message through her speeches and writing, according to historian Evers. She claimed it wasn't enough to establish an

Charlotte Perkins Gilman. Library of Congress. Circa 1900.

art colony or win voting rights for women. She was outspoken about the social and economic system requiring substantial adjustments. Gilman's 1898 publication of *Women and Economics: A Study of the Economic Relation between Men and Women as a Factor in Social Evolution* proposed substantial changes in marriage agreements, the family, and society, as well as dramatic shifts in the very nature of woman herself. Many valued a connection between art and social activism, including artist Hervey White from Woodstock. Like Gilman, artist Hervey White stepped out into the public arena with his provocative views and belief in the importance of a connection between art and social activism. Gilman was fond of Hervey White's novels, and she encouraged him to continue writing.

Charlotte Perkins Gilman's visits to Woodstock and her long-term friendship with White and Whitehead were documented in Alf Evers's book *The Catskills: From Wilderness to Woodstock* (1972), as well as in his 1987 work, *Woodstock: The Story of an American Town*. Even with the attention of a respected scholar and historian like Evers, Gilman remained relatively unknown in Woodstock during the twenty years I lived there. Alf referred to her as one of the nation's prominent and controversial social commentators and theorists of the period, in addition to being a substantial figure in local history.

Evers liked telling stories about how Woodstock dissident Hervey White mixed with socialists, anarchists, union organizers, artists, activists, and innovative writers like Gilman. Hervey and Charlotte met through Chicago, Illinois, community work with Jane Addams and Hull House. After one of Gilman's speeches in New York City, Ralph Whitehead introduced himself to her and a friendship between them developed.

White and Gilman visited Ralph Whitehead at his West Coast estate, Arcady, prior to the formal search for a site on the East Coast that led to the establishment of Woodstock, New York, as an art colony. Gilman supported women's voting rights, Alf said, but she also suggested that women might not be able to reach their potential without substantial changes in the social and economic structure. She advocated the establishment of cooperative kitchens. She believed women required personal freedom to reach their potential.

Woodstock was a supportive community for Gilman where she wasn't dismissed as lonely or dysfunctional or considered an inadequate mother because she allowed her young daughter to be raised by her ex-husband and a close friend who married each other. Freed from domestic obligations, Gilman devoted herself to social activism and writing. Woodstock developed a reputation as a retreat for activists during the second decade of the twentieth century. Gilman played a large role in creating an awareness of Woodstock as an artistic and cultural center.

Gradually the women's suffrage movement gained respectability. Because her suffrage activism was a form of social witness grounded in spiritual practice, Edna Kearns worked with a variety of votes for women organizations in New York State. Later she joined the National Woman's Party founded by Alice Paul, who also had a Quaker family history. Edna also served in elected positions in Long Island suffrage and women's clubs. She organized volunteers for parades, and attended state and national suffrage conventions. Edna served as a delegate to the forty-sixth annual convention of the National Woman Suffrage Association in Nashville, Tennessee, in 1914, where New York delegates like herself introduced state activists there to street soapbox speaking.

In my Woodstock home, I sorted through boxes of papers illustrating how my grandmother Edna had served on many Long Island civic boards. My grandparents opened their Rockville Centre home for suffrage meetings and fundraisers, as well as community organizing meetings. Edna lobbied for suffrage legislation on the state and national level, conducted study groups for women voters after the 1917 state election, participated in canvassing, and was active in the National Woman's Party after 1916. She served as editor of suffrage news for the *Brooklyn Daily Eagle* and as a columnist or press contact for numerous metropolitan New York City newspapers.

Active in New York City relative to nonviolence, my grandmother chided some Quakers for supporting World War I rather than affirming the Quaker peace testimony. This was spelled out in a letter to New York Quakers contained in her collection of primary documents passed down to me. My grandfather emphasized that Edna's participation in the women's rights movement went beyond her support for suffrage. Her Quaker background informed and inspired her involvement in a wide range of social issues, including race relations and gender equality. She placed a high priority on family history, as well as national and international affairs. As my grandfather explained it to me, Edna was a Quaker first and a women's rights activist second.

Activism had personal as well as broader implications. It would have been difficult, for example, for suffrage activist Charlotte Perkins Gilman to have written with humor, joy, and insight if she hadn't been able to rest in a lounging chair at Lark's Nest near Byrdcliffe in the town of Woodstock. She wasn't concerned that local residents and the larger world might not understand her. She realized that her thoughts and motivations were not always linear or close enough to the ground to capture and train. This didn't stop Gilman from her speaking and writing.

I was a sponge soaking up this kind of content from Alf Evers, a Woodstock institution. Those living locally recognized him on the streets even if they weren't acquainted with him. He established a practice of scholarly study of Woodstock and its population when serving as town historian and later when devoting himself to producing regional and local histories. Evers collected and studied women's history, integrating it into a comprehensive story of the past that included documenting those held in slavery in Catskill Mountain towns.

When Woodstock women increased their participation in local government during the latter part of the twentieth century, Alf Evers made sure this content was reflected in the historical record, and he emphasized the necessity of more research. In more than two hundred years of local government, only two women, Val Cadden and Tracy Kellogg, served as Woodstock town supervisors. An average of one woman per century, I thought. Then I wondered why other locations without Woodstock's reputation had more noteworthy records than this.

A visit with Alf Evers filled many afternoons when he presented me with exhaustive answers to my questions. His interest in history was infectious. He collected documents and facts like others might collect stamps and picture postcards. He told me how Charlotte Perkins Gilman retreated to Byrdcliffe and the Woodstock arts colony to write and visit with her friends. She interacted socially with the Whiteheads, Hervey White, and others when in residence.

Amelia Bloomer was an upstate newspaper woman who popularized the dress and pants garment that came to be known by her last name, Bloomer. What if Amelia Bloomer hadn't introduced Susan B. Anthony to activist Elizabeth Cady Stanton in Seneca Falls in 1851? Stanton and Anthony might have met each other some other way and still launched a women's rights collaboration changing the course of the nation's history. Just as likely, however, they might have worked as independent individuals facing an uphill challenge when advocating for equality between the genders.

A statue unveiled in 1998 in downtown Seneca Falls of Bloomer introducing Anthony to Stanton raised for me the possibility of a statue being created in Woodstock someday featuring Charlotte Perkins Gilman in the center, with Hervey White on one side and Ralph Whitehead on the other. Woodstock, a farming community in 1900, was ready for the art colony seed that Gilman soaked, planted, and tended. She realized the time had come for an arts colony there, one resistant to creative drought and with the potential of blossoming throughout the twentieth century and beyond.

Alf Evers made it his business to preserve as much of this women's history as possible. He modeled a practice of including women and their contributions in the larger story of Woodstock by emphasizing the role Charlotte Perkins Gilman played as integral to the chronology of Woodstock's art colony and community development. When I asked Alf, "Who was Charlotte Perkins Gilman?" so many years ago, I was reflecting the interest of others who, over the decades, have insisted on finding out as much as possible about the historical sweep of events and those involved. Alf Evers set the pace. Others like me have continued in his footsteps.

Chapter 32

Sojourner Truth in the Hudson Valley

I lived less than ten miles in Woodstock from where abolitionist, women's rights advocate, and minister Sojourner Truth grew up before the Civil War. Truth expressed courage and heart when she traveled up and down the East Coast during the mid-1800s as an evangelist and activist. She left Ulster County in the Mid-Hudson Valley behind and didn't look back.

Truth sold her personal portrait pasted onto cardboard, in addition to copies of her book, *The Narrative of Sojourner Truth, a Northern Slave, Emancipated from Bodily Servitude by the State of New York, in 1828*. Her life story was published in Boston in 1850, an "as told to" story compiled by Truth's friend Olive Gilbert.

It's one thing to be presented with the details of slavery in the deep South and quite another to recognize the Northern place-names associated with Truth's life. I drove throughout Ulster County and recognized where she had lived, suffered, and survived. The published narrative of her life highlighted the tragedies of bondage. This included the looming auction block that stole away Truth's brothers, sisters, and some of her own children. When young, she witnessed her parents sitting in the dark after the workday, their hearts bleeding and shattered when retelling stories of loved ones they'd never see again.

Sojourner Truth's life narrative demonstrated how the devil can be found in the details. Slavery was slavery, north and south. As my grandfather Wilmer suggested after I moved to the Woodstock area, slavery couldn't be reformed. A farm's upkeep in the Hudson Valley required long hours and endless toil, as documented in Truth's account. Similar stories were circulated in numerous memoirs in what has become a genre of slave narratives, heartbreaking accounts in the first and third person paralleling Truth's personal story.

Sojourner Truth was born and named Isabella Baumfree around 1797 in the town of Hurley, Ulster County, in the Mid-Hudson Valley of New York, the next town over from Woodstock. Isabella's owners sold her at age nine. She spoke the Low Dutch dialect of the Hudson Valley. This led to continual hardship and whippings. One Dutch master in particular was cruel because she couldn't always understand and follow his orders in English.

I SELL THE SHADOW TO SUPPORT THE SUBSTANCE.

SOJOURNER TRUTH.

Sojourner Truth, 1864. Library of Congress.

Later in life, Sojourner stood six feet tall, an impressive figure, even when wearing a simple bonnet. I imagined her barefoot and without a coat as a child trudging through the hills and valleys of the countryside to carry out one duty or another. Forced servitude involved long work hours, endless hardships, and restrictions. Pressure from abolitionists about New York State's large population of people in bondage before and after the American Revolution led to pressure at the state legislature to designate July 4, 1827, as the day of emancipation. Some freedom was legislated and set in motion immediately. For others, freedom was gradual and delayed.

As the impact of my reading Sojourner Truth's narrative settled, I protested Olive Gilbert's heavy hand in the text she created for the "as told to" narrative. I longed to listen to Truth's actual words. I expected her voice to be low, firm, direct, and unforgettable. Her words weren't in a Southern drawl but rather spoken with a Hudson Valley Dutch accent. Gilbert's adaptation of Sojourner Truth's story into conventional English left me little choice but to search for Truth's spirit between the lines.

Sojourner Truth was an activist. She was opinionated. She also knew why and when to keep her mouth open or closed. She became well known for her successful legal suit against Ulster County to return her young son Peter, kidnapped and sold into bondage in Alabama. She became famous for a spontaneous "Ain't I a Woman?" speech delivered before the 1851 women's rights convention in Akron, Ohio. It was a dynamic message, the record of which some scholars believe was an approximation, not a word-for-word representation.

Truth didn't wear fancy dresses or adopt false airs. She had scars of past whippings across her back. Yet all who heard her, from Abraham Lincoln to a wide range of women's rights activists and abolitionists, testified that they never forgot the impact she had on their lives. Someone like Sojourner Truth modeled the type of freedom that went beyond physical limitations. Like Frederick Douglass, she had a freedom of spirit, a message valuable for not only the times in which she lived but also with essential lessons for future generations.

I learned how to appreciate the range of Sojourner Truth's contributions after Ulster County residents installed a plaque dedicated to her in front of the county courthouse on Wall Street in Kingston during the years I lived in Woodstock. Sojourner Truth personified what it meant for a woman's spirit to run deep. She spread a message of how to "set the world right" through the use of humor, cold facts, spirituality, metaphor, and deep emotion. She valued the power of spiritual truth. Truth's vision of equal rights acknowledged the sacrifices, accomplishments, and limitations of her suffrage sisters. She emphasized that false pride, prejudice, and discrimination were as damaging as a social system designed to crush self-determination. Sojourner Truth spoke in public often. In her free time, she knitted with wool, a way of demonstrating, I imagined, that social change can occur overnight or be spread stitch by stitch.

Truth stayed overnight with the Stanton family in Seneca Falls, New York, when attending a women's rights convention there in 1866. Young Harriot Stanton, daughter of Elizabeth Cady Stanton and a later women's rights activist herself, took on the job of attending to the family's guest. Harriot Stanton Blatch wrote in her memoir published in 1940:

> The duty was assigned to me to read the morning papers to Sojourner as she sat smoking her pipe. One morning, greatly puzzled, I ventured the question, as my suspicions had been aroused as to why I was called in to shoulder this task, "Sojourner, can't you read?" "Oh no, honey," she answered quickly, "I can't read little things like letters. I read big things like men."[1]

Looking Back

In Their Own Words

Edna Buckman Kearns in Rockville Centre, circa 1915.

*E*xamples of writings from Edna Buckman Kearns, and at the ending of this segment, a selection by Wilmer Rhamstine Kearns:

1909

EDNA BUCKMAN KEARNS. NOTES. CIRCA 1909. FROM HER COLLECTION OF DOCUMENTS AND MEMORABILIA.

. . . It was my privilege to meet a Mary Keegan recently who was one of the 13 women who marched to the English Parliament to present their petition and Asquith sent 7,000 policemen to turn them back. This they would not do and so were arrested. In describing her arrest, she said: "A policeman told me to turn back. I said as politely as I could, No, thank you, I am going in this direction; again he asked me to go back; again I thanked him, but said I must go on." So the 7,000 policemen arrested the 13 women. When Suffragettes are arrested they are not allowed trial by jury; are not treated as political prisoners . . .

Mary Keegan in describing the prison fare said, for breakfast at 7 o'clock we had a jam jar of milk and a small piece of bread; for dinner 2 small potatoes and a small onion or carrot, no bread, nothing to drink; for supper at 4 o'clock the same as breakfast and nothing until the next morning at 7 o'clock. No change of clothing for a month and compelled to wear coarse woolen gowns much too large for them, which they had to almost double around their bodies. Nothing fitted them, not even their shoes. The matrons in charge are coarse and brutal . . .

. . . So much is said and written lately in regard to our suffragette sisters that while I am not an actual defender of their militant methods, I feel I may state a few facts regarding stone-throwing which so shocked our American sense of propriety.

In England when men want or disapprove of anything they throw stones at the windows of the public buildings. They do not send a committee or frame a petition to argue their point as our men do. Stone-throwing therefore is an old English custom.

Mrs. Pankhurst tells a story about a certain English mayor who removed a cannon from a public building. Instead of the men citizens sending a petition asking him to replace it, they threw stones and smashed all the windows of the mayor's house and the public building. The next morning the cannon was back in its old place. The argument being so effective, it is only natural that the English women follow the precedent established by the men . . .

1912

SUFFRAGIST WHIRLWIND CAMPAIGN—1912. BY MRS. WILMER R. KEARNS (HANDWRITTEN NOTES).

Those of us who joined the Brooklyn Suffragists at Lynbrook continued until the end of July 8 at Patchogue. We felt completely satisfied with the enthusiasm and interest shown at every village where we stopped to speak. On July 5 several automobiles joined us at Far Rockaway and went through with us to Woodmere, Lynbrook, Rockville Centre, Baldwin, and Freeport. We feel especially indebted to the kind friends who loaned their machines . . .

Large crowds met us in each village. In Rockville Centre, Mr. Richmond, a Baptist clergyman spoke for us, as did Mr. Dudley, pastor of the colored Baptist church. In Freeport, Captain Hause, the village president introduced the speakers, and traffic in Freeport was held up for a few minutes while our photos were taken for the *Brooklyn Times* and *Eagle* . . .

Women do not desire to make men play second fiddle. That is not the idea. We simply say, "Brother, you have been burdened with this tremendous governmental house cleaning for so long. Let us help you in this larger home. Together, we women and men can work shoulder to shoulder and together, as in the smaller home we can try to make it a better place for the children of the nation . . .

"MRS. W. R. KEARNS WRITES OF PLANS TO CONVERT THE REGULAR FAIRGOER— OPEN AIR MEETINGS WERE BIG FEATURE," SEPTEMBER 29, 1912, *BROOKLYN DAILY EAGLE.*

For miles on the roads leading to Mineola during the past week, one saw countless automobiles and teams bound for the same place—the Queens-Nassau Fair. Six or seven and sometimes ten trolleys on a track which usually has one, passed a certain point in a half hour. At the gates the crowds were so dense it was with great difficulty we obtained an entrance.

This was the largest and most attractive fair ever held at Mineola. The majority of the visitors were women; this not only because many men cannot leave business to attend, but the exhibits year after year are such that appeal particularly to the women . . .

Right in the midst of the lovely floral exhibits one could see from all points of the Exhibition Hall, the large yellow banners of the New York State Woman Suffrage Association and countless little flags with "Votes for Women." Right below them the Hicksville flags, the South Side Political

Equality League flags and the handsome banner of the Rockville Centre Suffrage Club with those of the Sea Cliff and Oyster Bay clubs.

All through the crowds one heard, "Why the Suffragettes are here!"

"Where?" "Over there; don't you see their yellow flags; let's go over and see what they're doing!"

So the interest was aroused, and the women sent by the seven Long Island clubs were kept busy each day selling literature, buttons, etc., and answering the questions of thousands of men and women eager for information . . .

1913

EDNA BUCKMAN KEARNS, MAY 1913. HANDWRITTEN NOTES.

. . . Let us then, you who earn, we who are mothers, and yes *every* woman, we wouldn't be true if we left so much as one woman out, let us stand shoulder to shoulder and demonstrate to the world, that its women are one in spirit. We must not only demonstrate by organizing. You women know better than I do the value of organizing, but let us put our organization into concrete form and march up 5th Avenue on May 4th and show the whole world that we really mean what we say when we say we believe in the sisterhood of women.

ROCKVILLE CENTRE, LONG ISLAND, NEW YORK. OCTOBER 27, 1913.
LETTER TO EDITOR OF *THE LEADER*, MR. E. G. GARDNER.

Dear Mr. Gardner:—

Kindly put the enclosed in your paper in answer to the criticism by Mr. Holthosen of Rockville Centre which appeared in your columns last week:—

After due deliberation and with a spirit of kindliness I hope toward all, I wish to deny the allegation of the ecclesiastical critic in your paper last week, that the Better Baby Movement as suggested by me is a "fad" or a desire for "notoriety . . ."

. . . It is not a "Fad" with me, because I am at heart a mother, anyone who knows me personally knows of my great love for children. It was because of my desire to help in the legislation for the welfare of the home and the little ones that I took any interest in the Suffrage Movement . . .

Edna Buckman Kearns

My dear Miss Lewis:—

It seems strange that Rosalie Jones doesn't tell you what is going on in Nassau County. She wrote to Miss Davison, saying that she was going to hold a meeting in Valley Stream in a week or so, so we felt it would not be wise to overlap.

I feel that she should have told you about the clubs here. Rockville Centre has had no club for over a year, since I was its President, I understand. Someone told me that they are going to start up again. I sincerely hope they do. Miss Davison can give you the information about her club—it is the oldest in the County, nearly 20 years old, not only that, the most alive and active. Miss Jones should have told you what clubs were in the County—it seems strange.

I do not know what you mean by my having to fall in line. If you understood me you would know at once that I never have to do anything. I positively refuse to be forced in any way. I have not ceased to work for Votes for Women and will help wherever and whenever I can, but, if you mean by "having to come under a Leader," then you do not know me. I think you will find that when you need help I will do all I can for the Cause; but last year I refused to have Miss Jones dictate to me, so you see it is not an individual feeling. It is simply that I am giving my time and money and strength for the Cause, as it is done gladly and freely. I don't have to obey anyone. I hope you understand.

Sincerely, Edna Buckman Kearns

1914

March 21st, Rockville Centre, New York. Letter to Mr. Leroy-Weed, Senate Chamber, Albany, New York.

Honored Sir:—

If not too late, I earnestly urge that you lend your support to the bill for Women Watchers at the polls.

Very truly yours, Edna Buckman Kearns

. . . Two hundred suffragists presented Dr. Anna Howard Shaw with an automobile. When she received it, tears came to her eyes. "This is a long way," said she, "from the days when Susan B. Anthony and I campaigned together, with one suitcase between us because we hadn't clothes enough to fill two, when we rode in buck-board, ramshackle wagons, any kind of a vehicle we could get. It is owing to the brave women with whom I am proud to work that we have bridged the gap and can travel in autos now."

Dr. Shaw has a passion for machinery. She says she will run the car herself. With characteristic humor she ended up saying: "I have a garage all ready for it. I built one three years ago, but at present it is occupied with two tons of the life of Susan B. Anthony."

1915

An acknowledgment by Edna Buckman Kearns.

April 28, 1915

RECEIVED from the Votes for Women baseball committee, 30 tickets at One Dollar each for the baseball game of May 18th. I hereby agree to try to sell these tickets for the Committee at no cost to myself and to return unsold tickets to the Committee on or before May 10th; but in case I fail to return such unsold tickets to the Committee by the date above I hereby agree to pay the Committee One Dollar for each of the unsold tickets.

I understand that the reason for this stipulation is that the Committee has paid cash for each of these tickets and cannot recover its money on unsold tickets unless such tickets are returned to the New York baseball league by a certain date.

Edna B. Kearns

"Current Gleanings: Shoulder to Shoulder for Principle" by Edna Buckman Kearns, *The Observer*, Rockville Centre, New York. June 18, 1915.

The hundred or more suffragists who ma`rched last Thursday in the suffrage division of the Southern New York Fire`men's parade at Hempstead were all women who meant everything to their various villages—women who do civic work, women who represent the brains and intelligence of their respective communities.

They kept step beautifully, all along the line, receiving applause. Many conservative home women came down to their gates and clapped and clapped. If these women walked to give others courage to take a stand for the thing they believed in, then they surely succeeded.

Quietly, never looking to right or left, never even speaking to each other, they demonstrated with their silent dignified appeal their marching, not because they wanted notoriety, but because of a principle. It requires more courage and bravery to march in your own village than to march on Fifth Avenue . . .

"Confessions of a Suffragist" by Edna Buckman Kearns, July 30, 1915, *The Owl*, Long Island, New York.

You have doubtless all read that extremely humorous book, *How it Feels to be the Husband of a Suffragette*, by Raymond Brown of Bellport, husband of the President of the State Suffrage Association; but you've probably never heard "How it Feels to be a Suffragist."

To use Billy Sunday's phraseology, "It's up to you to make good whether you want to or not." You simply have to be the best housewife and mother ever, and then some. You have to be above suspicion in all things. You have to constantly remind yourself that you are a soldier, fighting for a great cause. There is no playtime for you for the next three months.

If you should happen to glance at your neighbors sitting leisurely on their porches and envy them, just the least bit, you forget it the next moment, "for are there not bigger and better things to do," you chidingly ask yourself. If friends call you up and try to urge you to go on a trip with them for a rest; and you should be tempted to go, just for a fraction of a second, would anyone blame you? You look at your piled up desk and you say, "After November 2nd."

A suffragist must be the best manager in the world. She must be reasonable and just. Above all she must keep her temper even under the most trying circumstances. It's not an easy thing to be in the limelight. You know you are being criticized, scrutinized, and years ago you were ostracized. Happily that stage of it has passed away.

Now you are sought after by the very people who shunned you a couple of years ago. And you—oh!—you're glad and forgive and forget for is not that the wisest policy? And then deep down in your heart you know it is simply following the advice of a Great Teacher.

Do you remind your friends of the time they were opposed and rather disagreeable to you about it? You do not! You listen politely when they tell you they always believed in it—but—and murmur "I'm so glad." Do you try to ignore the woman of ability whose personality isn't pleasing to you? You do not! You try to push her ahead and do everything you can to bring out her best points. You really shut your eyes and try to see only the good in her.

Do you show dislike for a fellow worker? You do not! You simply work side by side with her keeping uppermost in your mind the "Big Thing" you are striving for. And you realize that she is as important if not more so than you. "She can" you say to yourself, "reach people whom I cannot."

Do you become conceited with the praise some people bestow upon you? You do not! You are as glad of praise as a weary, thirsty traveler in a desert is when he reaches an oasis. But is your head turned by it? It is not! You very soon meet some man or woman who in no uncertain manner tells you exactly what he or she thinks of you. And if perchance you had the slightest feeling that you were the "Great I Am," it is entirely knocked out of you in these decidedly heart-to-heart conferences with an opponent.

Do you scowl at the ice-man or the milk-man or answer your fellow suffragist crossly over the phone when they disturb your rest around eight in the morning, after you've been up till the wee morning hours of the night before (for, of course, thoughts come when all around you is still and quiet.) Do you, I say, greet these disturbers of your rest crossly? You do not! Somehow you've got the habit of trying to be pleasant, and while only half awake, it sticks to you.

Do you snap at a reporter, or fellow worker who calls you on the phone at twelve and one at night to ask for news? You do not. Do you tell editors and reporters exactly what you think of them? Do you carry out your inclination to shake them at times? You do not! You smile kindly, speak sweetly and chide them gently.

It's a habit—simply a habit—you get into when you are a suffragist. It's a bit trying at times. But then you smile within you and say, "Only three months more" and then—Freedom—freedom to vote, freedom of speech, freedom to smile to whom you please, freedom to ignore the telephone, freedom to speak crossly to the editor, freedom to enjoy life in a lazy way—I wonder! I wonder! Suppose the habit should stick! Suppose the "suffrage smile" should never go away! Suppose you're so accustomed to speak sweetly to editors, reporters, ice-men, fellow workers, husband, etc., that your freedom along these lines will never come. I wonder! I wonder!

It's a bit trying at times to be a suffragist, isn't it? But you say to yourself, "You know you are learning to love your neighbor as yourself, and after all, that's what you should do." And sometimes you are almost tempted to keep right on with the "Suffrage Habit" even after you get the vote. It's kind of nice to like people and be pleasant to people. It's pleasant to have their neighborly feeling toward everyone, you think. "Seems to me that if I could keep it up—if it isn't too much of a strain—why I'd do it. And a nice voice seems to say "Why not? Why not?"

Empire State Campaign Committee: Second Campaign District Comprising Nassau and Suffolk Counties. Mrs. Wilmer Kearns, Press Chairman.

Last Call for 1915

Dear Co-Worker,

Only four weeks left to get suffrage into local papers. For those of you who are having difficulty in getting "suff" in or where antis have paid advs., here are a few suggestions, at least try them, make a final effort—

1. Write up canvassing stories about local people whom you have interviewed, don't mention names unless they say you can. Get a sentence or two of propaganda. In your story make the canvasser answer the anti, etc.

2. Try going to all your big men. Give them literature, tell them we only have three weeks left, ask them to help by giving you a statement for local papers on why they think women should vote. If they will write letters to papers answering anti articles (you providing them material which I will send if asked for) so much the better. Also get prominent local women to write protesting that anti propaganda as advertising material is untrue and unjust.

3. Last, but not least MAKE news. DO THINGS—so that you can get suffrage in your papers, THEY JUST HAVE TO TAKE NEWS.

4. Every time you gather together to sew, can fruit, speak, hold luncheons, teas, card parties, where all are suffragists—write up a story about it, tell who were present. Do something—It's your only and last chance to help the cause we have worked for, for years.

5. If we fail it will be because of the lack of interest of the suffragists themselves. No one else will be to blame. Do your best to make us victorious on November 2. We have a chance if you will do your part.

Yours for victory, Edna Buckman Kearns

1917

Edna Buckman Kearns, *South Side Observer*, Rockville Centre, New York, August 24, 1917.

. . . When Rosalie Jones hiked, it called down a storm of criticism and comment from fellow Suffragists, as well as men. Today there isn't a Suffragist but feels that the publicity Miss Jones gave the cause pushed it forward by leaps and bounds. She once said, "I don't care what they say. I only want them to talk, and when you get them to talk either way, you prompt discussion. Discussion causes people to think—and then—well, there's hope.

EDNA BUCKMAN KEARNS IN HANDWRITTEN LETTERS TO SERENA KEARNS:
MARCH 4, 5, AND 11, 1919.

March 4, 1919

Dear Daughter Serena,

. . . If I am arrested tonight (just carrying a purple, white and gold banner),
I need not hunger strike here in New York. Dad can call on me in jail and
I can get good food—so don't Thee worry . . .

. . . Alice Paul called me up & told me to be prepared to go to prison
tonight. We may not though—There is a harbor strike on now so perhaps
the President can't sail tomorrow. People cannot get to Staten Island—all
ferries stopped . . .

Lovingly, Dearie

Edna and Serena Kearns at home in Rockville Centre, circa 1915.

March 5, 1919

Dear Daughter Serena,

. . . We had a battle on the streets last night, many women badly injured. Doris Stevens badly injured, hit in the head and eye blackened. Several women had black eyes. Several lost their hats, a gold watch was stolen from one and Alice Paul lost a pocketbook with a large sum in it. Thee sees she hadn't intended to picket for she was needed at Washington but she got into it and as several said, her face and occasional "Hold your banners" kept us up and gave us courage to hold on tighter even with six men to one little woman like me.

A woman aviator of Chicago had skin taken off her neck, choked by a policeman and a wound on her face and a sprained wrist. She was thrown by police to the ground and trampled. Miss Bugby of the Tribune said, "Mrs. Kearns was the most persistent there and the worst fighter." I didn't fight. I simply held my banner and resisted all attempts to have it taken from me.

. . . Well, dear. It was the biggest time in my life, somewhat like the parade in Washington. Thee remembers it when thee and I marched in Quaker garb on March 3, the day before Wilson was inaugurated the first time! Only this was shorter and fiercer . . .

. . . The newspaper reporters meanwhile were with us, but things happened so swiftly one said they couldn't get it all in. I was shouting that I was fighting for democracy. I realized I must shout in order to help me resist the men. It seemed to give me strength. I remember several times dimly hearing myself say something about my grandfather in '76 and '61 fighting for Liberty and Democracy. It somehow seemed to help me. Once Alice Paul got near to me and told me to stop talking and save my strength.

I remember a reporter saying "That's Mrs. Kearns who said that," something I said to some soldiers who were fighting me and I told them they freed German women but not to hinder us from fighting for American women. Then in the brawl a very dignified man turned to me and said, "You are such a splendid refined looking woman. Why do you do such disgraceful things?" And I said, "Sir, I had a grandfather in the '76 revolution and another in the Civil War. That's my answer, and he said, "But they didn't do such disgraceful things as this . . ."

. . . I was conscious of Alice Paul near me several times saying to women around her, "Hold your banners, break thru the line." It certainly inspired me to fresh effort. I heard one onlooker say, "It looks like a football game." Well, finally 6 women were arrested & sent to police station—there they refused to give their names & refused to answer all the questions talking in deaf and dumb on their fingers to themselves. They were released in a few minutes & taken in automobile to headquarters of our Party. The two police who brought them back I heard say, "Girls, please don't come down on our beat again." Meanwhile a big fat 6 ft. policeman threw himself on me—he had his temper up & then when his captain said, "Don't hurt them. Keep your temper," he hurled me to the ground. I arose & broke thru the police lines again & again. I rushed toward Broadway with several policemen after me . . .

. . . I yelled & women & men spectators yelled to him, "Officer, stop hurting that woman. You've got her cornered. Why hurt her, either stop hurting her or arrest her." Then he tried to twist my hands so people couldn't see he was hurting me. I took my loose thumb & turned back his little finger & he dropped my hand telling me to stop hurting him. I said, "But you are hurting me & I have just the very same right as you have. There is no law allowing me to twist my arms after you have me powerless." People saw he was hurting me again & again. They remonstrated with him; finally he pressed his thumbs and fingers across my wrists & stopped the circulation—my but it hurt—I shouted to him to stop. Several men said, "It's not necessary to hurt that woman." Well, he stood at the gate & I made speeches to the crowd & answered objections & won over many of the men, as well as some sailors . . .

March 11, 1919

Dear Girlie [Serena Kearns]:—

. . . Vida Milholland, sister of Inez Milholland, came down the center aisle at Carnegie Hall, all in white with gold crown carrying a beautiful lighted torch, with hall dark and spotlight only on her, then followed by women in costumes & flags of all nations whom she saluted, then followed lots of women in black with black veils over their heads, groping their way down the aisles & up to the platform pleading to "Liberty (Vida) & the free nations to liberate them—then followed a group of women in prison garb carrying the purple, white & yellow banners of the National Party . . .

"MEN TOO, LOVED FREEDOM" BY WILMER R. KEARNS (UNPUBLISHED NARRATIVE IN THE AUTHOR'S POSSESSION).

Never can it be said that the New York City police emergency squad was slow on the takeoff. In no time at all hardly, five a breast, fifty strong, they tore across town in March of 1919, broke ranks and lay siege on the headquarters of the National Woman's Party, 13 East 41st Street, where

Thursday morning.

Dearest:-

Thy letter received and read with much interest. Dandy. Thee
must behaving the time of thy life. Yes, the picture to which
thee refers is on the back page of the morning World. Why don't
you people make Wilson assert himself one way or the other; I
think I would be disgusted with that man.

Phoned Serena last night. Everything all right. Had cat to
the doctor last night. Also again I say everything all right.
Fine as silk. Yes, these are stirring times for thee. Enclosed
find your morning's mail. Will get to-day's Brooklyn papers
for thee, as requested. Will get some Worlds for thee. The
picture of thee might be plainer.

   MAKE HISTORY'

               Lovingly,

                  Wilmer.

Pardon typewriter.

Letter from Wilmer Kearns to Edna Kearns, circa 1914.

tranquility reigned supreme. Not their fault a slip occurred. Pity the poor
desk sergeant responsible for this wild goose chase.

The place was deserted, save for one lone occupant of the premises—
me, the mere husband of one of the pickets, looking for his wife Edna.

"Where's the riot?" the captain wanted to know.

"I wouldn't know," the mere man replied. It then went through his mind
that the women who were in distress and needed help, certainly they could
not rely on the police, for they, definitely were not on the women's side.

"What . . . the devil you say!" the captain bellowed. "You people are
the damndest . . ."

"You don't think well of us, do you?"

My question was ignored, with contempt. "Nothing we can break up
here, men, unless it's his neck!"

Strange how this mix up in location came about, but it did finally dawn on the captain that President Woodrow Wilson was in town and he gave his Reserves these orders: "Right about face, MARCH. Broadway and 39th Street and be quick about it."

This was the first clue the mere husband had as to his wife's whereabouts that night, having been detained at the office. Not finding her in their apartment, he naturally assumed she must have been held up at a committee meeting or something at their headquarters, as per usual. Himself an ardent male supporter of The Cause, yet, for one reason or another, this particular time she had not taken him into her confidence. Very much worried, he rushed over to Broadway . . .

WRITTEN 1960 BY WILMER R. KEARNS

Fellow-Americans:

May the validity of the ideas I have expressed contribute to better human relations, to the end that the goals of peace, universal freedom and the absence of poverty emerge triumphant in our time.[1]

Chapter 33

Pete Seeger's Aunt—Suffrage Activist Anita Pollitzer

"*C*ome on over and sit next to me," performer Pete Seeger called out as I searched for a seat at a Clearwater potluck held in the early 1980s in Beacon, New York, not far from the main office of the environmental organization's Hudson Valley office. I squeezed into a tiny space at the lunch table. No words came out when I opened my mouth. I was stumped about what to say to one of the nation's most beloved folksingers who was also a founder of the Hudson River Sloop Clearwater, a model throughout the US for environmental activism.

Then finally, I found my trembling voice.[1] "After you played a concert at my high school back during your blacklisting days, Pete, I turned into a teeny bopper fan of yours," I said. "The 'Kisses Sweeter than Wine' melody made my heart pound."

Pete Seeger on his way to perform at the Great Hudson River Revival, Croton Point, New York, circa 1982. Photo by Marguerite Kearns.

I expected Pete to laugh. Instead, he blushed. A heavy silence descended over the lunch table. Pete had interpreted my remark as idolizing him. I recovered, changing the subject. I was a Hudson River Sloop Clearwater employee back then, coeditor of the organization's membership publication. In the early days of my employment during the 1980s, I communicated with Pete through notes we exchanged in writing—messages appearing in my office mail box, such as, "Marguerite, can you cover this year's Clearwater pumpkin festival on Kingston's waterfront?"

"Sure, Pete," I would have replied.

The organization with a reputation as a "classroom of the waves" was represented in public by a replica sloop sailing the Hudson River since its 1969 launch. People from around the world recognized Clearwater's mission of welcoming folks of many backgrounds on board the boat for entertainment and education about the fragile river ecosystem.

Pete might not have mentioned his noteworthy aunt, Anita Pollitzer, who was prominent in the women's rights movement, if I hadn't made that faux pas. Prior to the potluck, Pete Seeger and I never had an occasion like this to visit—face to face and up close—until I placed my bowl of Stone Soup and salad on the potluck table next to him that day. Clearwater potlucks were a specialty of Toshi Seeger, Pete's filmmaker and environmental activist wife. Her signature Stone Soup started with a huge pot of water boiling on a stove or campfire. She dropped a clean stone into the water along with vegetables and spices contributed by volunteers. The pot's contents simmered for hours until delivered to the buffet table.

Pete set me up for a second helping of Stone Soup while we traded family stories. I told him about my grandparents Edna and Wilmer Kearns. He highlighted the votes for women activist in his family—Anita Pollitzer. In 1928 Anita married Pete's mother's brother, Elie Edson. The couple lived in New York City. Born and raised in South Carolina, Anita Pollitzer was a Southern gal who left her fingerprints on American history, even if a broader recognition of her life and contributions took decades to surface.

Anita made a mark in American art history in 1916 by introducing her friend Georgia O'Keeffe to well-known photographer Alfred Stieglitz. Anita and Georgia attended art school together in New York and corresponded over the years. This exchange of letters was preserved in *Lovingly, Georgia: The Complete Correspondence of Georgia O'Keeffe and Anita Pollitzer* (1990).

Pollitzer chose words and persuasion to fuel her social justice passion, much as O'Keeffe expressed herself in color, shapes, lines, and symbols on canvases. Although Anita was an extrovert, introverted Georgia relied on her friend Anita to send her news from Manhattan, especially after the artist moved to Northern New Mexico to paint.

Anita persuaded her friend to join the militant National Woman's Party. For the most part, Georgia stuck to her painting and Anita to her activism. As the years passed, Anita became more involved in the campaign to ratify the Nineteenth Amendment to the US Constitution. Georgia soaked up the solitude of the Southwest and made the region's dramatic flowers, sandstone cliffs, and high desert well known through her artistic expression. Alfred Stieglitz became O'Keeffe's mentor, husband, advocate, and business manager until his death in 1946. He spent considerable time and effort supporting American artists, and his wife in particular.

I told Pete Seeger about my grandmother Edna and her friend Bess, who chose not to marry, and how Edna Buckman married Wilmer Kearns and became an advocate for peace, justice, and women's rights. As it turned out, my grandmother Edna and Pete's aunt, Anita Pollitzer, knew each other. They both worked for the National Woman's Party based in Washington, DC. Anita was Gal Friday to leader Alice Paul while Edna served as Paul's congressional representative for the Nineteenth Amendment campaign on Long Island. Edna and Serena also picketed the White House with the National Woman's Party in 1917.

One of Edna's responsibilities on Long Island was to track down Theodore Roosevelt, who lived in Sag Harbor on the northern shore of Long Island. Her job was to bolster Roosevelt's support for women's voting rights. I didn't realize that Alice Paul and my grandmother Edna Kearns were close friends until I found a three-page single-spaced letter from Alice to Edna in my grandmother's papers. In the letter, Alice communicated with Edna in Quaker plain speech. Although the letter focused on the voting rights movement, Alice's references to "thee" was a significant element in their exchange.

I told Pete Seeger about the 1913 suffrage parade when Edna Kearns met Alice Paul in the parade formation. He listened intently when I spoke about my grandfather, Wilmer, one of many procession participants convinced there would be a "riot" on that freezing afternoon of March 1913 when women staged the first protest in the nation's capital. After refreshing the salad on my plate, Pete Seeger handed me a glass filled with ice and fruit juice. I wondered what stories Pete held close to his chest. Around Clearwater headquarters, I'd heard that not only had Pete been blacklisted professionally during the Senator Joe McCarthy era, but one branch of his family could be traced back to the *Mayflower*. Gossip or fact? I had no idea.

"Just sit down and get on with drafting your grandparents' story," Pete advised me. He told me about publishing projects he'd faced. Once his wife Toshi insisted he check into a hotel and stay in his room, order room service, and get something down on paper about his life that could be later revised or edited. Pete Seeger told me more about how his aunt Anita played an essential role in the process of ratifying the Nineteenth Amendment in 1920. This accomplishment was generally overshadowed by her involvement in Georgia O'Keeffe's artistic career.

According to Pete Seeger's version of the story, his aunt Anita "clinched the deciding vote in Tennessee in 1920," a claim he put in writing for me years later. If true, this was no small feat. Pete told me that this occurred during the well-publicized showdown associated with the Nineteenth Amendment's ratification during the summer of 1920. Tennessee stood to become the thirty-sixth and final state to ratify the constitutional amendment guaranteeing US women the right to vote.

Pete claimed his aunt Anita had dinner with twenty-four-year-old state legislator Harry T. Burn the evening before the Tennessee legislature's final vote. No record was ever made of what transpired that evening. However, this incident was when Anita allegedly convinced Harry to change his position from "no" on women's voting rights to "yes."

A widely circulated version of the tale told today features Harry Burn switching his vote after receiving a letter from his mother encouraging him to support the suffrage amendment's ratification. Many commentators and historians cite the message from Phoebe Ensminger Burn to her son as the reason why Harry finally threw his weight behind the federal amendment. Phoebe Burn's frequently quoted letter, now preserved in a Tennessee library, stated in part, "Hurrah and vote for suffrage . . . Don't forget to be a good boy and help Mrs. Catt put the 'rat' in ratification."

This letter from Harry's mother was only part of the story, according to Pete Seeger. He described Anita Pollitzer as a "firecracker" with a record of convincing many to support the federal suffrage amendment. Anita may have been short in stature, but she was personally powerful and an individual of stature highly successful in any task to which she was assigned.

Anita Pollitzer rose in the National Woman's Party ranks to become an organizer nationwide, as well as someone party head Alice Paul relied on as a close aide and adviser. Paul recruited Pollitzer to carry out special missions, especially her assignment to Nashville for the ratification vote the summer of 1920. Tennessee's elected officials couldn't have predicted the circus Nashville would turn into after a wide range of individuals and organizations showed up to either support or defeat ratification during the blistering summer heat.

The battle between those for and against ratification came to be referred to as the "War of the Roses" when suffrage opponents wore red roses and suffrage advocates displayed yellow roses. Representatives of alcohol producers and other business interests spent money lavishly in order to defeat the entry of women into politics. They were convinced that women voting would upset the social and political status quo. Powerful opponents were reportedly lurking in hotels and government buildings, tapping phones and eavesdropping in public spaces during the weeks prior to the state legislative vote. Both radical and mainstream suffrage groups sent organizers and activists to Tennessee from across the nation. A predicted tie in the vote brought Nashville to a boiling point.

From her office in Washington, Alice Paul kept in touch with Anita Pollitzer and other National Woman's Party organizers on the Tennessee front lines. Suffrage leader Carrie Chapman Catt and her crack lobbyists swung into action. They augmented Tennessee's own cadre of suffrage activists on the state and local levels. They filled legislative galleries and followed elected officials everywhere, including to and from their homes. It was said that Nashville reeled from one end to the other as advocates and opponents cornered anyone even remotely associated with the ratification process to inquire about their voting preferences.

Aware of the importance of breaking the vote deadlock, Anita Pollitzer took on the challenge of lobbying state legislator Harry Burn from McMinn County. His single vote in favor of votes for women broke the stalemate and opened the door for others supporting the suffrage amendment's ratification. Even into his old age during the 1970s, Burn was still controversial and visible among his former constituents and political associates. He claimed his mother's letter influenced his support of American women voting.

Harry Burn never publicly mentioned Pete Seeger's family narrative about dinner with Anita the evening before the ratification vote. However, the expression on Harry and Anita's faces as they shook hands in a vintage photo from 1920 lends substance to Pete's claim. It's possible that when Pete's aunt and Harry's mother leaned on him during the War of the Roses in Nashville, Harry knew what he should do.

The vote Harry Burn cast for women's suffrage, against the advice of his legislative superiors and pressure from every side, demonstrated that he had the same kind of courage and vision that defined other activists, including the Kearns family members and Pete Seeger's aunt, Anita Pollitzer. They set aside their regular lives and dedicated themselves to years in the service of winning equal rights.

Pete Seeger performed a song he wrote that I thought about whenever scolding myself for not yet completing the draft of a manuscript about my grandparents. In the song, "Turn! Turn! Turn!" based on Ecclesiastes 3: 1 from the Bible, Seeger tells his audiences that there is "a season" or a "time" for everything.

Anita Pollitzer and Harry Burn (*center, both wearing black*) after the 1920 ratification vote in Nashville. Photo courtesy of National Woman's Party at Belmont-Paul Women's Equality National Monument.

Chapter 34

Inez Milholland—US Suffrage Martyr

"Do you mind sharing a table with these nice folks from Florida? Or would you rather wait?" the host asked. I stood in line to be served at a thruway restaurant on my way driving from New York to Pennsylvania to visit my grandfather Wilmer. I noted my upcoming February birthday on the calendar at home and rushed to finish editing a last-minute article before leaving home during the late winter months of 1971. The highway restaurant was packed at one of those cookie-cutter establishments with contracts from the state thruway authority to serve bland and standard American food.

"I welcome some company at a table if they're okay with it," I said. I planned on a bowl of soup and something light to eat before continuing on the road. "In and out," I said silently to myself. "If I have to share a table, I can sit down and rest. I might even meet someone interesting."

"There's a nice couple from Florida over there, waiting," the host reported. They appeared to be folks with agreeable personalities. I wouldn't be there long. The man from Florida, with brown mustache fuzz directly under his nose, shifted from left to right. He used a gold hanky, lightly patted his neck, folded the cloth, and placed it back into his shirt pocket.

"I'm a housewife and grandmother from Sarasota," Mrs. Florida said, apparently pleased with the idea of sharing a table. "My husband manages an auto parts store. Where do you live?"

"Woodstock, the town. It's different from the 1969 music festival with the same name," I said in an attempt to put the context of location to rest.

"Sure, we've heard of Woodstock in the Catskill Mountains. Hasn't everyone?" she continued. "My niece and nephew went to the Woodstock Festival. Do you mind giving travel tips to hubby and me? Like where to go, eat, and shop when we drive by the town on our way to Montreal. We're off to see my Aunt Charlotte and Uncle Bob."

"Stop by Duey's coffee shop on Mill Hill Road," I suggested. "It's the greasy spoon where Woodstockers binge on hamburgers and French fries. You'll get an eye and ear full about the town there."

We studied the menu at our assigned table as I slipped off my winter coat, revealing my Indian embroidered shirt, bellbottom pants, and a necklace of bright beads and feathers to complement my mop of dark hair.

"Were *you* at The Festival?" Mr. Florida asked.

I wished I'd kept on my coat so my clothes wouldn't require me explaining that I'd moved to Woodstock in Ulster County not long after the 1969 famous music festival. During the years following the event, festival pilgrims wandered around the community hoping to run into musician Bob Dylan. He wasn't on the performer lineup, but he'd lived in the town of Woodstock once. I ordered soup of the day—cream of tomato—while waiting for another predictable question served with rolls and butter. Mrs. Florida's bright red flowered Hawaiian beach shirt attracted attention on this overcast day. Her husband wore the same design in gold.

Mr. and Mrs. Florida might take my advice and order a meal at Duey's in Woodstock. Unless they stayed for several days though, they'd miss witnessing events reflecting the local experimentation with art, music, meditation, fasting, chanting, and long hikes into the Catskill Mountain wilderness. They might not appreciate the wonder of predictable communal awakenings that left a tingling at the base of my spine. Some locals referred to the town of Woodstock as "magical." I didn't, but I acknowledged that there was something special about the community.

"Is it true Woodstock runs on slow because so many folks are getting high?" Mr. Florida persisted. I inhaled deeply and repeated to both Mr. and Mrs. what I'd explained to many others: "The artists moved in at the turn of the twentieth century to live side by side with the Dutch descendants who'd been there for generations. Native peoples were driven West. And then musicians moved to Woodstock in the nineteen sixties." I didn't respond to the question posed. I was in no mood to discuss getting high.

"And what do you do there to earn a living?" Mr. Florida continued.

"I work for the weekly newspaper—you know, reporting and editorial work."

"I didn't know they allowed women in news rooms."

"They do now."

"Are you on assignment?"

"I'm headed to Philadelphia to work on writing a family saga. My Quaker grandfather is up in years. My grandmother died in 1934. Both worked on women's voting rights campaigns from 1910 to 1920 on Long Island and in New York City."

"Oh, yes. Quakers—the ones who eat oatmeal, right?"

"No more than other Americans who love chocolate chip and oatmeal cookies."

I stopped there. Even though the 1969 Woodstock Festival left repercussions for decades after, new perspectives in art, literature, music, and science swept through the town when I started working for the first issue of *Woodstock Times* in 1972. I wrote about local affairs from my swivel chair at the newspaper office. Instead of squeezing into roles no longer appropriate in a fast-changing world, I joined with others to expand our perspectives, whether it included getting high or not. We discussed new cognitive patterns, inner and outer journeys, spirituality, plus visions in the dream world and ordinary reality.

I thought about this as Mr. and Mrs. Florida waited for me to reveal something personal about myself. What should strangers say to each other at a highway restaurant? I wouldn't have revealed my insecurities to them about writing well enough to complete the story about my activist grandparents. I might have told them the family legend of the Edgar Allan Poe chairs in my grandfather's living room that he claimed once belonged to the writer. I could mention to the Florida couple what I called the Soapbox Generation, with activists like my late grandmother Edna who stood on portable platforms—soapboxes—for spontaneous street speeches about voting rights and equality between the genders.

"I had the impression women could vote before 1920," Mr. Florida added to the conversation.

"A few could—like in New York State after 1917, as well as out West where Wyoming was the first state to hand women the ballot in 1869. Utah and Washington followed. 'Suffrage,' they called it. The right to vote," I told Mr. Florida in a mini-lecture.

"I wish you'd use another word than suffrage. It's hard to remember," Mr. Florida continued. "Gives the impression of being negative—you know—like suffering."

I sipped my glass of ice water slowly.

"And suffrage also strikes me as boring," Mr. Florida added. "No offense intended."

"The act of voting may strike you as dull, but it wasn't for American women who had doors to polling places slammed in their faces," I replied.

"You sure have a bee in your bonnet, don't you? Come on. This business is old hat because women can vote now," Mr. Florida said. "How's your chicken noodle soup, darling?"

"Tastes like it's fresh out of a can, hon," Mrs. Florida replied. She glanced around the dining room, as if expecting someone to join us. She waved to the server to bring us more paper napkins while I glanced out a restaurant window to track the progress of an incoming winter storm.

"The only reality is the present," Mr. Florida added. "Isn't that what you're doing? Following a trail of ghosts? Campaigning for women voting is over and done with. Face it. Why obsess over the past?" He clicked his tongue as if gearing up for an argument. I didn't respond. Mrs. Florida blew her nose.

"How can you stand this miserable weather?" Mrs. Florida asked me when slipping a sweater over her red Hawaiian beach shirt.

"Most everyone drives south during the winter months, in the direction of Florida—not north. On your way to Canada though, stop off in the town of Lewis, not far from Plattsburgh. Visit Inez Milholland's grave," I suggested.

"Who's Inez Milholland?" Mrs. Florida asked me.

"Our US suffrage martyr who died for women's voting rights in 1916."

"Never heard of her," Mr. Florida responded.

"People across the country adored Inez. My grandmother Edna worked with Inez on women's rights issues in New York State."

"I forgot to order ice cream with my apple pie," Mr. Florida interrupted. I stayed on topic by answering Mrs. Florida's questions. She moved closer to my chair to hear me explain more about Inez, who was born in Brooklyn before her family moved to Lewis, a community up north within New York's Adirondack Mountain region.

Inez Milholland at the head of the votes for women parade in Washington, DC, March 1913. Library of Congress.

"Many travelers make pilgrimages to Inez's grave," I added. "She carved out a special place in the hearts of Americans."

"Then how come we never heard of her?" Mr. Florida responded.

The topic of women's rights activism could be complicated. It wasn't like me to squeeze Inez Milholland into a conversation with strangers. But I figured that Mrs. Florida might enjoy hearing about these heroic figures from the annals of American history. The eyes of many people glazed over when I mentioned the word "suffrage." I could tell he'd never heard of suffrage or voting rights. If I persisted, I might be able to interest Mrs. Florida in Inez because of her high public profile. She'd been denied admission to law school because of her gender. Eventually she graduated from the law program at New York University.

I hurried to finish eating a slice of bread and pointed out how Inez had been headlined in newspapers across the nation during her lifetime from 1886 to 1916 because of her commitment to women's rights. Inez was distinctive because of her long curly hair, her engaging style, and her commitment to the cause. A popular athlete and all-around student at Vassar College in the Hudson Valley, where she earned an undergraduate degree, she died at age thirty when on a speaking tour of the West on behalf of women's voting rights. When riding a horse and leading parades, Inez reminded many people of Joan of Arc.

"Are your aunt and uncle expecting you on a certain day? If not, you'll have a great story to tell if you drive over to Lewis, New York, to see Milholland's grave," I suggested.

I spent the next few minutes telling Mr. and Mrs. Florida about Inez making history when riding her horse at the front of the 1913 suffrage parade in Washington, DC. Observers on the parade route yelled insulting remarks and assaulted marchers. My grandfather Wilmer was in line with the men's division. My grandmother Edna and my mother's older sister, Serena, marched in the Quaker division.

"You're beating a *dead* horse with that Inez lady," Mr. Florida announced.

"Maybe. But I don't think so," I replied, pulling a photo of Inez out of my pocketbook that I'd stored away to show Granddaddy. "Get a load of this."

"Don't tell me Inez was a rich kid who rode horses as a hobby," Mrs. Florida said when waving for a server to fill her water glass.

"When her grandfather got here from Ireland, he didn't have two nickels to rub together. Her own father made lots of money and then lost it all."

"Good grief," Mr. Florida responded. "Can't we talk about something else?"

I spoke quickly to wrap up the tale, describing Inez Milholland's collapse on a lecture platform in Los Angeles in 1916. Supporters transported her to a hospital where she succumbed to pernicious anemia. Her alleged last words on the lecture tour turned into a national rallying cry: "Mr. President, how long must women wait for liberty?"

Mr. Florida's ambivalence wasn't new to me. When I started asking questions about the early women's rights movement, it's possible that no one in my elementary school other than me, had ever heard the word "suffrage."

Mrs. Florida was relieved when our servings of apple pie arrived. I didn't elaborate about the challenges women faced from 1848 to 1920 when persuading men voters on local, state, and national levels to support voting rights for women. I figured that I didn't have the energy to persist.

"I'll get some folks together for a program at my women's church group. Do you ever visit Sarasota?" Mrs. Florida suggested. "My ladies would love to hear about Inez and your grandparents."

Mr. Florida sensed me staring at him. The bored and cynical expression on his face evaporated. He shifted to his usual "good husband and partner" persona. I checked out the restaurant window to monitor the progress of the storm as he glanced away. The corner of his mouth twitched as the scent of my cream of tomato soup and slice of apple pie merged with the aroma of the cheeseburger, potato chips, and dill pickle on his plate. I sighed and lamented silently to myself: "I should have settled for takeout."

My eyes watered, even though peace at the restaurant table had been restored. I worried about the blizzard moving into the Hudson Valley and questioned if I'd be able to make it from the New Jersey Turnpike to the bridge crossing the Delaware River that led to the Philadelphia area. I trembled at the sound of tires spinning on the outside frozen restaurant parking lot surface, wishing I were instead stepping gingerly on pine needles and branches in my Woodstock backyard. The thumping of my own heart took over in volume from what felt like a descent into a Florida swamp to wrestle with alligators.

Outside, snow flurries rapidly transitioned into a heavy snowfall. When I asked the server for my check, she told me about ice accumulating on regional highway surfaces. The storm would result in delays and school closings from the town of Hudson, south to the city of Newburgh. It made sense to postpone the trip to Philadelphia to visit Granddaddy and head home.

On the state thruway north, I skidded on icy road surfaces. The streets of Woodstock were deserted as I drove up Mill Hill Road. My shoulders relaxed after realizing I'd won over Mrs. Florida by telling her about Inez Milholland. I still had to convince two hundred million other Americans about the significance of generations of American women putting themselves on the line for voting rights. When I was young, the story of the early women's rights movement wasn't presented to us students learning about US history. We did, however, learn about George Washington's cherry tree and Abraham Lincoln's insistence on returning the correct change.

Why had awareness of early women's rights movement activists disappeared from the nation's collective memory? How could I have allowed women's rights movement activities to pass by me without becoming more involved after reaching my twenties? I could have done more. Why didn't the ballot provide US women with the political power they believed would sweep the nation after the ratification of the Nineteenth Amendment to the US Constitution? Why didn't more women run for political office? Where did I fit in the ongoing human rights struggles around the world? How could I celebrate the accomplishment of winning the franchise by my grandparents' generation and yet be so cynical and distrustful of much associated with partisan electoral politics in contemporary times?

"Speak to me, Grandmother Edna," I said out loud, but only the dull banging of my Studebaker's frozen windshield wipers replied. My teeth chattered. I barely got my Studebaker's tires pointed into the direction of my driveway. At home, I dragged out my journal and jotted notes about Mr. and Mrs. Florida before collapsing for a nap on the living room couch.

"I should give Mr. Florida the benefit of the doubt," I said to myself after loading more wood into the living room's Franklin stove.

I expected Granddaddy to tell me not to give up, to hang on, during our next visit. He'd predict that I'd wake up one morning and discover more layers of freedom struggles in a rapidly changing world. It was just like my grandfather to suggest that someday Americans would expect women to play a decisive role in the affairs of the nation. He was convinced that men would finally realize that women were more interested in becoming equal partners than in reversing the power equation. Granddaddy was of the opinion that people all over the world would become increasingly impatient with hierarchies, power struggles, and social injustices.

I wasn't clear about my place in history. Like many others in the Woodstock Nation, I gravitated toward practical solutions before committing myself to address limited reforms. I witnessed too many of the same old gender power struggles while the inevitable name calling and accusations associated with gender, class, race, and more continued.

"Remember what Edna wrote in one of her newspaper columns about how 'it is glorious to stand up for truth, even if one does suffer unjustly,'" my grandfather mentioned on my next trip to visit him in Pennsylvania when we spoke for hours.

"What did Inez Milholland tell audiences during her lecture tour before she passed into history?" I asked.

Granddaddy opened a file on his bookshelf to find a quote he'd saved.

"Liberty must be fought for. And women of the nation . . . This is the time to demonstrate our sisterhood, our spirit, our blithe courage, and our will."

I held my breath.

"Edna wrote in one speech that the day would arrive, finally, when everyone would know firsthand 'the peaceful feeling that comes when doing right,'" Granddaddy added.

"Oh," I said, in my seasoned and objective newspaper voice. "I hope so."

Chapter 35

The Struggle Continues

*A*fter my mother called to tell me about Granddaddy's death in 1972, I drove immediately to a Woodstock café. Customers crowded me from all sides. I missed the sooty aroma of Granddaddy's cigar stub grown stale in his kitchen air overnight. I remembered the musty smell of old yellowed newspaper clippings about the Spirit of 1776 wagon pasted onto Edna's scrapbook pages.

I surveyed the Woodstock café and couldn't recognize any one who would have noticed the grooves around both sides of my mouth deepening and my brows pressing together in grief. I cringed when a man at the next table blew cigarette smoke into my face. I could complain to management, but that wouldn't help. The irritation had more to do with the realization that I'd have to face writing about the early women's rights movement without Granddaddy's help. My mother was the only one left in my immediate sphere who'd been close to Edna.

"I take medication for my mental problems," the café server told a nearby patron. "It's a preexisting condition. I don't qualify for most medical insurance." The server placed her hands on her hips, with little awareness of others in close proximity.

"Plan A with dental is more than I can afford," she added. "Classic Margherita pizza is our special tonight. All you can eat."

The juicer motor screamed as raw carrots slid toward the graters. The café menu offered ten varieties of pasta dishes. Servers carried trays of red and white wine in wide thin-stemmed glasses. A cross section of locals crammed the bar area, in addition to a sprinkling of tourists eager to find out more about the residents of Woodstock. The longer I stayed, the more the café filled with loud talk and laughter. The sun disappeared from view on the border of the thick Catskill Mountain forest outside. After the wind died down, I drove home.

My kitchen absorbed the cool light of a full moon, its surface enormous and loaded with pockmarks. I imagined my own face staring down at me from above, first as a sixth grader, and then as an adult. I remembered how Granddaddy's face perked up when I first told him I'd be moving to Woodstock from the Southwest in 1971.

"Artists and visionaries live in Woodstock," he mused, "like Elbert Hubbard and his cronies up in Roycroft near Buffalo."

"Right."

I bit the rough edge of my right hand's thumbnail. I couldn't come to terms with my inability to complete the story of my grandparents. I'd learned a great deal about my family, my grandfather, my parents, and myself. But I'd barely scratched the surface of Edna. I'd followed her around for years, collected and read her newspaper columns, and appreciated the glow of her face in photos. I marveled over her raw spirit, what she did and where she went. But I didn't know her, really, except when reading her written words. One tender letter to Granddaddy penned on the eve of one of her hospitalizations reminded him of how he'd been responsive to her goal of becoming a women's rights activist. Then she elaborated on who qualified to inherit the living room rug. She survived the surgery even if the nature of it remained a mystery to me.

The stages of grief, as laid out by Swiss-American psychiatrist Elisabeth Kübler-Ross, surfaced in my awareness. I recognized denial, and the foolish notion that Granddaddy would always be "there" for me. Anger bubbled up within for not anticipating that my writing might continue as unfinished. Bargaining represented another phase of the stages of sadness. Unless I worked with my mother to continue documenting our family history, the drama of Wilmer and Edna wouldn't manifest by itself. Depression came next. I worked late at the Woodstock newspaper so I could return home and fall into bed and not think about this crisis of loss. Acceptance represented a final stage. I needed almost a year to bounce back after accepting that my grandfather had left me behind.

What about the old suffrage wagon stored in Granddaddy's garage? The clandestine relationship between Charles and Angela that forced itself out into the open at Wilmer and Edna's 1904 wedding? The rumor my mother heard that Bess married late in life? Was it true? And what was the significance of Edna and Serena picketing the White House in 1917, carrying a sign appealing to the US president, Woodrow Wilson, for his support of women's voting rights?

Was our family story worth telling? Perhaps it was only an article and not a book. The drama included my mother following in Edna's footsteps during the 1960s when holding a picket sign to protest nuclear testing with her activist group, Women Strike for Peace. She participated in a family tradition of protest. So did I. Edna's involvement in the peace movement started well before 1917 when the US declared war on Germany. She agreed with suffrage leader Alice Paul that campaigning for women's rights should not be laid aside, even during wartime. Edna continued her involvement in groups supporting Quaker testimonies, women's and social issues. Edna, Wilmer, and Serena moved from New York State back to the Philadelphia area in 1920 when Edna was pregnant with my mother. They took the Spirit of 1776 wagon to Pennsylvania with them.

The governor of Pennsylvania appointed Edna to a commission supporting aid to dependent children. Serena Kearns, my aunt, spent her working years employed as a social worker. During the national bicentennial celebration, she collaborated with my grandfather to write a short article about Edna published in a booklet of prominent local women.

Edna and Serena Kearns picketing the White House for women's voting rights, 1917.

At home in Woodstock during the 1970s, I pressed my nose against the living room window glass in the direction of Tinker Street and counted the number of pickup trucks passing by. The bed springs creaked. The floorboards groaned. Windows rattled when Trailways buses roared down Woodstock's main street toward Bearsville, Mount Tremper, and Phoenicia. I still hadn't come to terms with the memoir and family history challenge before me. The past wasn't a separate realm of its own, but an amorphous beast flowing around me, lifting me in and out of the present and crossing borders of time and space.

I sensed a hand reaching out to me.

"Edna?" I asked out loud. "Dearie?"

I settled on the lower step of the staircase headed upstairs and heard a tree limb crack in the back yard. I lifted my head in the direction of where I imagined Edna. I sensed her squeezing my hand as if to say, "I loved Wilmer too. He was a good man, my best friend. Now we are together again."

Granddaddy hadn't left me. Nor had she. They had passed into me. I felt it, but this personal experience didn't constitute proof of anything. Nor did my mother's claim that I was, to her, a replica of my grandmother and how she insisted on writing newspaper articles. This didn't translate to Edna's soul passing into me. I reflected on the many occasions when I'd chased after facts, memories, and stories, only to reach the conclusion that I'd been born too late. I'd simply been a visitor from a distance, a stranger in a stage set of the early women's rights movement. And what had been accomplished after the activist torch was passed from my grandparents to my mother's generation and then to mine?

My grandmother's friend Bess wouldn't have been surprised at the glacial pace of social change. She would have repeated her previous prediction that the transformation of American culture wouldn't be significantly different after women voted in 1920. She may have continued insisting that the hierarchy of male privilege had to be disrupted or destroyed. Edna would have been disappointed at the gradual decline in Quaker membership and how the theological divisions among Quakers required substantial healing. And Wilmer wouldn't have liked hearing about my researched revelations and facts about the legendary tale of Edgar Allan Poe and his alleged chairs displayed in his living room.

At the Woodstock Library I discovered Poe's collected writings. I entertained myself by reading the usual poems, including "The Raven," "Lenore," and "Anabelle Lee," followed by several short stories. Three tales starred Poe's detective Dupin in Paris. I stood frozen in a library aisle after spotting an essay he published in May 1840, "The Philosophy of Furniture," written when Poe lived in Philadelphia, a selection featured in *Burton's Gentleman's Magazine*.

There it was, the evidence I'd been searching for, an account in Poe's own words expressing the author's preference for certain types of chairs—the seating best adapted to a home setting. The library cleared as I read to the essay's conclusion and realized that Poe depended on satire and parody to air the subject I desperately needed to find out about. He laid out his style choices for parlor chairs and furniture, expressed deadpan in the writer's exaggerated and highly opinionated style.

"There is reason, it is said, in the roasting of eggs, and there is philosophy in furniture," Poe stated in the essay's first paragraph. He continued writing seriously until throwing in one statement or another to reinforce the essay's underlying satiric sentiment. Poe resumed his argument in an amusing professorial tongue-in-cheek style: "The Dutch have merely a vague idea that a curtain is not a cabbage." Poe claimed furniture arrangement reflected emotional and intellectual states. Such a thought would have never occurred to my grandfather.

Poe didn't spare the reader about furniture styles then in vogue. He stomped his feet. He scorched his literary enemies by mentioning their names. He made his case clear. Poe would have hated the chairs in Granddaddy's living room. And in his distinct style, Poe made sure his words galloped from the page. I hoped that future scholars wouldn't question my conclusion. Poe never sat in the chairs my grandfather called the Edgar Allan Poe chairs.

I opened one of my old notebooks, and there was my written account of a story my mother told me. I'd kept myself from overreacting when she first told me about my own baby book. The memory of her telling me this tale lingered, and suddenly it popped to the surface of my awareness. When Wilma spoke about my own baby book, she described how as a teenager she'd packed for attending the Quaker boarding school after Edna died.

As a child, my mother said she once climbed to the top shelf of Edna's bedroom closet, searching for Valentine's Day chocolates or a preview of the next holiday gift exchange. And there it was: an empty baby book. Were my grandparents planning for another infant after my mother's birth? I didn't know. Nor did my mother. Who was the baby book meant for? Before leaving home after Edna's death, she lifted the baby book from the high shelf and wrapped it in her sweatshirt. Then the bank foreclosed on the family home, Echo Dale. Wilma told me she felt alone and abandoned, except for the baby book she carried, saved for her first child—me. She speculated years later that Edna had set aside the baby book for me.

I opened the baby book recording my birth, my first steps and words. I had proof of so much else, including the realization that our family legends hadn't resulted in fame, recognition, or extra cash. The boxes of photos, documents, and memorabilia included stacks of papers with Edna's faded handwriting and writings about the struggle for women's rights. During my childhood I sensed Edna following me, staring over my shoulder, pointing me in various directions. I couldn't have gained a perspective on my life if my grandparents hadn't been part of it. What if others labeled me as sentimental? Relatives and my neighbors in Woodstock might remark that I'd acquired a new roommate—my grandmother's ghost. I could no longer concern myself with uncovering new notes for Edna's speeches about women's equality until I'd written the last words of the story about myself, my mother, Wilmer and Edna.

I'd spent years searching for evidence that my grandmother cared about me, that she believed that her years of intense work in the early women's rights movement should be passed on to future generations. For so long, my baby book represented something old-fashioned, a relic of the Edwardian era, something I once believed my mother had purchased at a yard sale. But instead, Edna had purchased and saved another baby book, as if she suspected something more.

And why did this matter? I didn't have all the answers to my family's mysteries. Our family history had too often stressed an underlying theme of "almost," but not quite. As a family, we were caretakers of a horse-drawn wagon General George Washington never used to inspect his troops. As a woman in my late twenties, I moved to the Hudson Valley after the famous 1969 music festival, rather than before it. And I was

Marguerite, as an infant, 1943.

definitely the reporter who told countless pilgrims to Ulster County that the Festival wasn't held in the town of Woodstock itself, but instead about fifty miles away in the Catskill Mountains on a dairy farm in the town of Bethel of Sullivan County. So many almosts, so many might-have-beens.

I moved to New Mexico from Woodstock in 1992 after my life radically changed following a relationship breakup. I've lived in the Southwest since, working on the Wilmer and Edna story in phases. I was revising a draft of the memoir and family history when I dressed for the women's march scheduled in Santa Fe during January of 2019. I held high a poster-size image of Wilmer, Edna, and little Serena Kearns marching north from New York City in a women's rights parade toward the state capital of Albany.

Edna, Wilmer, and Serena set off with activist Rosalie Jones and others during the first week in January of 1914. To the right in the photo, Granddaddy walked with a cane and wore a dark hat. Serena and Edna marched to his left, not far from an American flag. I carried this reproduced image stretching from my neck to my waist and headed to the historic Santa Fe plaza to show off my family. I wanted to

March from New York City to Albany, January 1914. The Kearns family is near the flag, to the right. Bain Collection, Library of Congress.

demonstrate that Americans had been marching in support of women's rights for more than a hundred years. The women of this nation, I believed, were too stubborn to quit.

I adjusted my eyes to the shifting light on the plaza platform. There, those with activist credentials waited next to politicians to greet the crowd on a women's march in Santa Fe. It represented another demonstration of support for equality and civil rights, joining other women's marches held in other locations throughout the state and nation.

Participants in the 2019 Santa Fe women's march lined up on the sidewalk outside the state capitol building to gather for the event. They carried provocative signs and messages. Men marched too, like in 1914, with family members and others joining the procession to represent churches, places of employment, and numerous organizations. Edna, Wilmer, and Serena accompanied me on this round, virtually. They marched in both 1914 and 2019. I was a reminder that the ground on which they walked had also been covered by prior generations expressing similar concerns. I asked how long women in the US and around the world would continue to march. How much longer—150 or 200 years? How long would the resistance to equality continue? How much longer would more than half of the US population continue to allow toxic fallout to be tossed into their faces and across their paths?

Marguerite, self-portrait, 2015, holding a 1921 image of her mother, Wilma, as a baby (*far right*), her grandmother Edna (*middle*), and her step-great-great-great-"grandmother" Mary Ann Buckman (*far left*). Four generations of women in one family.

The air of Santa Fe's plaza filled with the scent of pinon wood burning in fireplaces close by and across the city. It was the kind of January morning best spent curled up in bed, not circling the plaza with my feet tapping to drumming and chanting.

"Will this never end?" I asked myself and no one in particular. I held tight to my optimism. "It's another day in the front lines of social change," I told those marching beside me. After the introductory speeches were delivered at the grandstand, I adjusted my floppy hat, buttoned my coat, and marched in a circle around the plaza once more before the spell of the moment could be broken.

The chairs bearing Edgar Allan Poe's name are stacked in my storage unit in Santa Fe. Mice have chewed the seats and the chair legs wobble. The wood frames are pale and fragile showing the wear and tear of decades. I am completing the telling of the story about my grandparents' contributions to the service of expanding the rights and participation of women and others in politics and the mainstream culture.

Edna and Wilmer Kearns, circa 1919.

Although some folks in previous years have dismissed the early women's voting rights movement, it has been studied enough by historians to ensure its place in history. The early women's rights movement is now considered a major milestone in social and political history, an unfinished revolution continuing into the twenty-first century and beyond.

Activists from my grandparents' generation eliminated numerous barriers in their journey toward freedom. I'm sure Wilmer and Edna would have said: "Protest is patriotic" and "a luta continua." The struggle continues, grounded for me in the story of my grandparents and their spirits filtering through the generations as more windows and doors are opened wide to equality and freedom:

> All the great issues of life have been the outcome of "small things" . . . All along our way little openings occur, and to be faithful to our higher natures, a desire will arrive in our hearts for a reaching out to others . . .

Edna Buckman Kearns

In this ongoing effort toward justice and freedom, I no longer stand alone.

Acknowledgments

An earlier version of chapter 29, "The Wagon in Woodstock," was published in *Woodstock Times* on March 8, 2017, entitled "Woodstock's Wagon Women." An earlier version of chapter 31, "One Woman per Century," was published in *Woodstock Times* on July 18, 2017. An earlier version of chapter 33, "Pete Seeger's Aunt—Suffragist Anita Pollitzer," was published by *Woodstock Times* on August 25, 2017. An earlier version of chapter 30 was published in *New York Archives* in the fall of 2013.

Writing a memoir and family history required years of commitment, as well as an enormous amount of effort. Without my grandfather, Wilmer Rhamstine Kearns, and my mother, Wilma Buckman Kearns (Culp), this work would not have been possible.

I appreciate the valuable contributions of Dr. Susan Goodier for her research and writing about Edna B. Kearns, as well as her friendship, direction, and encouragement in the indexing of the Buckman-Kearns archival collection during 2010.

My niece Tara Bloyd and sister Winnie Culp provided considerable ongoing editorial support over decades. As readers, they have kept me focused throughout many drafts and revisions. Working with Olivia Twine of Woodstock, New York, has been an essential part of producing this memoir and family history in terms of her research and editorial support.

A list of those who have supported me on this journey is longer than I could ever hope to assemble. I must express my appreciation to a friend, writer, and former journalism colleague, Frank Yacenda. In the spring of 2019 he stepped forward during a phase of editing the manuscript. His writing background, perceptive edits, suggestions, and ongoing support were invaluable.

Over the past decade there has been an outpouring of volunteer efforts by thousands of US volunteers determined to build support for the 2020 centennial of the Nineteenth Amendment to the US Constitution in the US, as well as the 2017 suffrage observances of one hundred years of women voting in New York State. This effort has contributed to a more complete understanding of the early US women's rights movement and has included documentaries, panel discussions, conferences, books, educational materials, research, an activist database, and more, funded by individuals, and public and private sources.

The larger Kearns family group, circa 1922–1924, with Wilmer, young daughter Wilma, and Edna Buckman Kearns at the left near the top of the image. Serena Kearns is in the second row to the left of her paternal grandfather John P. Kearns.

The following organizations and individuals have been generous with their encouragement and participation in supporting the continuing exhibition of the Spirit of 1776 suffrage wagon at the New York State Museum, and the sharing of an enormous amount of support work involved in such an endeavor.

Organizations and institutions providing valuable input and support include the New York State Museum, SUNY Press, National Women's History Alliance, Buckman Family Reunion, Santa Fe Library (Interlibrary Loan), Ulster Publishing, the Kolb-Kulp-Culp Family Association, Plymouth Monthly Meeting (PA), Penington Friends House, Puffin Foundation, Pendle Hill (a Quaker study, retreat, and conference center), State

Museum of Pennsylvania, Collected Works of Santa Fe (NM), Suffolk County Historical Society, Friends Historical Library, League of Women Voters of New York State and New Mexico, Española Public Library, Abiquiú Public Library, Santa Fe Community College, Northern New Mexico College, Mertz Library of New York Botanical Garden, the Stephen Watts Kearny DAR chapter, Historical Society of Woodstock, Free Library of Philadelphia, Heritage Museum of Orange County (California), the Office of New York State Governor Andrew Cuomo, *Santa Fe Literary Review*, Historical Society of Woodstock, *Friends Journal, Western Friend*, William G. Pomeroy Foundation, public radio KSFR, New York State Lieutenant Governor Kathy Hochul, Peirce College, NEA-NM, Turning Point Suffragist Memorial, Quaker House (Santa Fe, NM), Long Island Woman Suffrage Association, public radio WAMC, Renesan Institute for Lifelong Learning, Long Island Museum, the Roaming Writers, National Votes for Women Trail, New York Cultural Heritage Tourism Network, the Woodstock Byrdcliffe Guild, Women's Vote Centennial Initiative, Christiansen Memorials, Vision 2020, New York State Women's Suffrage Commission, Votes for Women 2020, Suffrage Wagon News Channel, Library of Congress, How Women Won the Vote *Gazette*, the Office of New York State Governor George Pataki, National Collaborative for Women's History Sites, the National Park Service, Town of Huntington (NY), Santa Fe Monthly Meeting, New Mexico Press Women, the New York History blog, and the Kate Besser Award.

The following individuals have made a significant difference in terms of their interest, support, and participation in preserving the Spirit of 1776 wagon, as well as contributing to the support of this memoir and family history: Miriam Sagan, Mary Wachs, Robert P. J. Cooney Jr., Rosalie Morales Kearns, Jennifer Lemak, Amanda Lanne-Camilli, James Peltz, Eva Burrows, Marilyn Mitchell, Kenneth Florey, Eleanor Ortiz, Emily Stern, Brian Hollander, Geddy Sveikauskas, David Lindblom, Ann Pfau, Robert Weible, Meredith Monk, Jone Miller, Hofstra University professor emerita Dr. Natalie Naylor, Allison Dunn, Jane Van De Bogart, Margaret R. Johnston, Bettina Raphael, Hana Ransom, Alf Evers, Janet Sadler, Alan Sussman, Robert F. Keeler, Judy Keeler, Jean Houston, Pat Medvick, Theodore Bloyd, Neil Norby, Peter Norby, John Warren, Robin Kunz, Richard Kearns Jr., Carlos T. Kearns, Nancy Brown, Karie Diethorn, Pete Seeger, Toshi Seeger, Safiya Bandele, Russell Whiting, Deborah Begel, Richard L. Kearns, Robert Hughes, Meneese Wall, Judy Ribble, Robert Rand, Jeanette Wittman, Daniel Kilpatric, Devin Lander, Carol Ricken, Don Bittner, Kate McCahill, Dr. Julia Deisler, Sibel Malik, Diane Surresco, Teri Gay, Pauline Rand, Kathleen Kelly, Alicia Frink, Deborah Hughes, Spike Herzig, Sabra Moore, David Schiller, Maurice Hinchey, Antonia Petrash, Jack Petrash, Ellen Povill, Ruth Simpson, Tom Udall, Martin Heinrich, Marilyn Perez, Kai Qu, Elisabeth Rothenberger, Joel W. Culp, Meg Smith, Tony Smith, Virginia Stephenson, Gerri Gribi, Meredith Machen, Carolyn Dechaine, Eighty Bug, Jamie Hiber, Senta Hoge, Thomas B. Culp, Marc Black, Susan Black, Jo Sgammato, Michael Barnett, Ted Hallman, Wendy Polhemus-Annibell, Richard Breen, Betsy Breen, Bill Blyer, James Kindall, Denise Ireton, Monica Roman Gagnier, Jon Povill, Zoe Nicholson, Martha Wheelock, Yuyu Cheng, Meg O'Brien, Susan Zimet,

Lynn Rollins, Charles Goodmacher, Dare Thompson, Joshua Ruff, Emily Buckman Milford, Abby Sheckley, Jan Sanders, Christy Dammen, Maya Sutton, Susan Nilsen, Norm Ziegler, Jude Ziegler, Peggy Medina Giltrow, Sandra Weber, Tisha Dolton, Andrew Fuller, Maureen Millar, Nancy Minon, Regis McCann, Stacey Murphy, JoAnn Margolis, Sally R. Wagner, Elsie Wright, Beverly Miller, Peter Sinclair, Rebecca Cecil, Lei Isaacs, Barbara Irvine, Coline Jenkins, Zita Jefferson, Roberta Jeracka, Pat Hastings, Marylou Butler, Marj Burton, Ken Burton, Thomas Paine Cronin, Sandy Dunn, Molly Murphy MacGregor, Yva Momatiuk, Lisa Mercurio Fullard, Ellyn Okvist, Janet Hicks, Graham Johnson, Tobias Bloyd, Brock Knez, Mary Leonard, Sue Lean, Mindy Brown, Heather Winterer, Brenda McGivern Mercurio, Nancy Mercurio, Tom Armstrong, Joyce Rouse, Neil Trager, Geoffrey Stein.

Any errors or omissions are entirely mine.

Genealogy Chart for Marguerite Kearns

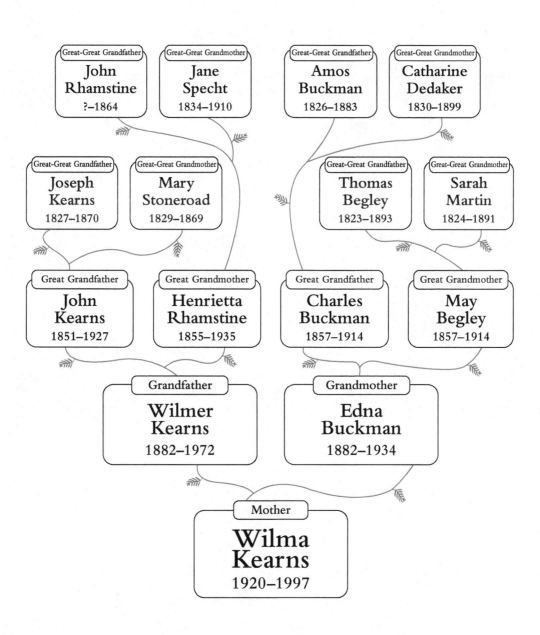

Great-Great Grandfather
John Rhamstine
?–1864

Great-Great Grandmother
Jane Specht
1834–1910

Great-Great Grandfather
Amos Buckman
1826–1883

Great-Great Grandmother
Catharine Dedaker
1830–1899

Great-Great Grandfather
Joseph Kearns
1827–1870

Great-Great Grandmother
Mary Stoneroad
1829–1869

Great-Great Grandfather
Thomas Begley
1823–1893

Great-Great Grandmother
Sarah Martin
1824–1891

Great Grandfather
John Kearns
1851–1927

Great Grandmother
Henrietta Rhamstine
1855–1935

Great Grandfather
Charles Buckman
1857–1914

Great Grandmother
May Begley
1857–1914

Grandfather
Wilmer Kearns
1882–1972

Grandmother
Edna Buckman
1882–1934

Mother
Wilma Kearns
1920–1997

Timeline of the Spirit of 1776 Suffrage Wagon

Spirit of 1776 suffrage campaign wagon on exhibit at the New York State Capitol Building, Albany, 2012. Photo by Marguerite Kearns.

July 1848

Women's convention in Seneca Falls, New York. The delegates of women and men approve the Declaration of Sentiments based on a rewrite of the nation's Declaration of Independence of 1776, with an emphasis on how men *and* women are created equal.

September 1852

A call for women to engage in tax resistance in support of votes for women at the National Woman Rights Convention in Syracuse, New York. This argument justifies women and their organizations taking a stand. Tax resisters in the early days of the early women's rights movement have mixed results. This is due to an uneven application of suffrage in the nation, including school elections and less resistance to women voting in the West.

July 1876

Votes for women activists protest at the Philadelphia Centennial Exposition when five suffrage activists read their Declaration of Rights of the Women of the United States, a proclamation prepared by Susan B. Anthony, Elizabeth Cady Stanton, and Matilda Joslyn Gage. At the same event, artist Archibald Willard unveils his painting *Yankee Doodle*, later renamed *The Spirit of '76*. These two definitions of patriotism—the military version and patriotic protest—compete for support from the public.

1882

The birth of Edna May Buckman on Christmas Day 1882. The birth of Wilmer Rhamstine Kearns in January 1882. They marry in June of 1904 at Echo Dale, near Norristown, Pennsylvania.

July 1913

The I. S. Remson firm, a Brooklyn wagon company, presents the Spirit of 1776 horse-drawn wagon to the New York State Woman Suffrage Association in Manhattan. State president Harriet May Mills assigns Edna Kearns to coordinate the organizing journey of the suffrage campaign wagon as a symbol of taxation without representation in support of the votes for women cause. The US in 1913 ratifies the Sixteenth

Amendment to the US Constitution establishing a federal income tax, a key link in the suffrage argument of "no taxation without representation" that the Spirit of 1776 wagon symbolizes.

July and August 1913

The Spirit of 1776 suffrage campaign wagon is involved in the organizing of New York City and Long Island. It is used in parades, as well as at exhibits, speeches, fundraisers, and other events, including the Mineola Fair on Long Island.

Fall 1913

Harriet May Mills, the outgoing president of the New York State Woman Suffrage Association, in a letter presents the Spirit of 1776 wagon to Edna Buckman Kearns of Rockville Centre, New York, to use with her ongoing suffrage campaigns.

November 1917

New York State women win the right to vote following a state referendum on the issue in 1917.

1920

On Tuesday, November 2, 1920, millions of US women vote for the first time. Although the Nineteenth Amendment to the US Constitution guarantees all women voting rights, it takes decades for voting restrictions on the local level, especially in the South, to be challenged and overturned. During 1920, the Spirit of 1776 suffrage wagon is transported to the Philadelphia area when Edna, Wilmer, and Serena Kearns move from New York back to Echo Dale, the Buckman family home near Norristown, outside of Philadelphia. There, Edna and Wilmer open a flower nursery business, Echo Dale Gardens. Wilma Buckman Kearns, the author's mother, is born on November 12, 1920.

1920–1930

The suffrage campaign wagon, the Spirit of 1776, is on exhibit at Echo Dale Gardens, the Kearns family nursery business.

1934

Edna Buckman Kearns dies on June 1, 1934, of breast cancer. She is buried in the Quaker burial ground in Plymouth Meeting, Pennsylvania, with her parents, May and Charles Buckman.

1930–1960

Wilmer Kearns stores the Spirit of 1776 wagon in his garage in the Philadelphia area. Wilmer works on preserving the suffrage movement artifact and promoting its history. With a friend, Wilmer Kearns drives the wagon during 1943 throughout towns and villages in the Philadelphia area.

1971

The author moves to Woodstock, New York, from the Southwest, where she is closer to her parents and can complete the family interviewing and research with her grandfather, Wilmer Kearns, and aunt, Serena Kearns. She accepts a position as a reporter and coeditor of the Hudson Valley newspaper *Woodstock Times*.

1972

The death of Wilmer R. Kearns, when responsibility for family storytelling and research shifts to the author's mother, Wilma Buckman Kearns (Culp), who inherits the Spirit of 1776 wagon and the women's rights archival collection of Edna Buckman Kearns.

1984

Acceleration in the pace of the family research and genealogy study. Author's participation in the Buckman Family Reunion in Pennsylvania.

1985

The Spirit of 1776 wagon is transported to Woodstock, in the Hudson Valley, from the Philadelphia area.

March 1986

The Spirit of 1776 suffrage campaign wagon is on exhibit at the Mansion House in Kingston. *The Victorious Coalition: Votes for Women in New York State* is sponsored by the Floating Foundation of Photography of High Falls, New York, under the direction of Jone Miller and Steven Schoen. The exhibit features suffrage activists Elisabeth Freeman and Edna Kearns. Jane Van De Bogart and Marguerite (Culp) Kearns are curators, with assistance from Margaret R. Johnston (Peg). The exhibit is funded, in part, by the decentralization program of the New York State Council on the Arts.

1992

Marguerite Kearns moves to the Southwest, and she takes the votes for women archival materials with her.

1992–1997

The Spirit of 1776 wagon is stored in Ulster County, New York, including locations in the town of Olive and the hamlets of Bearsville and Shady.

1997

Wilma Buckman Kearns (Culp) dies, and research materials are consolidated, in preparation for the final writing of the memoir and family history.

2000

The Spirit of 1776 suffrage campaign wagon is donated to New York State, first to the Museum of Women: The Leadership Center in New York City, and then, later, to the New York State Museum in Albany.

2008

New York State Museum transportation curator Geoffrey N. Stein writes in the *Legacy* magazine of the state museum that the Spirit of 1776 suffrage campaign wagon is "a prime artifact of the women's suffrage movement."

2009

The research and suffrage wagon advocacy takes the form of an award-winning blog, publishing weekly to advocate for the suffrage wagon's exhibition in New York State, as well as a platform for education about the early US women's rights movement.

2010

The Spirit of 1776 wagon is the centerpiece of a Women's History Month exhibit, *Women Who Rocked the Vote*, at the New York State Museum in Albany.

2011

US Congressman Maurice D. Hinchey from New York State's 28th District calls the Spirit of 1776 suffrage campaign wagon "an outstanding example" of how New York women forged a path to the passage of the Nineteenth Amendment. He expresses confidence that voters will "welcome the opportunity to see this part of our history on permanent exhibition."

2012

The Spirit of 1776 suffrage campaign wagon is featured in governor Andrew Cuomo's exhibit at the State Capitol in Albany, New York, during Women's History Month, entitled *From Seneca Falls to the Supreme Court: New York's Women Leading the Way*.

2013

Both houses of the New York State Legislature acknowledge the centennial of the 1913 wagon's suffrage community organizing by passing bipartisan resolutions designating July 1, 2013, as the Spirit of 1776 Wagon Day in New York. Votes for Women 2020 organizes the legislative resolution.

2016

Marguerite Kearns takes on the position of cochair of the Inez Milholland centennial national observance for the National Women's History Project with Robert P. J. Cooney Jr. Inez Milholland (1886–1916) is nationally recognized as the US suffrage martyr after she collapses and dies from pernicious anemia when on a votes for women speaking tour in the West in 1916. Edna Kearns worked with Inez Milholland in the New York State suffrage campaigns.

2017

State centennial observance of New York women winning the vote in 1917. The Spirit of 1776 wagon is on display at the State Capitol Building during Women's History Month in 2017, followed by exhibition in the lobby of the New York State Museum where it promotes the museum's exhibit *Votes for Women: Celebrating New York's Suffrage Centennial* that runs from November 2017 through May 2018.

2018

A road maker is installed on the main street of Huntington, New York, to commemorate a crowd of a thousand witnessing a confrontation between suffrage supporters and those opposing women voting that erupts in a 1913 Huntington parade where the Spirit of 1776 wagon takes part and becomes a focal point of the controversy.

2019

Marguerite Kearns participates in the January 2019 women's march in Santa Fe, New Mexico, carrying a poster-size vintage photograph of Edna, Wilmer, and Serena Kearns marching in a January 1914 women's rights "hike" to the New York State capital. Her message reminds march participants that women have been demonstrating for their rights by way of marches and parades for more than one hundred years.

2020 and Beyond

The 2020 national centennial observance of American women winning the right to vote due to the passage and ratification of the Nineteenth Amendment to the US Constitution on August 26, 1920. The Spirit of 1776 wagon used by Edna Kearns and others is included in plans for the state museum's permanent exhibition. Long Beach, New York, is installing a historic marker under the auspices of the National Votes for Women Trail to commemorate the suffrage organizing of Edna Buckman Kearns in Long Beach in 1913. A gravestone marker is installed at the Quaker burial grounds in Plymouth Meeting, Pennsylvania, where Edna Buckman Kearns and her parents are buried. And Kamala Harris is inaugurated in January 2021 as the first female and the first woman of color to serve in the White House.

Notes

This memoir and family history highlights the experience of one family during the early women's rights movement. It is not intended to be a complete history of organizing for women's rights in the United States. The research for this work relies on Buckman-Kearns oral family history and folklore, Quaker records and documents, spiritual and secular scholarly sources, reference books of social and demographic history, deeds, spiritual journals, diaries, maps, photographs, marriage certificates, birth and death records, correspondence, scrapbooks, legal and business papers, the results of fact-finding trips, and the study of related collections and archives. Appreciation is extended to Richard L. Kearns and Margarita M. Kearns for sharing access to Kearns family history and images collected over the years from 1900 to 1920.

Draft copy of a telegram from Edna Buckman Kearns to US president Woodrow Wilson, 1917.

Part I

CHAPTER 1: THE MARCH OF THE WOMEN

1. "Suffrage Parade a Unique Affair," *Nassau Post*, Freeport, New York, July 16, 1915. This article confirms what I heard from family members—that Edna Kearns was a quiet, forceful, and effective speaker.

2. Patricia Greenwood Harrison, *Connecting Links: The British and American Woman Suffrage Movements, 1900–1914* (Westport, CT: Greenwood Press, 2000), 153.

CHAPTER 2: WILMER MEETS EDNA

1. George E. McCracken, *The Welcome Claimants Proved, Disproved and Doubtful with an Account of Some of Their Descendants* (Baltimore, MD: Genealogical Publishing Co., 1970).

This resource documents the Buckman family of Quakers from Sussex, England (the largest family group on the ship *Welcome* with William Penn), from whom Edna May Buckman was descended. Informal Buckman family reunions were held at the home of Thomas Buckman and Mary Ann Brooke Buckman in Rydal, Pennsylvania, until Mary Ann Brooke Buckman formalized the family reunion in 1913. The Buckman family gatherings continued for more than seventy-five years during the twentieth century. This particular Buckman family reunion brought together one branch of the Buckman family in Pennsylvania. During the 1970s when the practice of holding annual family reunions was on the decline, Caroline Watson Warner (daughter of Jenny Buckman) and Warner's cousin, Hazel Buckman Errico, poured effort into the annual family gatherings until Caroline Watson's death in March 1986. Then Elsie Warner Wright of Yardley, Pennsylvania, and her sister Jean Nolte took over organizing the annual sessions until the reunion gatherings ended during the 1980s. Over the years, the Buckman Family Reunion met at various Quaker Meeting Houses in Bucks County where ancestors had been members, in addition to other locations, including Buckman-related family farms, Pennsbury Manor (the home of William Penn), as well as the Bucks County family farm of Elsie Warner Wright. There, Buckman descendants continue to live on one of the five remaining working farms in Makefield Township, Bucks County, as of 2019. This Buckman working farm has been operational since 1928. The last Buckman Family Reunions of the twentieth century were held at Makefield Monthly Meeting in Dolington, Pennsylvania, as well as the Wright farm. The family reunion collection at Friends Historical Library at Swarthmore College contains a list of Buckman descendants gathered by reunion volunteers, as well as an anniversary newsletter issue of seventy-five years with highlights of prior reunions, a reunion recipe of lemon butter, and profiles of key reunion participants. Marguerite Kearns served as president of the Buckman Family Reunion for two years during the 1980s, as well as its newsletter editor.

2. The National Society Daughters of the American Revolution, Office of the Registrar General, confirmed the American Revolution ancestors of Wilmer R. Kearns and relevant genealogical records in an approved application for DAR membership by Wilma Buckman Kearns (Culp) during the 1980s. Proven American Revolution ancestors for Wilmer Kearns include Privates William Frampton, Adam Specht, and Thomas Kern(s).

3. "Small Things," from the Edna Buckman Kearns archival collection. Dr. Susan Goodier and Marguerite Kearns indexed the papers of Edna Kearns (December 25, 1882–June 1, 1934) in 2010. These primary sources are in the author's possession.

CHAPTER 3: GRANDDADDY WILMER

1. Midge Mackenzie, *Shoulder to Shoulder: A Documentary* (New York: Knopf, 1988).

2. Primary documents relative to the Penington Friends House at 215 East Fifteenth Street in New York City are available at Friends Historical Library. The Penington remains in operation as a Quaker institution in New York City serving the needs of long-term and overnight guests.

CHAPTER 4: "DISH RAGS" AND "SHE-MEN"

1. Brooke Kroeger, *The Suffragents: How Women Used Men to Get the Vote* (Albany: State University of New York Press, 2017), focuses on the history of the Men's League for Woman Suffrage, active in New York starting in 1909. Wilmer Kearns was a member and supporter.

2. Unpublished selection from Edna Buckman Kearns's collection of documents and memorabilia in the author's possession.

3. US Senate, *Suffrage Parade: Hearings before a Subcommittee of the Committee on the District of Columbia, Part I* (March 4–17, 1913).

4. Susan Goodier and Karen Pastorello, *Women Will Vote: Winning Suffrage in New York State* (Ithaca: Three Hills, an imprint of Cornell University Press, 2017), 3. After the 1917 votes for women victory in New York State, a direction was set toward the ratification of the Nineteenth Amendment to the US Constitution. The New York support network consisted of a "patchwork" of suffrage organizations and programs until Carrie Chapman Catt centralized the New York organization for the 1917 women's voting rights referendum campaign that passed, although the 1915 referendum failed.

5. The Library of Congress has in its collection numerous photographs documenting the early US women's rights movement. The majority of images in the George Grantham Bain Collection date from 1900 to the mid-1920s.

6. More news coverage of the 1913 suffrage parade by Edna Buckman Kearns is available from her collection of correspondence, newspaper columns, and memorabilia. She wrote articles about women's voting rights published in New York City, as well as the metropolitan area news media. The selection quoted here was pasted in a scrapbook. There is no information as to the date or the name of the publication.

CHAPTER 5: AN UNLIKELY COUPLE

1. Elizabeth Cady Stanton, *Eighty Years and More: Reminiscences 1815–1897* (New York: T. Fisher Unwin, 1898).

CHAPTER 6: "WHEN IS PAPA COMING HOME?"

1. Therese Oneill, *Unmentionable: The Victorian Lady's Guide to Sex, Marriage, and Manners* (New York: Back Bay Books / Little, Brown and Company, 2016), 53–74.

2. Hattie A. Burr, *The Woman Suffrage Cook Book* (Boston: Printed by the author, 1886), 98.

3. "Conferences, Associations, Etc.," *Friends' Intelligencer* (June 8, 1901): 365.

4. Margaret Hope Bacon, *Valiant Friend: The Life of Lucretia Mott* (Philadelphia: Friends General Conference, 1999), 159.

5. Edna May Buckman Kearns, "The Wanamaker Diary—1904." Unpublished diary handwritten by Edna, in the author's possession.

6. *The Furniture Trade Review and Interior Decorator* 15 (April 1895). This and other trade publications of the period confirm the history of Boll Brothers and its prominence in the industry, in addition to catalogs and other information sources

"Where All the World Sleeps: Beds and Bedding Made by the Boll Brothers Manufacturing Company," *Patriot* (Harrisburg, Pennsylvania) 88, no. 15 (January 20, 1903): 13. This article includes an overview of the Boll Brothers' manufacturing plant in Harrisburg, its range of products, and the claim that it was the second largest firm of its type in the nation with offices and showrooms in New York City and San Francisco.

7. "Boll Bros. Plants Destroyed by Fire; The State Printery Badly Damaged," *Harrisburg Telegraph*, October 13, 1903, 1.

8. Genealogical family history of Buckmans compiled by Wilma Buckman Kearns (Culp) during the 1980s.

CHAPTER 7: THE SECRET

1. Henrietta Rhamstine Kearns, Wilmer's mother, demonstrated love for family members by her mastery of Pennsylvania Dutch cooking, according to Kearns family members still living in Beavertown, Pennsylvania. The recipe for dried beef gravy, for example, was handed down in the family from Henrietta Kearns to her daughter-in-law Edna, to Edna's daughter Wilma, and then to, Marguerite Kearns.

2. Ellen Carol DuBois, *Harriot Stanton Blatch and the Winning of Woman Suffrage* (New Haven: Yale University Press, 1997), 88.

CHAPTER 8: "DON'T FALL IN LOVE WITH CURMUDGEONS"

1. The Samuel S. Fleisher Graphic Sketch Club of Philadelphia that Edna May Buckman attended was one of the nation's first community centers offering art classes, free or at a minimal cost. It was named for Samuel S. Fleisher, a graduate of the Wharton School at the University of Pennsylvania.

2. *The Journal of George Fox*, revised edition by John L. Nickalls with an epilogue by Henry J. Cadbury and an introduction by Geoffrey F. Nuttall (Philadelphia: Religious Society of Friends, 1997), 2–21.

3. Henry W. Wilbur, *The Life and Labors of Elias Hicks* (Philadelphia: Friends' General Conference, 1910). The importance of the Inner Light as described in the ministry of Long Island resident Elias Hicks. The ministry of Quaker Elias Hicks led to the Hicksite-Orthodox schism of the late 1820s.

4. Margaret H. Bacon, *The Quiet Rebels: The Story of Quakers in America* (New York: Basic Books, 1969), 3–8.

5. Frederick B. Tolles and E. Gordon Alderfer, eds., *The Witness of William Penn* (New York: Macmillan, 1957), 15.

6. Carol Faulkner, *Lucretia Mott's Heresy: Abolition and Women's Rights in Nineteenth-Century America* (Philadelphia: University of Pennsylvania Press, 2011), 75–86. The burning of Pennsylvania Hall in Philadelphia in 1837 was an example of the mainstream resistance at that time to interracial social justice gatherings.

CHAPTER 9: THE SPIRIT OF 1776 WAGON

1. Juliana Tutt, " 'No Taxation without Representation' in the American Woman Suffrage Movement," *Stanford Law Review* 62, no. 5 (May 2010): 1473–1512.

2. "Leading Tories on Long Island Came from Upper Social Class; Names Are Familiar Now; How They Aided the British Cause," *Brooklyn Daily Eagle*, May 2, 1928, 12.

3. Henry Steele Commager and Richard B. Morris, eds., *The Spirit of Seventy-Six: The Story of the American Revolution as Told by Participants* (Edison, NJ: Castle Books, 2002), 1.

4. Hugh Cunningham, "The Language of Patriotism, 1750–1914," *History Workshop*, no. 12 (Autumn 1981): 8–33.

5. Simon Hall, *American Patriotism, American Protest: Social Movements Since the Sixties* (Philadelphia: University of Pennsylvania Press, 2011), presents the argument that patriotic protest was a theme influencing various social movements during the twentieth century.

6. When the Spirit of 1776 wagon was donated to the New York State Woman Suffrage Association in 1913, I. S. Remson, who purchased the wagon, was deceased. The following letters, in the author's possession, address the wagon's origins and reflect the involvement of the Remson firm after making the donation: A. F. Wilson, President, The I. S. Remson Manufacturing Company, 740–750 Grand Street, Brooklyn, NY, to Mrs. Lee, NYS Woman Suffrage Association, June 19, 1913. Letter from the archives of Edna Buckman Kearns. A. F. Wilson to Amos Veritzen, June 28, 1913. Letters from A. F. Wilson to Mrs. Edna B. Kearns dated June 28, 1913; July 11, 1913; August 9, 1913; and October 14, 1913.

7. "Out with the Cutters: Brooklynites Who Handle the Ribbons over Famous Flyers—A Century Old Vehicle and Still Serviceable—The Music of Sleigh Bells," *Brooklyn Daily Eagle*, February 3, 1895, 8.

8. Email, September 28, 2010, from Joshua Ruff, Deputy Director of Collections and Interpretation, Long Island Museum, Stony Brook, New York. Reply to information request about the type and probable date of construction of Spirit of 1776 suffrage wagon. Ruff commented: "Carriage makers were not always careful or knowledgeable about design or construction features of wagons from much earlier periods. That's a similar story with furniture makers and makers of other kinds of material culture. They knew the variations but they may not have realized exact periods. And in the same way, exact origins and provenance sometimes get very confused over the decades. . . . I think the wagon could be anywhere from 1810 to 1830, so 'about 1820' seems accurate. . . . The other thing I noticed was that the Spirit of 1776 wagon appears to be on an elliptic spring and those weren't around until the early 1800s."

Ronald Ducharme, *Treatment Report: A New England Pleasure Wagon*, submitted to Kit Moseley, the Museum of Women: The Leadership Center, New York, December 2, 2000. This three-page wagon report by New York State preservation specialist Ronald Ducharme highlights the conservation methods utilized following the donation of the Spirit of 1776 wagon from the Kearns family to the State of New York. It also provides an overview of the wagon's style and probable construction as a nineteenth-century pleasure wagon. The Spirit of 1776 was first donated to The Museum of Women: The Leadership Center, a state-sponsored initiative in Manhattan during the Governor George Pataki administration. The wagon was later transported to the New York State Museum in Albany, New York, to become part of its permanent collection.

9. Tutt, " 'No Taxation without Representation,' " 1473.

10. The link between the "taxation without representation" theme and the Spirit of 1776 wagon's symbolism is addressed in this representative sampling of news articles published in the summer of 1913 about the suffrage campaign wagon's organizing tour in New York City and on Long Island: "Suffragists Out for a Stir," *New York Times*, July 1, 1913; "Get a One-Horse Shay," *New York Times*, July 2, 1913; "Off on Caravan Tour to Win Long Island," *Brooklyn Daily Eagle*, July 2, 1913, 4; "Suffragists Off for Farms in Garb of '76," *Sun*, July 2, 1913; "Suffrage Talk amid Waves," *New York Times*, July 5, 1913; "Suffragists Tour Island," *Brooklyn Daily Eagle*, July 9, 1913, 5; "From Wagon's Tail Woman Spreads Gospel," *San Diego Union*, July 20, 1913, 23; "Gen. Jones' Mother a Belligerent Anti," *Brooklyn Daily Eagle*, July 31, 1913, 4; "Suffragists Finish Tour of the Island," *Daily Standard Union*, August 6, 1913, 12; "Suffragists to Be Present," *Daily Star* (New York City), September 23, 1913. 1. The patriotism link is addressed in a letter from Alice Carpenter, chairman of the National Woman's Party (New York City committee), to Edna Buckman Kearns dated March 14, 1917, in the author's possession. Carpenter says that the "appeal of patriotism, always strong" was never more significant than between Edna Kearns and Rosalie Jones's "anti" mother (Mary Elizabeth Jones), who challenged the suffragists on their right to use the Spirit of 1776 wagon as the caravan arrived in Huntington, New York, for a parade and open-air meeting during July 1913.

11. There is some question as to the actual name of the I. S. Remson employee responsible for riding in the old wagon to advertise the Brooklyn wagon firm. He is referred to in letters both as Amos Veritan as well as Amos Veritzen.

CHAPTER 10: GETTING TO KNOW THE FAMILY ON EDGAR ALLAN POE'S CHAIRS

1. The interviewing and discussion about Echo Dale, the Buckman family home, was recorded on March 21, 1984, in Woodstock, New York, by Marguerite Kearns and her mother Wilma Buckman Kearns (Culp). This document is in the author's possession.

2. The exact street location of the building Poe rented in the Northern Liberties section of Philadelphia has been confused over the years in various references. This is due, in part, to the City of Philadelphia renumbering street addresses. Karie Diethorn, chief curator for the Independence National Historical Park, related the following in an email to the author on March 11, 2019. In this communication, Diethorn said the street address of the property (Thibaut Map 5, p. 477) for the Poe house (that fronted onto Wistar Street) was perpendicular to North Seventh Street. The actual building at 234 North Seventh Street wasn't built until after the Poe family left Philadelphia in 1844. After the City of Philadelphia consolidated its boroughs in 1855, buildings were renumbered, and the former Poe house lot became 530 North Seventh Street (rear). These facts were collected by the author to test the authenticity of the Buckman family legend of the Edgar Allan Poe chairs.

3. According to Karie Diethorn, there is no definitive source confirming what Poe wrote when living at any particular residence. Poe may have started writing "The Raven" when living in Northern Liberties in Philadelphia. "The Raven" was published in New York City in January 1845. An important source document, *Edgar A. Poe: The Years in Philadelphia, 1838–1844* by Jacqueline Thibaut (appendix D, p. 416), states that Poe may have written

"The Gold Bug," "The Black Cat," "Raising the Wind," "The Spectacles," and "A Tale of the Ragged Mountains" at what is now the Poe house in Philadelphia administered by the National Park Service. Poe didn't keep a journal documenting when each literary piece was started or completed.

4. The source document, *Edgar A. Poe: The Years in Philadelphia* by Thibaut, presents documentary evidence that the Buckman family distant relatives may have been Poe's landlords briefly when the poet and his family rented there. The work questions if certain documents filed with the City of Philadelphia actually represent who Poe's landlord was at any particular time.

5. A "leading" refers to a spiritual decision by a Quaker to contemplate an interest or "concern" to take action on a particular topic or social issue. Such a commitment goes through a process of "discernment" to determine if the possible leading is grounded in spiritual reflection and tested as originating from a divine source. Leadings are individual decisions that may or may not reflect the concerns and direction of the larger Quaker worship community. A leading is a serious personal spiritual matter tested by prayer and contemplation.

6. "The way will open" is a Quaker expression suggesting that there may appear to be barriers to an action or reaching a certain outcome or goal. However, with appropriate "waiting," accompanied by prayer and reflection, the "way will open." This refers to the process of testing and reaching toward clarity and action based on a divine source, thus allowing the issue or concern to be dealt with in a spiritual manner.

7. Donna McDaniel and Vanessa Julye, *Fit for Freedom, Not for Friendship: Quakers, African-Americans, and the Myth of Racial Justice* (Fitchburg, MA: QuakerBooks of FGC, 2009). By 1761, Quakers were barred from owning slaves in both the United States and England, the outcome of years of debate and conflict resolution from within the Religious Society of Friends. This work documents the inconsistencies and challenges associated with consensus and unity among Quakers and the overall impact of the dominant culture on its citizens.

8. Elwood Roberts, ed., *Biographical Annals of Montgomery County, Pennsylvania* (New York: T. S. Benham and the Lewis Publishing Company, 1904). Biographical resource from 1904 that contains references to Thomas Buckman, his first and second wives, and how he earned a living.

Part II

CHAPTER 11: THE TELEPHONE PARTY LINE

1. The US presidential election of 1956.

2. Carolyn Keene, *The Hidden Staircase* (New York: Grosset & Dunlap, 1987, 1959, 1930).

3. Gunlög Fur, *A Nation of Women: Gender and Colonial Encounters Among the Delaware Indians* (Philadelphia: University of Pennsylvania Press, 2012).

CHAPTER 12: JUST FRIENDS

1. Faulkner, *Lucretia Mott's Heresy*, 140.

2. Patricia A. Cooper, *Once a Cigar Maker: Men, Women, and Work Culture in American Cigar Factories, 1900–1919* (Urbana: University of Illinois Press, 1992).

3. Letter circa 1903 from Edna Buckman to Wilmer Kearns. Collection of primary documents in the author's possession.

Chapter 13: Dinner at Delmonico's

1. Judith Choate and James Canora, *Dining at Delmonico's: The Story of America's Oldest Restaurant* (New York: Stewart, Tabori & Chang, 2008).

Chapter 14: Many Women, Many Views

1. Clayton L. Farraday, *Friends' Central School; 1845–1984* (Philadelphia: Friends' Central School, 1984).

2. Nellie Bly, *Around the World in Seventy-Two Days and Other Writings* (New York: Penguin Books, 2014). The quotation about being a "doll" or a "drudge" is from the 1896 interview news reporter Nellie Bly conducted with Susan B. Anthony.

3. Poem from Edna May Buckman's collection of documents and memorabilia in the author's possession.

Chapter 16: "Is It Always Like This?"

1. Example of a letter from Wilmer Kearns to Edna Buckman, 1904, in the author's possession.

2. David L. Greene, *The Kearns Family of Decatur and Derry Townships, Mifflin County, Pennsylvania* (Demorest, GA: D. L. Greene, 1979).

Chapter 17: "Will Thee Marry Me?"

1. Selection from Edna Buckman Kearns's collection of documents and memorabilia in the author's possession.

Chapter 18: Rumblings at the Dinner Table

1. The unpublished 1904–1905 diary of Edna Buckman Kearns includes the Quaker "clearness" committee of her marriage to Wilmer R. Kearns and the Green Street Monthly Meeting's discussions associated with it.

Chapter 19: "Happy New Year to Thee and All"

1. Selections from January 1 through January 10, 1904, from the unpublished diary of Edna Buckman Kearns in possession of the author.

Part III

Chapter 21: Charles, Angela, and the Wedding Scandal

1. The unpublished 1904–1905 diary of Edna Buckman Kearns highlights Joseph Wharton's contacts with her, March through May of 1904. Diary entry of March 13, 1904, confirms his agreement to serve as an overseer for the June 1904 Quaker wedding.

2. Kevin Kenny, *Peaceable Kingdom Lost: The Paxton Boys and the Destruction of William Penn's Holy Experiment* (New York: Oxford University Press, 2009).

3. Phillips P. Moulton, ed., *The Journal and Major Essays of John Woolman* (Richmond, IN: Friends United Press, 2001).

Chapter 22: Honeymoon in St. Louis

1. The unpublished 1904–1905 diary of Edna Buckman Kearns contained lists of wedding gifts, the names of some invited to the wedding, and details of the wedding's planning and preparation.

Chapter 24: Civil War Orphan School

1. The school records of Henrietta Kearns at the McAlisterville Soldiers' Orphan School are from the collection of the Kearns family in Beavertown, Pennsylvania.

2. The recipe book Henrietta Kearns made for her daughter-in-law Edna Buckman Kearns has been lost over the years, even though some recipes were shared among family members and treasured.

3. Military service of John Rhamstine, who served in the Union Army during the Civil War, is confirmed by original enlistment documents in the Kearns family possession and by notes taken by Wilma Buckman Kearns (Culp) during a 1962 visit to relatives in Beavertown, Pennsylvania.

Chapter 26: Holly, Mistletoe, and Evergreens

1. Handwritten letter from Edna Buckman Kearns to Wilmer Kearns about the imminent birth of Serena from the Buckman-Kearns collection of letters, photos, memorabilia, and news clippings in the author's possession.

Part IV

Chapter 29: The Wagon in Woodstock

1. Partial text of a handwritten letter from Marguerite Kearns to Wilmer Kearns, circa 1971.

2. Marguerite Kearns, "Wagon Women for Suffrage Had Woodstock Ties," *Woodstock Times*, March 8, 2017. An earlier version of chapter 29 was printed on March 8, 2017, by *Woodstock Times*. Reprinted with permission from publisher Geddy Sveikauskas and Ulster Publishing, Woodstock, New York.

3. State University of New York at New Paltz professor Amy Kesselman presented a program on New York's women's suffrage movement to accompany the 1986 exhibit that featured the Spirit of 1776 suffrage wagon. Hundreds of people attended the exhibition and programs about Edna Kearns and Elisabeth Freeman. Joel W. Culp, with the assistance of Thomas B. Culp, transported the Spirit of 1776 wagon from Pennsylvania to New York State for the 1986 Mansion House exhibition in Kingston, New York.

4. Handwritten notes for a speech from the archival collection of Edna Buckman Kearns in the possession of the author.

5. Hall, *American Patriotism, American Protest*.

CHAPTER 30: UPROAR IN HUNTINGTON

1. The Kearns motor car was manufactured in Beavertown, Pennsylvania, by Charles Maxwell Kearns, family members and employees from 1907 until 1929. A Kearns vehicle, the Lulu model, is part of the permanent collection on exhibit in the industry and transportation section of the State Museum of Pennsylvania in Harrisburg, according to Curt Miner, chief curator. Lulu Kearns, Wilmer Kearns's sister, worked with Edna Buckman Kearns in the 1913 votes for women organizing campaign on Long Island. The Lulu model of the Kearns car on exhibit at the State Museum of Pennsylvania is named after Lulu Kearns.

2. Marguerite Kearns, "The Spirit of 1776," *New York Archives* (Fall 2013): 28–31. An earlier version of the 1913 confrontation with Edna Kearns, the Spirit of 1776 suffrage wagon, and Mary Livingston Jones was published by *New York Archives*.

3. Hilda R. Watrous, *Harriet May Mills, 1857–1935: A Biography* (Syracuse, NY: n.p., 1984).

4. Letter from A. F. Wilson to Mrs. Edna B. Kearns, July 11, 1913. From the family archive in the author's possession.

5. The use of the Spirit of 1776 campaign wagon in 1913 to promote the "taxation without representation" argument in support of women's voting rights was only part of Edna Kearns' women's rights activism. See endnotes in "Looking Back: In Their Own Words" for a listing of articles about Edna Buckman Kearns and her women's rights work.

6. "Gen. Jones' Mother a Belligerent Anti," *Brooklyn Daily Eagle*, July 31, 1913, 4.

CHAPTER 31: ONE WOMAN PER CENTURY

1. Marguerite Kearns, "A Woodstock Founding Mother," *Woodstock Times*, July 18, 2017. An earlier version of chapter 31 was printed by *Woodstock Times* on July 18, 2017. Partial reprint with permission from Geddy Sveikauskas, Publisher, Ulster Publishing, Woodstock, New York.

CHAPTER 32: SOJOURNER TRUTH IN THE HUDSON VALLEY

1. Harriot Stanton Blatch and Alma Lutz, *Challenging Years: The Memoirs of Harriot Stanton Blatch* (New York: G.P. Putnam, 1940).

LOOKING BACK: IN THEIR OWN WORDS

1. Edna Buckman Kearns, from family collection in author's possession, 1909–1919. Wilmer Kearns, unpublished piece of writing from documents in the author's possession dated 1960.

Sources for suffrage work by Edna Buckman Kearns include: "Suffs Assembled at Kearns' Home," *South Side Observer*, February 23, 1918; " 'Suffs' to Go Canning," *Brooklyn Daily Eagle*, July 20, 1915; "Suffrage Fans Next," *Brooklyn Daily Eagle*, April 19, 1915, 15; "Suffrage Notes," *Brooklyn Daily Eagle*, July 14, 1915; "Suffragists Active," *Oswego Daily Palladium*, August 31, 1915, 4; "Suffragists at War Over Better Babies," *Brooklyn Daily Eagle*, October 31, 1913, 4;

"Suffragist Gets Woodmere," *Brooklyn Daily Eagle*, January 6, 1915, 12; "Suffragist Invades Sea to Plead Cause to Crowd at Beach," *Cleveland Leader*, July 5, 1913, 1; "Sugarless Candy Pleases Farmers," *Brooklyn Daily Eagle*, December 21, 1917; "'Army' Invades Patchogue," *Brooklyn Daily Eagle*, February 16, 1915, 8; "Barefoot Dance to Be Feature of Suffrage Pageant," *Evening World*, April 26, 1913, 6; "Better Babies' Aim of Nassau Contest," *Brooklyn Daily Eagle*, October 15, 1913, 4; "Brooklynite's Impression of Suffrage Convention," *Brooklyn Daily Eagle*, November 28, 1914, 4; "Busy Southside Suffs," *Brooklyn Daily Eagle*, October 19, 1915; Edna Buckman Kearns, "Confessions of a Suffragist," *Owl*, July 30, 1915, 2; "Children at Fair Have a Merry Time," *Brooklyn Daily Eagle*, September 25, 1915; "Cupid Joins the Suffragist Army," *Daily Argus*, January 2, 1914, 12; "Daughter for Mrs. W. R. Kearns," *Brooklyn Daily Eagle*, November 19, 1920; "Dramatic Fete for Suffrage," *Brooklyn Daily Eagle*, February 10, 1915, 5; "Did 'Suffs" Hiss at 'Anti' Meeting?" *Brooklyn Daily Eagle*, June 29, 1915, 5; "Woman's Suffrage Forum," *Jersey Journal*, January 29, 1913, 4; "Garden City [News]," *Hempstead Sentinel*, n.d., 8; "Governor Stands in Pouring Rain to Hear Rockville Centre Speaker," *Owl*, November 20 1914; "Grieved at Stand: Women's Peace Society Distributes Leaflets," *Boston Herald*, December 26, 1921, 12; "Husbands of Suffragists Eager for Victory," *Owl*, September 17, 1915, 6; "In Nassau County 25 Years Ago," *Nassau Daily Review-Star*, September 9, 1937 (about EBK advocating for the Progressive Party in 1912); "In Nassau County 25 Years Ago," *Nassau Daily Review-Star*, November 20, 1942, 8 (about Wilmer and Edna Kearns hosting a community meeting at their home about a new train depot in 1917); "L.I. Women Active at Nashville Meeting," *Brooklyn Daily Eagle*, November 19, 1914, 10; "Long Island Men on Suffrage," *Friends' Intelligencer*, June 20, 1915, 407 (Wilmer Kearns quote, Congressman Hicks quote, also Robert Seaman, Quakers; over six thousand copies mailed to Nassau and Suffolk; that canvassers noticed a shift in attitude of men voters); "Long Island Women Active at Nashville Meeting," *Brooklyn Daily Eagle*, November 19, 1914; "Lynbrook Suffragists Hold a Picnic," *Brooklyn Daily Eagle*, August 10, 1912; "Mere Man Is Shy, Suffragists Learn," *Brooklyn Daily Eagle*, April 15, 1915; "Mere Men for Suffrage," *Brooklyn Daily Eagle*, September 14, 1915, 4; "Mothers and Daughters Invited to Reception," *Owl*, July 23, 1915; "Mrs. Kearns Appointed," *Brooklyn Daily Eagle*, December 11, 1916, 5; "Mrs. Kearns Makes Good-Bye Campaign," *Brooklyn Daily Eagle*, September 15, 1915; "Mrs. Kearns Risks Life to Speak at Fair," *Brooklyn Daily Eagle*, September 16, 1915; "Mrs. Kearns Tells of Hike," *Brooklyn Daily Eagle*, January 6, 1914; "Mrs. Kearns Urges Action in Senate," *Hempstead Sentinel*, May 2, 1918; "Name E. N. Edwards for the Assembly," *Brooklyn Daily Eagle*, August 20, 1912, 5; "Nassau Suffrage Events," *Brooklyn Daily Eagle*, July 20, 1915; "Nassau Suffragists in Mineola Parade," *Brooklyn Daily Eagle*, May 25, 1913, 5; "Not for Tariff Reduction," *Brooklyn Daily Eagle*, July 24, 1912; "Oceanside [News]," *South Side Observer*, January 25, 1915; "Oceanside [News]," *South Side Observer*, March 1, 1918, 3; "Oceanside [News]," *South Side Observer*, March 18, 1918, 3; "Political Paragraphs: From Nassau County," *Brooklyn Daily Eagle*, August 30, 1912, 9; "Political Pot Simmering," *Daily Long Island Farmer*, August 20, 1912, 1 (EBK is Progressive alternate); "Progressives Pleased," *Hempstead Sentinel*, October 22, 1912 (Progressive Party meeting and endorsements, and EBK as alternate delegate to convention); "Questions at Union Square," *New York Times*, May 3, 1914; "Races Are Feature at Mineola Fair," *Brooklyn Daily Eagle*, September 22, 1915 (EBK and the antis, also suffrage workers at the country fair report); "Rockville Centre [News]," *Owl*, September 3, 1915 (that EBK spoke in seventeen villages during the previous week); "Rockville Centre [News]," *Owl*, May 21, 1915 (Ina Buckman or Mrs. T. Smith Buckman was EBK's guest at large NYC suffrage event); "Rockville Centre

[News]," *Southside Observer*, April 5, 1918 (that EBK attends farewell dinner in Washington, DC, for NWP, Ann Martin of Nevada, vice chairman and woman candidate for Senate); "Says Murphy Is 'Poor Politician," *Brooklyn Daily Eagle*," November 1, 1915; "Split in Suffrage Camp," *Daily Long Island Farmer*, November 1, 1913, 1; "Six Year Old Campaigner," *Brooklyn Daily Eagle*, October 20, 1912; "Study Class," *South Side Observer*, December 28, 1917 (visit by Max and Peg Kearns from Beavertown, Pennsylvania, and Edna's work with the Farm Bureau and the Mineola Fair on Long Island); "Suffrage Day Is Widely Kept: Questions at Union Square," *New York Times*, May 3, 1914; "Suffrage News," *Brooklyn Daily Eagle*, January 17, 1914 (in this, Edna is identified with working for the New York State Woman Suffrage Association while representing the Hippodrome event in 1914); "Suffrage Notes," *Owl*, June 7, 1913; "Suffragists at Exhibits," *Brooklyn Daily Eagle*, April 14, 1915; "Suffragist Campaigners at Freeport," *Brooklyn Daily Eagle*, July 12, 1912, 4; "Suffragists Celebrating Lucy Stone Day Today," *Miami Herald*, August 13, 1915, 2; "Along the South Shore with a Suffrage Party," *Brooklyn Daily Eagle*, 1912; "Times Suffrage Edition Monday," *Long-Islander*, June 4, 1915, 5; "Tournament Aftermath," *South Side Observer*, June 2, 1913; "Votes for Women: The Long Island Movement," edited by Mrs. Wilmer R. Kearns, *Brooklyn Daily Eagle*, October 11, 1912; "Want to Volunteer for Housework to Release a Woman for War Aid?" *Brooklyn Daily Eagle*, January 10, 1918; " 'We Haven't Lost Yet,' Says L.I. Suffragist," *Brooklyn Daily Eagle*, November 3, 1915; "With Suffrage Workers," *Evening Post*, January 10, 1913, 4; "Women Appeal for Financial Assistance," *South Side Observer*, May 30, 1913; "Will Movie 'Suffs' Burn Houses? Not if Mrs. Kearns Knows It!," *Brooklyn Daily Eagle*, August 25, 1915, 3; "With the Suffragists: Brooklyn Women at Hammerstein Celebration," *Brooklyn Daily Eagle*, August 31, 1912, 8; "What the Suffragists Are Doing," *Owl*, September 10, 1915; "Woman Suffrage on Long Island," *Brooklyn Daily Eagle*, October 9, 1912, 4; "Women Want to Preach," *Daily Long Island Farmer*, August 14, 1912, 1; "Women Will Vote Says D. F. Malone," *Brooklyn Daily Eagle*, July 17, 1915.

CHAPTER 33: PETE SEEGER'S AUNT—SUFFRAGIST ANITA POLLITZER

1. Marguerite Kearns, "Pete Seeger, Anita Pollitzer, and the 'War of the Roses,' " *Woodstock Times*, August 25, 2017. An earlier version of chapter 33 was published on August 25, 2017, by *Woodstock Times*. Reprinted in part with permission from publisher Geddy Sveikauskas, Ulster Publishing, Woodstock, New York.

Selected Bibliography

Long Island suffrage publicity photo arranged by Edna Buckman Kearns, circa 1913.
Part of her head is visible above the vehicle's front flags.

Adams, Katherine H., and Michael L. Keene. *Alice Paul and the American Suffrage Campaign.* Champaign: University of Illinois Press, 2008.

Ambler, Rex. *The Quaker Way: A Rediscovery.* Winchester, England: Christian Alternative, 2012.

Anderson, Kristi. *After Suffrage: Women in Partisan and Electoral Politics before the New Deal.* Chicago: University of Chicago Press, 1996.

Bacon, Margaret H. *The Quiet Rebels: The Story of Quakers in America.* New York: Basic Books, 1969.

Bacon, Margaret Hope. *Mothers of Feminism: The Story of Quaker Women in America*. San Francisco: Harper & Row, 1986.

Bacon, Margaret Hope. *Valiant Friend: The Life of Lucretia Mott*. Philadelphia: Friends General Conference, 1999.

Barber, Lucy G. *Marching on Washington: The Forging of an American Political Tradition*. Berkeley: University of California Press, 2002.

Blyer, Bill. "Women's Groups Petition N.Y. State Museum to Display L.I. Suffrage Leader's Wagon." *Newsday*, June 27, 2015.

Brinton, Howard H. *Friends for 350 Years: The History of the Society of Friends Since George Fox Started the Quaker Movement*. Wallingford, PA: Pendle Hill Publications, 2002.

Brown, Elisabeth Potts, and Susan Mosher Stuard, eds. *Witnesses for Change: Quaker Women over Three Centuries*. New Brunswick: Rutgers University Press, 1989.

Cassel, Daniel Kolb. *A Genealogical History of the Kolb, Kulp or Culp Family and Its Branches in America*. Norristown, PA: Morgan R. Wills, 1895.

Catt, Carrie Chapman, and Nettie Rogers Shuler. *Woman Suffrage and Politics: The Inner Story of the Suffrage Movement*. New York: Charles Scribner's Sons, 1926.

Chapman, Mary. *Making Noise, Making News: Suffrage Print Culture and U.S. Modernism*. New York: Oxford University Press, 2014.

Chapman, Mary, and Angela Mills, eds. *Treacherous Texts: U.S. Suffrage Literature, 1846–1946*. New Brunswick: Oxford University Press, 2011.

Comly, George Norwood. *Comly Family in America: Descendants of Henry and Joan Comly Who Came to America in 1682 from Bedminster, Somersetshire, England*. Philadelphia: J. B. Lippincott, 1939.

Commager, Henry Steele, and Richard B. Morris, eds. *The Spirit of Seventy-Six: The Story of the American Revolution as Told by Participants*. Edison, NJ: Castle Books, 2002.

Cooper, Patricia A. *Once a Cigar Maker: Men, Women, and Work Culture in American Cigar Factories, 1900–1919*. Urbana: University of Illinois Press, 1992.

Cunningham, Hugh. "The Language of Patriotism, 1750–1914." *History Workshop*, no. 12 (Autumn 1981): 8–33.

Dublin, Thomas, and Margaret Johnston. "How Did Elisabeth Freeman's Publicity Skills Promote Woman Suffrage, Antilynching and the Peace Movement 1909–1915?" *Women and Social Movements in the United States, 1600–2000s*, 2008. Document Projects, Alexander Street Documents, https://documents.alexanderstreet.com/browse/document_project?page=1.

Dubois, Ellen Carol. *Harriot Stanton Blatch and the Winning of Woman Suffrage*. New Haven: Yale University Press, 1997.

Dubois, Ellen Carol. *Suffrage: Women's Long Battle for the Vote*. New York: Simon & Schuster, 2020.

Durham, Geoffrey. *The Spirit of Quakers*. New Haven: Yale University Press, 2010.

Falk, Candace. *Love, Anarchy and Emma Goldman: A Biography*. New Brunswick: Rutgers University Press, 1990.

Farraday, Clayton L. *Friends' Central School; 1845–1984*. Philadelphia: Friends' Central School, 1984.

Faulkner, Carol. *Lucretia Mott's Heresy: Abolition and Women's Rights in Nineteenth-Century America*. Philadelphia: University of Pennsylvania Press, 2011.

Finnegan, Margaret. *Selling Suffrage: Consumer Culture and Votes for Women*. New York: Columbia University Press, 1999.

Flexner, Eleanor. *Century of Struggle: The Woman's Rights Movement in the United States*. Cambridge: The Belknap Press of Harvard University Press, 1975.

Florey, Kenneth. *American Woman Suffrage Postcards: A Study and Catalog*. Jefferson, NC: McFarland & Co., 2015.

Fur, Gunlög. *A Nation of Women: Gender and Colonial Encounters Among the Delaware Indians*. Philadelphia: University of Pennsylvania Press, 2012.

Goodier, Susan. *No Votes for Women: The New York State Anti-Suffrage Movement*. Urbana: University of Illinois Press, 2013.

Goodier, Susan, and Karen Pastorello. *Women Will Vote: Winning Suffrage in New York State*. Ithaca, NY: Three Hills, an imprint of Cornell University Press, 2017.

Gordon, Ann D., ed. *The Selected Papers of Elizabeth Cady Stanton and Susan B. Anthony: In the School of Anti-Slavery, 1840–1866*. Vol. 1. New Brunswick, NJ: Rutgers University Press, 1997.

Greene, David L. *The Kearns Family of Decatur and Derry Townships, Mifflin County, Pennsylvania*. Demorest, GA: D. L. Greene, 1979.

Hall, Simon. *American Patriotism, American Protest: Social Movements Since the Sixties*. Philadelphia: University of Pennsylvania Press, 2011.

Harrison, Patricia Greenwood. *Connecting Links: The British and American Woman Suffrage Movements, 1900–1914*. Westport, CT: Greenwood Press, 2000.

Hubbard, Elbert, and Sam Torode. *Elbert Hubbard: A Treasury of Insights, Inspirations, and Provocations*. East Aurora, NY, 2016.

Irwin, Inez Hayes. *The Story of the Woman's Party*. New York: Harcourt, Brace and Company, 1921.

Kearns, Bob, and Anne Kearns. "Charles Maxwell Kearns, Automobile Pioneer: 1907 to 1929." Privately printed, 2009. Copy in author's possession.

Kearns, Marguerite. "Artifact NY: The Spirit of 1776 Suffrage Wagon." *New York History* 101, no. 2 (2020): 366–371. doi: 10.1353/nyh.2020.0022.

Kearns, Marguerite. "Hitch a Ride on the Women's Suffrage Wagon." *Newsday*. March 18, 2010.

Kearns, Marguerite. "The Spirit of 1776." *New York Archives* (Fall 2013): 28–31.

Kearns, Marguerite. "Suffrage History: Long Island's Three Wagon Women." *New York History Blog*, April 9, 2014. https://suffragewagon.org/WagonWomen.pdf.

Kearns, Serena, and Wilmer Kearns. "On Edna Buckman Kearns (1882–1934)." In *Prominent Women of the Wissahickon Valley Area: Bicentennial Perspective for Women*, 52–54. Ambler, PA: Ambler Business & Professional Women's Club, 1976.

Keene, Carolyn. *The Hidden Staircase*. New York: Grosset & Dunlap, 1987, 1959, 1930.

Kimmel, Michael S., and Thomas E. Mosmiller, eds. *Against the Tide: Pro-Feminist Men in the United States, 1776–1990—A Documentary History*. Boston: Beacon Press, 1992.

Kraditor, Aileen S. *The Ideas of the Woman Suffrage Movement, 1890–1920*. New York: W.W. Norton & Company, 1981.

Kroeger, Brooke. *The Suffragents: How Women Used Men to Get the Vote*. Albany: State University of New York Press, 2017.

Lemak, Jennifer A., and Ashley Hopkins-Benton. *Votes for Women: Celebrating New York's Suffrage Centennial* (New York State Museum). Albany: State University of New York Press, 2017.

McCammon, Holly J., Lyndi Hewitt, and Sandy Smith. "No Weapon Save Argument: Strategic Frame Amplification in the US Woman Suffrage Movement." *Sociological Quarterly* 45, no. 3 (Summer 2004): 529–556.

McCracken, George E. *The Welcome Claimants Proved, Disproved and Doubtful with an Account of Some of Their Descendants*. Baltimore: Genealogical Publishing Co., 1970.

Milford, Emily Buckman. *Ancestors and Descendants of Joseph Comly Buckman and Caroline Nice (Livezey) Buckman*. Self-published, 1981.

Murphy, Stacey, ed. *NY Votes for Women: A Suffrage Centennial Anthology*. Ithaca: Cayuga Lake Books, 2017.

Naylor, Natalie A. "In Deeds of Daring Rectitude: Winning Votes for Women in Nassau County and the Nation." *Nassau County Historical Society Journal* 50 (1995): 30–44.

Naylor, Natalie A. *Women in Long Island's Past: A History of Eminent Ladies and Everyday Lives*. Charleston: History Press, 2012.

Nickalls, John L. *The Journal of George Fox*. Revised edition with an epilogue by Henry J. Cadbury and an introduction by Geoffrey F. Nuttall. Philadelphia: Religious Society of Friends, 1997.

Oneill, Therese. *Unmentionable: The Victorian Lady's Guide to Sex, Marriage, and Manners*. New York: Back Bay Books / Little, Brown and Company, 2016.

Petrash, Antonia. *Long Island and the Woman Suffrage Movement*. Charleston: History Press, 2013.

Roberts, Rebecca Boggs. *Suffragists in Washington, DC: The 1913 Parade and the Fight for the Vote*. Charleston: History Press, 2017.

Sheppard, Walter Lee. *Passengers and Ships: Penn's Colony*. Vol. 1. Baltimore: Genealogical Publishing Co., 1970.

Slaughter, Thomas P. *The Beautiful Soul of John Woolman, Apostle of Abolition*. New York: Hill and Wang, 2008.

Stein, Geoffrey N. "Suffrage Wagon: Rolling for Women's Right to Vote." *Legacy: The Magazine of the New York State Museum* 4, no. 1 (Summer 2008): 16.

Stevens, Doris. *Jailed for Freedom: American Women Win the Vote*. New York: Boni and Liveright, 1920.

Stanton, Elizabeth Cady. *Eighty Years and More: Reminiscences 1815–1897*. New York: T. Fisher Unwin, 1898.

Stillion Southard, Belinda A. *Militant Citizenship: Rhetorical Strategies of the National Woman's Party, 1913–1920*. College Station.: Texas A&M University Press, 2011.

Stovall, James Glen. *Seeing Suffrage: The Washington Suffrage Parade of 1913, Its Pictures, and Its Effect on the American Political Landscape*. Knoxville: University of Tennessee Press, 2013.

Terborg-Penn, Rosalyn. *African American Women in the Struggle for the Vote, 1850–1920*. Bloomington: Indiana University Press, 1998.

Thibaut, Jacqueline. *Edgar A. Poe: The Years in Philadelphia, 1838–1844*. Research prepared for Independence National Historic Park superintendent Hobart G. Cawood, 1981.

Tetrault, Lisa. *The Myth of Seneca Falls: Memory and the Women's Suffrage Movement, 1848–1898*. Chapel Hill: University of North Carolina Press, 2017.

Tutt, Juliana. " 'No Taxation without Representation' in the American Woman Suffrage Movement." *Stanford Law Review* 62, no. 5 (May 2010): 1473–1512.

US Senate. *Suffrage Parade: Hearings before a Subcommittee of the Committee on the District of Columbia, Part I*. March 4–17, 1913.

Weigley, Russell F., ed. *Philadelphia: A 300-Year History*. New York: W.W. Norton & Company, 1982.

Weiss, Elaine. *The Woman's Hour: The Great Fight to Win the Vote*. New York: Viking, 2018.

Wellman, Judith. *The Road to Seneca Falls: Elizabeth Cady Stanton and the First Woman's Rights Convention*. Urbana: University of Illinois Press, 2004.

Wilbur, Henry W. *The Life and Labors of Elias Hicks*. Philadelphia: Friends' General Conference, 1910.

Williamson, Elizabeth, and Haruka Sakaguchi. *New York Times*. "Legacy of Suffrage: 100 Years Later, These Activists Continue Their Ancestors' Work." August 11, 2020.

Yates, W. Ross. *Joseph Wharton: Quaker Industrial Pioneer*. London: Associated University Presses, 1987.

Zahniser, Jill, and Amelia R. Fry. *Alice Paul: Claiming Power*. London: Oxford University Press, 2014.

Index

Page numbers in italics refer to illustrations.

About the Author

Marguerite Kearns. Photo by Michael Weisbrot.

*M*arguerite Kearns is the granddaughter of women's rights activists Edna B. Kearns and Wilmer R. Kearns. She grew up in the Philadelphia area learning about her family history and lived in New York State for twenty years. A former journalist and teacher, Marguerite's award-winning writing in literary journals, blogs, and other publications has contributed to a support base for her storytelling about American history. Marguerite follows the matrilineal convention of using her mother's family name, Kearns. She lives in Northern New Mexico.